Comrade Sister

New World Studies
Marlene L. Daut, Editor

# Comrade Sister

## Caribbean Feminist Revisions of the Grenada Revolution

Laurie R. Lambert

University of Virginia Press
Charlottesville and London

University of Virginia Press
© 2020 by the Rector and Visitors of the University of Virginia
All rights reserved
Printed in the United States of America on acid-free paper

*First published 2020*

9 8 7 6 5 4 3 2 1

Library of Congress Cataloging-in-Publication Data
Names: Lambert, Laurie R., author.
Title: Comrade sister : Caribbean feminist revisions of the Grenada Revolution / Laurie R. Lambert.
Description: Charlottesville : University of Virginia Press, 2020. | Series: New world studies | Includes bibliographical references and index.
Identifiers: LCCN 2019047998 (print) | LCCN 2019047999 (ebook) | ISBN 9780813944258 (hardback) | ISBN 9780813944265 (paperback) | ISBN 9780813944272 (epub)
Subjects: LCSH: Grenadian literature—Women authors—History and criticism. | Grenadian literature—20th century—History and criticism. | Women in literature. | Sex role in literature. | Feminism and literature. | Grenada—History—Coup d'état, 1979—Influence.
Classification: LCC PR9275.G7 L36 2020 (print) | LCC PR9275.G7 (ebook) | DDC 820.9/9729845—dc23
LC record available at https://lccn.loc.gov/2019047998
LC ebook record available at https://lccn.loc.gov/2019047999

Cover art: *In Search of Self,* Susan Mains, 2001. Acrylic and mixed media; 60 × 56 inches. (Courtesy of the artist)

*To my parents, Rita Lambert and the late Lawrence Lambert, C.B.E.*

# Contents

| | | |
|---|---|---|
| | Acknowledgments | ix |
| | Introduction: (En)Gendering Revolution | 1 |
| 1. | Generational Ties, Revolutionary Binds: Family as Archive in the Writing of Merle Collins | 37 |
| 2. | After the Invasion: Masculine Authority and the Anxiety of Revolution | 77 |
| 3. | "Comrade, Sister, Lover": Dionne Brand and the Limits of Radical Movements | 110 |
| 4. | Legacies of Mercy: Neoliberalism and the Disavowal of Revolution | 151 |
| | Conclusion: In Search of Our Mothers' Revolutions | 173 |
| | Notes | 183 |
| | Bibliography | 205 |
| | Index | 217 |

# Acknowledgments

THE IDEA for this book first took shape as a dissertation in the English Department at New York University. I am grateful to my advisers, Robert J. C. Young, Michael A. Gomez, Aisha Khan, and the late J. Michael Dash, for the training and mentorship they offered. I have continued to benefit from their guidance throughout my early career as they have remained steadfast supporters of this project.

At the University of California, Davis, I was fortunate to be part of a vibrant community of scholars. I thank the faculty and staff of the Department of African American and African Studies for their support. It was a privilege to be part of the Hart Hall community. I am especially grateful to Danielle Heard Mollel, Danny C. Martinez, Elizabeth Montaño, and Bettina Ng'weno for their friendship.

Since joining Fordham University I have had the pleasure of working with wonderful colleagues in African and African American Studies, History, English, Comparative Literature, and beyond. I thank Amir Idris and Fawzia Mustafa, in particular, for their assistance in helping me access crucial resources for the completion of this book.

I benefited tremendously from a postdoctoral fellowship in Critical Caribbean Studies at Rutgers University. Yolanda Martínez-San Miguel was an inspiring mentor, reading and providing feedback on my dissertation and chapter 1 of the manuscript. I thank the Critical Caribbean Studies faculty, the Department of Latino and Caribbean Studies, and the faculty and fellows at the Institute for Research on Women for welcoming me to their seminar that year.

Staff at the T. A. Marryshow Library at the University of the West Indies Centre in Grenada, especially Curtis Jacobs and Margaret Roberts, were of tremendous assistance. I am also grateful to the librarians and staff of the Grenada Public Library, the National Archives and Records

x  *Acknowledgments*

Administration in College Park, Maryland, the Thomas Fisher Rare Book Library at the University of Toronto, and the University of the West Indies special collections on the St. Augustine and Mona campuses. Andaiye, Michael Ellis, Genifer Francis, Neil Martin, Dickon Mitchell, Nicole Phillip-Dowe, Shalini Puri, Ray Roberts, David Scott, Sekou Stroude, Tessa Stroude, and Marva Victor provided timely insight and assistance as I conducted archival and field research. Puri also graciously agreed to serve as the external reader on my dissertation committee. Interviews with Clive Nunez, Gloria Payne-Banfield, Ann Peters, Leslie Pierre, Shirley Robinson, and Kathy Sloane were illuminating; I am grateful for their time and patience.

David Austin, Ronald Cummings, Ana Dopico, Ada Ferrer, Aisha Finch, Natasha Lightfoot, Harvey Neptune, Anton Nimblett, Lisa Outar, Sonya Posmentier, and Michelle Stephens have engaged my ideas and challenged me in wonderful ways. Aisha Khan, Faith Smith, and Deborah Thomas commented on earlier drafts of the manuscript. I am grateful for their feedback. I also received generous comments from participants in the Black Atlantic Graduate Seminar at the University of Delaware's African American Public Humanities Institute and the Caribbean Epistemologies Seminar at the City University of New York's Center for the Humanities. I thank Laura Helton and Herman Bennett, respectively, for invitations to these collegial venues. One of the best experiences in writing this book was a manuscript workshop with Donette Francis, Mark Jerng, Donna V. Jones, Brian Meeks, and Bettina Ng'weno. Their feedback changed the shape of my work for the better. I thank Génesis Lara for her notetaking during the workshop. Carol Lawes provided expert editing at a crucial moment.

Academic life can feel itinerant at times, and I thank the following people for the consistency of their friendship across the miles: Magalí Armillas-Tiseyra, James Cantres, Uzoma Esonwanne, Ebony Jones, Evelyne Laurent-Perrault, Tyesha Maddox, Bridget McFarland, Yuko Miki, Alison Okuda, Chandani Patel, Nathalie Pierre, Amaury Sosa, Jonathan Square, Shauna Sweeney, Jini Kim Watson, and Shirley Wong. Daily writing accountability with Nikki Traylor-Knowles, Shawnita Sealy-Jefferson, Lynn Itagaki, June Chung, Diane Bassham, and Anna Agbe-Davies helped me stay on track. Kris Alexander, Aurora Anaya-Cerda, Janelle Charles, Julie Crooks, Negin Dahya, Reza Dahya, Darren Downes, Neeya Jacob, JR Kanu, Parveen Kaur, Christine Mohan, Cherril Pierre, Xania Pitt, Rochelle Roberts, Erica Shaw, and Raymond Yee have been a tremendous circle of support. A special shout-out to Rochelle for providing invaluable research assistance as I prepared the final manuscript.

I thank the late J. Michael Dash, Marlene L. Daut, Eric Brandt, Helen Chandler, and everyone at the University of Virginia Press for shepherding this project through its final stages. Eric's and Helen's professionalism and kindness brought ease to the process. I am grateful to two anonymous readers for their enthusiastic endorsement of this work and their constructive critique, which has sharpened my analysis.

Financial support for this project was provided by the UC Davis Academic Senate, the UC Davis Humanities Institute, the University of California Consortium for Black Studies, Rutgers University Institute for Critical Caribbean Studies, and Fordham University's Office of Research.

Earlier versions of chapter 3 appeared as "The Sovereignty of the Imagination: Poetic Authority and the Fiction of North Atlantic Universals in Dionne Brand's *Chronicles of the Hostile Sun*," *Cultural Dynamics* 26, no. 2 (2014): 173–94, and "When Revolution Is Not Enough: Tracing the Limits of Black Radicalism in Dionne Brand's *Chronicles of the Hostile Sun* and *In Another Place, Not Here*," in *The Postcolonial Contemporary: Political Imaginaries for the Global Present*, edited by Jini Kim Watson and Gary C. Wilder (New York: Fordham University Press, 2018), 55–76. They are reprinted by permission of Sage Publications and Fordham University Press, respectively. A short selection on the *Torchlight* newspaper in chapter 2 appeared in "The Revolution and Its Discontents: Grenadian Newspapers and Attempts to Shape Public Opinion during Political Transition," *Round Table: The Commonwealth Journal of International Affairs* 102, no. 2 (2013): 143–53, and under the same title in *Grenada: Revolution and Invasion*, edited by Patsy Lewis, Gary C. Williams, and Peter Clegg (Mona, Jamaica: University of the West Indies Press, 2015), 81–96. It is reprinted by permission of Taylor and Francis Limited. I thank Kathy Sloane for providing the images found throughout this book and Damani Baker for granting permission to use the image of Alimenta Bishop in the conclusion. Kathy and Damani have both photographed Grenada with love and care. Thank you to Dionne Brand for permission to use material from *Chronicles of the Hostile Sun* (Toronto: Williams-Wallace, 1984), Merle Collins for permission to use material from *Lady in a Boat* (Leeds: Peepal Tree Press, 2003), and the Derek Walcott Estate for permission to use material from "Good Old Heart of Darkness." I am grateful to Susan Mains for permission to use her painting *In Search of Self* for the cover art.

My family anchored me during the writing of this book. Members of the Lambert and Redhead families, the Francis and Ellis families, the Taylor family, and the Wedderburn family have hosted me in Grenada, Jamaica, Trinidad, and Maryland as I completed archival research and fieldwork. When I needed a break, they welcomed me back home to Toronto or made me feel at home in New York. My brothers, Raymond and Lancelot, deserve special mention for their loving friendship and good humor, and for gifting me with wonderful nieces and nephews. I draw such inspiration from my grandmothers, Theresa Francis and the late Myrtle Lambert, exemplary Caribbean feminists. My parents, Rita and Lawrence Lambert, made every sacrifice to ensure that I would have the privilege of doing this kind of work. It was painful to lose my father in the months before I finalized the manuscript, but I know he would have reveled in its publication. Words cannot describe the love, joy, faith, and fun that have come from building a life with Junior Wedderburn. I thank him for the gift of a divine partnership. Finally, I thank God, from whom all my blessings flow.

Comrade Sister

# Introduction
(En)Gendering Revolution

WHAT WOULD it mean to reimagine the Grenada Revolution with women at its center? How do women influence political movements? How do they shape the ideology of revolution, and how do they make themselves the beneficiaries of political power? These are questions I came to after reading a 1979 article titled "Caribbean Women and Politics," by the Trinidadian writer Merle Hodge, one of many internationalist workers who lived and worked in Grenada from the late 1970s to the early 1980s.[1] Hodge's first sentence sums up the premise of the piece: "Caribbean women have yet to properly enter politics."[2] Her critique is not that women have failed to play a role in the history of Caribbean politics but rather that until the late 1970s, despite their constant support for and involvement in major political movements, Caribbean women had yet to achieve the kind of representation in political office that would reflect the depth of their efforts. She outlines how movements led by men such as Uriah Butler and Eric Gairy, as well as the People's National Movement and the Black Power movement in Trinidad, provided some progress for Caribbean men but less relief from oppression for Caribbean women. She further argues that the few women in political office often found themselves conforming to the party line in order to maintain their positions. As she puts it, these women politicians were too often "hopelessly manipulated and neutralized by the male majority."[3] What Hodge describes is the classic postcolonial condition in which women contribute to anticolonial struggles, only to be excluded from true leadership positions and rendered invisible in the retellings of these histories.[4] She calls for Caribbean women to abandon their usual position as the "backbone" of these battles and to take on front-and-center roles on the political landscape: "For as long as women consent to carry out decisions and never make them, for as long as they fail to influence the thinking of political movements and help shape the ideology of the causes they support, they will find that they are liable to be used by movement after movement. They will continue to be the instruments but never the beneficiaries of political power."[5] But what if the question were not whether women influence political movements but rather *where* we look to find this influence?

This book is a literary analysis of the politics of gender and sexuality of the Grenada Revolution (March 1979–October 1983). It examines how Caribbean writers represented gender in the revolution and how they have documented the struggles of the region's women to participate in and process the consequences of the political radicalism of this period. It also examines the strategies of representation employed by Caribbean women writers, in particular as they evaluate the place of Grenada in a pattern of political resistance that expands across the region. Through close readings of literature—essays, novels, poems, and memoirs—and documentary film, I affirm that the narration of the Grenada Revolution opens up new meanings about how the political trauma of Caribbean radicalism is processed. This book examines how Caribbean women—their experiences, memories, and work—are key to understanding these new meanings, with implications for how Caribbean revolutions are understood.

The impetus behind writing this book is both personal and political. For many years a framed photograph of Grenada's second prime minister, Maurice Bishop, dressed in military fatigues, hung in a place of honor in my grandmother's home. In family conversations, Bishop, a chief architect of the Grenada Revolution, was remembered fondly and praised for his leadership. These conversations were dominated by the women in my family: one of my aunts had worked as Bishop's secretary for a time, and others knew him or his family. Men in my family had lived through the revolution as well; one was even a member of the revolution's military branch, the People's Revolutionary Army (PRA), but somehow had less to say about it. In these conversations everyone agreed both that the revolution was a progressive period in Grenada's history and that the 1983 U.S. invasion of Grenada was necessary, that it had saved the nation from some unexplained calamity. Perhaps it was in the way these points were made that, even as a child, I understood them to be contradictory. I accepted these fragments as part of a history that might never coalesce into a coherent narrative. Today I know that these perspectives, contradictory though they may seem, are held simultaneously by a large number of Grenadians. The revolution emerges in Grenadian consciousness in the form of conversations broken off and unanswered (or unanswerable) questions. Memories of the revolution persist, in gestures large and small—the renaming of the airport in Bishop's honor, the plastering of his name and image in public graffiti, the careful placement of his photograph in the private homes of Grenadians across the diaspora. Bishop's is the name most associated with the revolution, and perhaps second is that of Bernard Coard, the deputy prime minister. Many women were also involved in the making of this political process in Grenada, though they remain less known. Within the revolution women were often referred to as "comrade sister," "comrade" being a popular form of address in socialist circles, with "sister" added to recognize a gendered difference. Both comrade and sister were meant to denote a sense of equality. From the beginning of the revolution, Bishop's rhetoric, including his use of "comrades" or "brothers and sisters" to address his fellow revolutionaries and Grenadians, focused on creating a political system for and of the people. Grenadians were meant to feel that they were finally in control of their destiny, the revolution having rid them of their first prime minister, Eric Gairy, an authoritarian father figure. The rhetoric of revolution and nationalist pride called on Grenadians to think of themselves as a unified collective.[6] But there remained a serious power differential between genders during the revolution. I focus on literary representations by Caribbean women writers because their work places readers at the intersection of gender and politics in the public and private spheres, opening up a view of how Caribbean women have constructed their most significant contributions to the revolution. Thus much of what follows is a careful examination of the discursive distance between comrade and sister.

## Revolution and Gender: Keywords for Caribbean Studies

*Revolution* is one of the foundational terms on which Caribbean studies as a discipline has been forged. Scholars of the region have long grappled with how revolutionary formations shape the politics and culture of the Caribbean, tracing a genealogy between the Haitian Revolution and myriad other slave revolts to later uprisings such as the Cuban Revolution. This idea of revolution forming the basis of a regional identity was famously outlined by the historian and theorist C. L. R. James in his essay "From Toussaint L'Ouverture to Fidel Castro," which serves as the appendix to the 1963 edition of *The Black Jacobins,* his history of the Haitian Revolution. James writes that as it relates to revolution, what we see in the Caribbean "is an original pattern, not European, not African, not a part of the American main, not native in any conceivable sense of that word, but West Indian, *sui generis,* with no parallel anywhere else."⁷ The genealogy that James lays out is not only distinctly Caribbean but also exclusively masculine-identified in its gender politics. He names Jean Price-Mars, José Martí, Antonio Maceo, Fernando Ortiz, Marcus Garvey, George Padmore, Aimé Césaire, Arthur Andrew Cipriani, Juan Bosch, Fidel Castro, George Lamming, Vic Reid, Wilson Harris, and even V. S. Naipaul (who dismissed much of Caribbean culture) as formidable political and cultural leaders. These figures traverse the anglophone, francophone, and hispanophone Caribbean in terms of their origins; however, aside from James's nod to the Haitian peasantry, each of the figures he names as key to the timeline of cultural and political resistance in the region is a Caribbean man. James is not alone in his formulation. The historiography of Caribbean revolution, in particular, is filled with narratives of men (mainly heterosexual), who are represented as bold and charismatic figures. They include Toussaint L'Ouverture, Jean-Jacques Dessalines, and Henri Christophe in Haiti, Simón Bolívar in Venezuela, and Fidel Castro and Che Guevara in Cuba. In Grenada, the image of Maurice Bishop fits the mold of the iconic revolutionary male subject. He was the revolution's most visible and charismatic leader.

Caribbean writers have been fascinated by this history of revolution, resistance, and male leaders. As such, the masculine iconography of revolution, sovereignty, and political independence has also informed the development of the region's national literatures.⁸ In the anglophone Caribbean the quest for sovereignty and political independence, framed as resistance to colonial domination, has run parallel to the rise of national literatures, especially in Jamaica, Trinidad, and Barbados.⁹ Literary nationalism in these countries has been typically, though not exclusively, represented as the purview of male authors. Figures such as George Lamming and Derek Walcott, as well as Kamau Brathwaite, C. L. R. James, V. S. Naipaul, and Andrew Salkey, dominated Caribbean letters during the period just before and immediately after independence, indexing literary nationalism as a key site of masculine authority. In *Making Men* (1999), Belinda Edmondson argues that male writers of the anglophone Caribbean took up a project of narrating the nation while inspired by a Victorian sensibility of gentlemanliness.¹⁰ They wanted to prove that they could master English social codes and mores at the same time as they explored representations of their Caribbean surroundings. Because of their education, training, and, in many instances, travel, these men had an intimate understanding of English subjectivities, at the same time as they claimed for themselves a distinctly Caribbean sensibility. Even as they rejected English colonialism, however, they internalized some of its cultural forms. This is not to suggest that women are absent from the literature of this period, either as subjects or as authors, but rather to notice that men dominated the literary scene and that they were fascinated by representations of revolution. Edmondson finds that male Caribbean writers consistently write black women out of narratives of revolution in this body of literature because the black woman's presence threatens the assumed relationship between Caribbean masculine authority and revolution.[11] Caribbean women writers, however, from this period and later write their own interpretations of nation-building and revolution.

Edmondson's work builds on the groundbreaking collection of essays *Out of the Kumbla: Caribbean Women and Literature,* published in 1990 and edited by Carole Boyce Davies and Elaine Savory Fido. The volume addresses the importance of accounting for women's experiences in literary and historical representations of Caribbean life. "I know they are there, but, it seems there is no history of women's participation in struggle in the Caribbean," Boyce Davies writes, noting that the existing histories that touched on women's experience were "merely scratching the surface."[12] The essays in this compilation of postcolonial feminist literary criticism were written in the early to mid-1980s, just as the Grenada Revolution was coming to an end. They focus on the 1970s and 1980s as Caribbean women writers responded to the conditions of imperialism and decolonization.[13] Boyce Davies and Savory Fido define a "feminist literary criticism of Caribbean literature" as one that addresses the then dearth of texts representing women's perspectives on a range of issues germane to the region.[14] One of their main concerns is the seeming "voicelessness" of Caribbean women in literary criticism up to the late 1970s, which they identify not only as the lack of texts written from women's point of view but the difficulties women writers experienced getting their work published and their exclusion from the "critical dialogue" of the field.[15] Some of the earliest literary texts on the revolution were published by the Caribbean women writers Dionne Brand and Merle Collins and addressed concerns similar to those raised by Boyce Davies and Savory Fido and other third world feminist literary critics, including Gayatri Spivak and Chandra Talpade Mohanty.[16] Reading their writing, it is impossible to simply accept the masculine genealogy laid out by James and others. Instead it becomes imperative to think about what we learn when we change our minds and envision revolution, and specifically the Grenada Revolution, from the perspective of the region's women.

Following the work of Edmondson, Boyce Davies and Savory Fido, and other scholars of feminist literary criticism of the Caribbean, I am interested in analyzing the politics of gender that surrounds revolution in

Grenada, in examining how Caribbean women writers help us see anew the patterns of trauma that accompany both imperialist oppression *and* the Caribbean's revolutionary drive. Literary and political norms were transformed around the time of the Grenada Revolution. A different kind of masculine authority, one informed by the Black Power movement, arose in the late 1960s and 1970s. It was not Victorian. It was a more macho form of masculinity, one tied to black consciousness, and it marked a generational difference between Bishop and writers such as Lamming and Walcott. Bishop and his party comrades in the New Jewel Movement (NJM) represented a younger generation that did not care to prove that they were as English as the English. They wanted to express pride in their Caribbean identities. They were rebellious. They wore shirt jackets and military fatigues instead of suits. People found Bishop magnetic, even sexy. These young radicals prided themselves on being both cosmopolitan and connected to the grass roots. They were educated abroad but spoke plainly in the kind of "nation language," to borrow a term from Brathwaite, with which the general public could identify.[17] Crucially, they were openly critical of capitalism and drew inspiration from both socialist and communist political ideologies. The NJM's actual economic practice during the revolution could best be described as "noncapitalist." Party members embraced a mixed economy with state, private, and cooperative sectors. Their path was neither socialist nor capitalist in any strict sense.[18] Still, in much of the rhetoric and, later, the literature surrounding the revolution, actors inside and outside the Caribbean have used the term "communism" to describe the NJM's ideological position. This misnomer for the NJM's activity is an example of how the Grenada Revolution was often caught in a Cold War binary that was only partially related to what Grenadians were building at home.

At the same time that the NJM was getting stronger as a party, women were taking more radical and public positions on the issues they found important. For example, beginning in 1970 a group of Grenadian nurses led a series of protests and sit-ins at the Ministry of Health to bring attention to the government's mismanagement of the General Hospital.[19] This coordinated stance against the government of Eric Gairy, led by women, was unprecedented, and the nurses drew support from across the public. In the early 1980s the coordinated efforts of NJM women to lead a Women's Desk and to build the National Women's Organization, which included Grenadian women of all ages and from all walks of life, were also part of the expanding role of women demanding radical changes, as a collective and in the public sphere.[20]

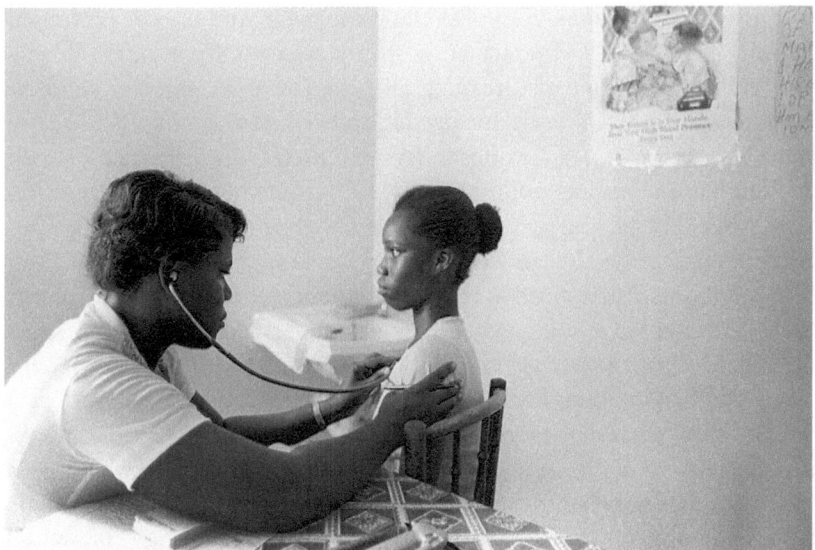

**Figure 1.** A Grenadian girl receives care at the Medical Station in Perdmontemps, St. David's, Grenada. (© Kathy Sloane, courtesy of the photographer)

I have chosen to adopt a Caribbean feminist methodology to analyze the literature of the revolution because I was struck by the difference in gender representations between the archival record of the Grenada Revolution and the literary oeuvre inspired by that revolution. So many more Caribbean women achieved voice and context in the creative literature produced about this revolution than is discernible in the archives. In the literature of the Grenada Revolution, women turn up in all kinds of ways that normally escape archival preservation. To date, Merle Collins and Dionne Brand are the major writers on this revolution, having published extensively on the topic since 1984: between them, three novels, four poetry collections, two nonfiction books, and numerous nonfiction essays that deal with some aspect of that moment in Grenada's history.[21] The women they write about work in cane fields on rural estates; serve in homes, tending to children and grandchildren; write letters to friends on other islands and in the Caribbean diaspora; attend college; endure abusive relationships; debate political legacies with their fathers, brothers, and lovers. They also write about themselves and how the revolution and its aftermath shaped them as writers. Reading this literature felt like coming upon a counterbalance to the archival record, which skews heavily toward representations of men as the principal actors of the revolution. A Caribbean feminist literary criticism focuses attention on Caribbean women authors while also reading all texts (by writers across genders) intersectionally, accounting for gender and sexuality alongside race and class. As a critical tool, Caribbean feminist literary criticism can be used to illuminate texts and testimonies by authors of any gender or generation, while recognizing how different forms of oppression are particularly compounded in Caribbean women's experiences.[22]

My analysis is grounded in the work of black feminist scholars such as Kimberlé Crenshaw, who coined the term "intersectionality," and Patricia Hill Collins, whose groundbreaking essay "Mammies, Matriarchs, and Other Controlling Images" identified black women's literature as a site for the "emergent woman" whose life experiences and worldview defied the stereotypical images produced by mainstream society to keep black women oppressed in racialized and gendered binaries.[23] Scholars of feminism in the Caribbean have much in common with U.S.-based black feminist thinkers, often overlapping in terms of method, critique, and diasporic engagement across borders. Grenadian American Audre Lorde perhaps best embodies this overlap. Lorde was an activist for the rights of all black people, but, as she detailed in her essay "I Am Your Sister," she was in the struggle for black queer women in particular. "I Am Your Sister" is especially instructive for the way it outlines the importance of addressing difference within communities of black resistance. Lorde decried homophobia among her fellow activists and organizers in the U.S. civil rights movement and Black Power movement. Taking other black activists to task for not recognizing the contributions of black queer activists such as herself, Lorde sought to build spaces where black people could work together "across difference."[24]

This book takes up a similar task of identifying fault lines within the Grenada Revolution, where the pervasive sexism and patriarchal thinking inherited from the colonial period continue to influence how postcolonial radical movements dealt or deal with gender. The contributions of contemporary scholars of Caribbean feminism such as M. Jacqui Alexander in *Pedagogies of Crossing* (2005), Donette Francis in *Fictions of Feminine Citizenship* (2010), Tonya Haynes in "Interrogating Approaches to Caribbean Feminist Thought" (2017), Gabrielle Jamela Hosein and Jane Parpart, editors of *Negotiating Gender, Policy and Politics in the Caribbean* (2017), Kamala Kempadoo in *Sexing the Caribbean: Gender, Race and Sexual Labour* (2004), Patricia Mohammed, editor of *Gendered Realities: Essays in Caribbean Feminist Thought* (2002), Rhonda E.

Reddock, editor of *Interrogating Caribbean Masculinities* (2004), and Faith Smith, editor of *Sex and the Citizen: Interrogating the Caribbean* (2011) help locate feminism in the context of a region whose colonial and postcolonial formation includes histories of slavery, indenture, apprenticeship, independence, migration, and diaspora in a multiracial context. A Caribbean feminist analysis produces a more nuanced understanding of the conditions that led to the Grenada Revolution and of the unique forms of oppression, exclusion, and violence visited on the women who lived through and helped create this revolution. Whether it is articulated explicitly or not, revolution always has a politics of gender and sexuality. Writers such as Collins and Brand have chosen to foreground the roles played by Caribbean women, across various positions of age, class, and sexuality, in fomenting and responding to radical action. Paying attention to these politics transforms how we decide which authors and texts have valuable things to say about revolution.

## Authorizing Revolution's Narratives

It was from the radio station, arguably the most important target of the paramilitary attack launched by a secret cell within the NJM on March 13, 1979, that Bishop initially addressed the island in a speech now known as "A Bright New Dawn." His voice played over the Grenadian airwaves, bringing a message of optimism and change: "People of Grenada, this revolution is for work, for food, for decent housing and health services, and for a bright future for our children and great-grand-children."[25] For Caribbean and Latin American listeners, Bishop's use of "revolution" immediately put Grenada in a tradition, at least rhetorically, with Haiti, Venezuela, Mexico, and Cuba. What these other revolutions had in common, however, was protracted violent struggle involving significant sectors of the population. The violence preceding the revolution in Grenada was on a smaller scale: Gairy's quotidian bullying, punctuated by the occasional flagrant episodes. On Sunday, November 18, 1973, six members of the NJM leadership, including Bishop, Unison Whiteman, and Selwyn Strachan, were beaten by the police on Gairy's orders. Weeks later, on Monday, January 21, 1974, Bishop's father, Rupert Bishop, was shot and killed by police during a public protest on the Carenage, a portside area near Grenada's capital, St. George's.[26] These events were later known as Bloody Sunday and Bloody Monday, respectively. While the Grenadian masses had participated in strikes and demonstrations protesting the ineffectiveness of Gairy's government, they had not responded violently to his abuse.²⁷ The NJM coup was planned and executed by a small vanguard within the party and was designed to elicit mass participation only after the NJM had secured its position in power. While masses of Grenadians turned out in support of the party's takeover, making it a fait accompli, all but a tiny minority in the NJM were surprised by the March 13 move. It was not yet a collective action. What the Grenada Revolution had in common with other revolutions from Caribbean region, however, was a predominantly male leadership.

As Grenadians learned, the revolution was for freedom, for the improvement of schools and villages, for the building of roads and the establishment of farming cooperatives, and for bringing women's rights to the fore. The revolution was for renewed pride in Grenadian music, dance, theater, and literature, for a more expansive understanding of Grenada's radical history. The anti-imperialist, social-democratic vision of the revolution cannot be separated, however, from the means through which this vision was pursued and some of the more troubling outcomes it produced. The Grenada Revolution, while freedom-making, also carried with it a thread of violence visited on some of the most oppressed and vulnerable members of the population—the folks in whose name revolutionary change was sought. Some of these instances of silencing, oppression, and aggression were unique to the revolution and circumstances in Grenada after 1979. Others represented the unintentional continuation of patterns of oppression first visited on Grenadians during the colonial period. As Grenadians tried to focus on the progressive values espoused by the NJM, they also learned that revolution could continue the subordination of women's voices, the silence around sexual difference and queerness, and the generational conflict between the older "Gairyites" and the younger radicals. This last kind of conflict set up the expectation that new, modern forms of revolutionary knowledge, including Marxism, could replace wisdom passed down from elders and ancestors. Grenadians also learned that the People's Revolutionary Government (PRG), led by Bishop, would harass its critics. Between 1979 and 1983, Bishop signed orders for hundreds to be imprisoned without trial.

The end of the revolution traumatized Grenada and, arguably, the entire anglophone Caribbean. At least seventeen Grenadians were killed on Fort Rupert on October 19, and as many as 160 were killed during the invasion. These numbers are estimates only, as several persons were reported missing around this time and never found. During the invasion, nineteen Americans were killed. Estimates of Cubans killed range from twenty-five to seventy-one.²⁸ The bodies of Bishop and eight other

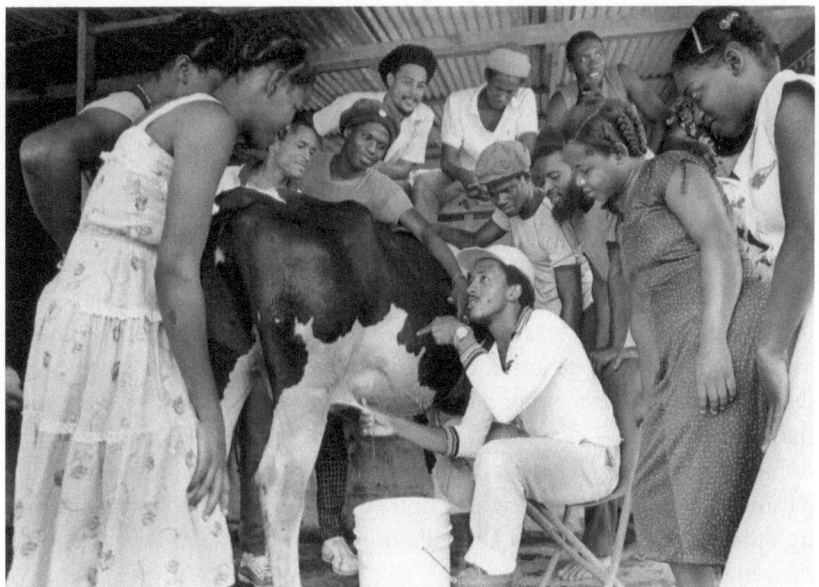

**Figure 2.** Students receive agricultural science training at Mirabeau Farm School, St. Andrew's, Grenada. (© Kathy Sloane, courtesy of the photographer)

ministers have never been recovered.[29] While the death count may seem small relative to other instances of political violence, for an island of 100,000 people it was horrific. Many of the nation's best and brightest minds were either dead or imprisoned. The revolution that was once a source of pride was now a disgrace, and a distinct sense of shame and trauma dominated its literary imaginary. But long before the U.S. invasion, the revolution brought an increased focus on militarization, which served to prepare Grenadians to defend their right to revolution but also became a source of aggression, in some cases disrupting existing family structures as parents became concerned about the militia training their teenage children were receiving. Detentions and physical abuse at the hands of the PRA were part of how the revolutionaries maintained their authority.[30]

To study this revolution and its effects requires examining this thread of fear flowing through and alongside Grenada's radical politics if we are to understand how revolutionary authority was constructed and maintained in Grenada, as well as how it collapsed. State-sponsored violence was not the exclusive practice of the PRG, however. Before 1979 Gairy had been responsible for similar violations. This was, therefore, a pattern that had carried over from colonial governance to the postcolonial governance of Grenada.[31] The pattern of violation and silencing that undergirded aspects of the Grenada Revolution was symptomatic of a form of structural violence that arose as a result of and in response to colonial violence.[32] If we acknowledge that a particular violence and trauma stem from imperialism, then we must also recognize the different but related violence and trauma that stem from revolution as a response to imperialism. The murder of Bishop by members of his own military presented the Caribbean with the unavoidable reality that the Grenada Revolution was both freedom-making and traumatic. This fratricidal outcome to an internal party conflict was a sign of the corruptive potential of revolution and power. On the one hand, revolution was a collective process of self-determination. On the other hand, the conditions of revolution were such that an individual's rights and dignity could be violated at any time, if doing so was deemed by the leadership to serve the greater good of the nation. The leadership's fear of failure and the threat of destabilization by the U.S. government led Grenadian leadership to keep a tight grip on the reins of power.

In the daily life of Grenadians living through the revolution, these circumstances combined to create what the anthropologist Veena Das, writing about Partition in India, calls an "ecology of fear in everyday life."[33] This experience of fear is itself a form of violence and complicates the narrative of revolution as entirely freedom-making. It is my contention that it is experienced more vividly by women when the structure of a society remains fundamentally patriarchal, as it did during the Grenada Revolution. This form of violence surfaces not only as bodily harm but also as the experience of having one's voice violated or deemed suspect by the state. This is what Das calls a denial of "context."[34] Throughout the course of the Grenada Revolution, the denial of context for the voices of some citizens was waged in the name of protecting the revolution. If you were not explicitly pro-revolution or if you questioned or critiqued the actions of the government, you could be targeted for surveillance, censorship, or detention.

That this revolution is part of a relatively recent Caribbean history means that many of the participants are still alive today. However, some who witnessed it, including key figures in the NJM, have been reticent about pivotal aspects of the political process. Attempts to recount the past are still unbearably painful for some. Shame ensures unbroken silences around various parts of the history. In the face of this shame and silence, creative literature offers maps to a political period that thus far has resisted the conventions of historical narration.[35] This literature is not a substitute for history but rather a constitutive part of the story of the Grenada Revolution, helping readers understand how the revolution has been remembered, ignored, and in some ways forgotten.[36] Especially people wish to forget its violent ending. Long before the horrific assassination of Bishop in October 1983, however, violence surfaced in many ways in the daily lives of the women who lived the revolution. Women's writings thus help readers confront the effects of this quotidian violence while putting into context the more publicly acknowledged betrayal of Bishop's death.

In analyzing Caribbean women's writing on the Grenada Revolution, it becomes apparent that living through this violence over a sustained period of time and passing it down to the next generation leads to patterns of repression and festering psychic wounds.[37] These wounds are opened again and again with each new violation or memory of past violation. They are seemingly unable to heal. They can cause the development of certain kinds of disruptive behavior. Trauma in this Caribbean context is linked to several violent histories and their legacies. These histories include the genocide of the indigenous peoples who first inhabited the region's islands, the slave trade and plantation complex, and indentured servitude. These histories inspired forms of resistance such as warfare, suicide, and infanticide, which themselves added to the suffering of oppressed communities even as they produced certain freedoms. In other words, the atrocities of the plantation and its legacies, combined with the decolonization process, have compounded the experiences of collective trauma in the region.

Accounting for the pain the Grenada Revolution visited on so many Caribbean people requires taking on trauma studies from a postcolonial perspective.[38] Conventional trauma studies, with canonical work by Cathy Caruth, Shoshana Felman, and Dori Laub, among others, fails to think through trauma outside a Eurocentric framework. In response to the limitations of this work, postcolonial trauma studies aim to move away from the Eurocentric, event-based school of thought, known to focus heavily on Freudian psychoanalysis.[39] Instead, postcolonial trauma studies interrogate the historical and political contexts that determine what gets recognized as trauma, calling attention to the power imbalances created by colonialism. This work analyzes how trauma unfolds as a process over time. It adopts a more sociological approach that does not rely on techniques derived from deconstruction or psychoanalysis to state its case. Under the rubric of postcolonial or decolonial trauma studies, scholars have considered different methods for dealing with trauma, such as examining the roles of religion, spirituality, and ritual in trauma recovery, particularly in non-Western societies.[40] Postcolonial trauma studies shift the focus away from the individualized experience of trauma to the collective experience, which is critical to survivors of the Grenada Revolution, whose unfolding process affected a nation and a region.

The "top-down" approach to political authority used by the NJM as it executed its initial coup produced both fear and enthusiasm in different sectors of the Grenadian public. In *Caribbean Revolutions and Revolutionary Theory: An Assessment of Cuba, Nicaragua and Grenada*, first published in 1993, Brian Meeks determines that the secrecy that pervaded the NJM's initial plans for the revolution also affected the party's maneuvers in those final months as government leadership deteriorated.[41] Notwithstanding the parish council meetings the revolutionary government set up across the island to promote participatory democracy and receive local feedback on plans for infrastructure and development, the party often obscured its goals and workings from the Grenadian public. In his analysis, Meeks, who was a participant-observer of the revolution, draws attention to the physical exhaustion that fell on the NJM leadership as its exclusivity and secrecy meant that much of the organizational work of the revolution was taken on by a small cadre of the NJM vanguard. Meeks identifies "the deeply-entrenched structure of hierarchy" within the NJM as one of the key components of its downfall, and links it to a failure on the part of the NJM leaders to fully distance themselves from the models of political authority previously practiced in Grenada.[42] I am similarly interested in the persistence of practices of authority that echo the patriarchal order of colonialism because the recurrence of this oppressive form transformed Grenadians' affective responses to the end of the revolution. This transformation shows up in the creative literature in the characters' sense of déjà vu regarding this kind of violence, which in some cases renders them able to anticipate in advance how the revolution might unfold. The retrospective work of narrativizing this history in literature presents a further entanglement for the figure of recurring traumatic oppression as it depends in part on memory, which is its own form of recurrence.

Shalini Puri's *The Grenada Revolution in the Caribbean Present: Operation Urgent Memory*, published in 2014, strikes at the heart of public memory of the revolution. She analyzes monuments, graffiti, calypso, literature, and geography as archives of the revolution's complex legacies. Puri builds a balanced examination of the revolutionary process that attends as much to the parts of the revolution that warrant memorial as it does to the aspects that beg critique. Foundational to her inquiry is a refusal of the generic categories most conveniently at hand for narrativization—epic, romance, or tragedy—to conceptualize Grenada. Instead she draws on metaphors of stone, hurricane, and straits, putting the geography of the region to work in identifying local frameworks for the particularities of remembrances this revolution has wrought. While David Scott's embrace of tragedy to understand related issues of memory in *Omens of Adversity: Tragedy, Time, Memory, Justice,* also published in 2014, presents a contrast to Puri's approach, I share with both these writers an interest in the temporal binds that seem to foreclose on the possibilities the revolution promised. Underlying Scott's analysis is an effort to grasp how and why the antisocialist sentiment that has dominated politics in the West for much of the late twentieth century and early twenty-first century has stymied our ability to offer a fair evaluation of Grenada's revolutionary period. Moving deftly among philosophy, literature, history, and politics, Scott argues that the American imperialist drive for transitional justice puts Grenadians, and Caribbean people more broadly, in the conflicting position of renouncing their radical past in order to embrace a neoliberal world order. Before arriving at this point, however, Scott works through the theoretical equations that mark the hopeful beginnings of the revolution as "messianic time," the immediate collapse as "catastrophic time," and the tragic aftermath of its end as "ruined time." For Scott, the revolution's multiple temporal logics are central to the hold it has on the collective Caribbean psyche.[43] Plotting how these temporal modes affect different generations of Caribbean people, he traces the cycles of colonial and postcolonial violence that repeat themselves and resurface in the revolution and in representations of the revolution.

In the pages that follow I argue that this repetition is structured specifically by a patriarchal order and that an analysis of gender and sexuality is key to articulating the complexity of what transpired in Grenada during those four and a half years. *Comrade Sister* thus focuses on gender and sexuality as central to the analysis of the Grenada Revolution and its literary representations, thinking through the different roles women take on in this history. I examine the different ways women found joy in the revolution through self-expression, while also recognizing the heavier burden of trauma women bore as they were deemed subordinates to men in both colonial and postcolonial political frameworks. The neglect of women's voices in the public sphere when men dominate journalism and positions of political leadership is also a form of silencing. Even the women who held leadership positions within the NJM were still saddled with domestic work, and this additional burden weakened their ability to move up through the party ranks successfully.[44] Grenadian women of all walks of life were uniquely positioned to see all the ways the revolution itself was in need of revolutionizing. Much can be learned, therefore, from studying how Caribbean women writers grapple with the contradictory character of the Grenada Revolution. By focusing on narratives written by Caribbean women and highlighting the gendered contours of some of the writing on Grenada by Caribbean men, I hope to elucidate how deeply gender affects the way revolution is lived, imagined, and remembered. The representations of revolution under examination here help me illustrate the necessary associations between gender and political trauma. Accounting for the healing and reconstructive contexts that Caribbean people have created to survive so many cycles of colonial and neocolonial oppression and anticolonial resistance requires keen attention to the work of women.

## A Literary Archive of Revolution

There are myriad gaps in the archival documents available on the Grenada Revolution. The reasons for these omissions are not arbitrary. During the American invasion in October 1983, thousands of government documents were destroyed when the island was bombed. The United States seized thousands more documents, returning them to Grenada only more than a decade later, during the administration of U.S. president Bill Clinton. Currently the Grenadian government does not have the resources to archive these materials properly and they are not freely accessible to the public. One must travel to the U.S. National Archives in Maryland to read what survives of these documents. Other colonial records are accessible only in London.

One reason to turn to literature is that creative writers have the ability to create accounts of the revolution that shift readers' attention to perspectives that may have escaped archival preservation. The archive is a patriarchal construct that depends on knowledge production from such sources as courts, newspapers, and government records. These documents are created in places where women have traditionally been underrepresented. Literature affords the possibility of countering the masculinist logic of the archive, and as such, my desire is not to ignore the archive but rather to read alongside it. Read together with oral histories and archival sources, the creative literature of the Grenada Revolution offers new ways to interpret the contradictions and silences inherent in Grenada's political history. These texts contribute to our historical understanding of the revolutionary period in Grenada by drawing our attention to the very limits of historical convention and the necessary dialogue between memory, historical narrative, and literary imaginaries. Literature provides images and speculative directions for how new archives might be constructed and read in places like Grenada, where the violent trauma of imperialism silenced key populations in some instances and rendered the historical record opaque in others. Literature captures the cadence and quality of Grenadian voices; it shows readers how the revolution changed intimate spaces and relationships; and it acknowledges the everyday people who lived and shaped the revolutionary process. It recognizes the contributions of women and the complexities of gender in shaping revolutionary spaces and ideas. This is vital work that makes sense of this revolution and redefines the kinds of narratives of revolution we produce to understand Caribbean life. The attention to multiple viewpoints means there is no one master narrative to be sought; rather, there are many stories to be heard and countless hopes and fears to be accounted for in any retelling of the Grenada Revolution. By accepting multiple narratives and genres as a guiding principle rather than viewing them as a roadblock to storytelling, I acknowledge that Caribbean writers have located a rich literary response to the problems presented by the Grenada Revolution's complex archival sources. This literature is not only a response to the archive. It is an invitation to reevaluate the methods by which we think through Caribbean history.

Dionne Brand's *Chronicles of the Hostile Sun,* published in 1984, was the first literary text about the revolution that I read. Picking this book up in my early twenties was a revelation because I felt for the first time that the contradictions in my family's oral histories about the period finally made sense. The messiness of the U.S. involvement in Grenada and the tensions between north and south are fully explored in her writing. Brand's narratives of the revolution cross borders, with connections running far north to the Canadian cityscapes of Toronto and Ottawa and back south to Cuba and Trinidad. She is interested in how black women live these diasporic connections. In her work, revolution is as much about gender equality and sexual freedom as it is about workers' rights and the promotion of democratic socialism. Writing about a revolution that had no public stance on the rights of queer people, Brand explores relationships between women who love other women, making same-sex love visible.

Joan Purcell's writing highlights the experiences of a woman who moves into politics in the wake of the revolution. In contrast to Collins and Brand, Purcell writes from the perspective of someone who was wary of the revolution for almost its entire duration. She occupies a position of lower-middle-class respectability and religiosity. She writes as a politician, having held political office in Grenada in various roles after 1983. Central to Purcell's political and spiritual struggle is her gender identity, and her writing is filled with references to how being a woman had a specific impact on her ability to lead in government. She fulfills, in many ways, Hodge's earlier call for meaningful roles for women in elected office; however, she is not a leftist vision of black feminism. Still, her voice is necessary to help develop a picture of the diverse perspectives held by women who lived through the revolution. Her combination of political engagement and evangelical Christianity stands opposite the secularism of the PRG, but it plays a tremendous role in how she managed key parts of the aftermath of the revolution on behalf of Grenadians. When Brand and Collins approach spirituality, it is as a way of appreciating the land and connecting the realm of the living to the realm of the ancestors. Purcell is explicitly religious, however, and brings evangelical Christianity to every aspect of her work and home life. As a result, she sees many of the changes both in her life and in the nation as a matter of divine intervention.

Few archival texts could give readers the same kind of access to women's lives in Grenada during the periods represented in the work of these writers. The authors offer significant and necessary revisions of the dominant narratives of the Grenada Revolution, and of the black radical tradition more broadly. They use their authorial power to narrate subjects who too often fall out of the frame of black radicalism and political trauma as imagined in their most frequently circulated forms. Analyzing these works through a Caribbean feminist lens, I see a challenge to the heroic masculinity trope so prevalent in writing on Caribbean revolutions. This literary archive highlights how women have had to create their own spaces (discursive and otherwise) in the midst of revolution. It shows how Caribbean radical politics has depended on the labor of women even as this labor has been ignored and many Caribbean women have been let down. The texts I consider underscore the importance of new ways of thinking about the culture and politics of Caribbean revolution. By demonstrating what feminist visions of radicalism look like, authors such as Brand and Collins revise and renew the Caribbean and black radical traditions.

I am also interested in the diversity in form and expression of gender politics more broadly in the literature of the revolution. To this end I include the work of George Lamming, Andrew Salkey, and Derek Walcott, as their work too illuminates the interplay of gender and revolution.

These male writers are of a different generation from that of Brand, Collins, and Purcell. While their writing on Grenada is at times constrained by their own assumptions about masculinity and revolutionary authority, the fact that they are men does not mean that their work is not at times engaged with feminist principles or the illumination of important gender critiques. The gender and generational differences are hugely important in how they respond to the Grenada Revolution. Moreover, the generational difference means that the male writers I discuss have a unique relationship to colonial authority. Though Lamming, born in 1927, Salkey, born in 1928, and Walcott, born in 1930, are of the same generation, they came from different islands, and their political stances varied, from full support of the revolution to open disdain for it. From each of them we learn something different about Caribbean gender politics broadly, and black masculinity in particular. These men were part of a Caribbean literary establishment even before the revolution began. As adults they witnessed the transition from colonialism to decolonization and the arrival of the postcolonial period in the Caribbean. Lamming had the closest relationship to the PRG, traveling to Grenada during the revolution and speaking at conferences there. It is not clear whether Salkey ever traveled to Grenada during the period; however, his writing makes clear that he was an admirer of Bishop and felt strongly that the U.S. invasion was a gross violation of the country's sovereignty. Walcott was the most ambivalent about the state of affairs in Grenada. He despised the PRG's detention of individuals without trial, particularly writers such as the journalist Leslie Pierre. Walcott did not travel to Grenada during the revolution because he disdained the government, finding it authoritarian. Nonetheless, after 1983 he wrote scathingly of the U.S. invasion and lamented the misrepresentation of Grenada in American media.

During the 1970s and 1980s, American neocolonialism limited the effectiveness of revolution as a gateway to political sovereignty in the Caribbean. When the Grenada Revolution failed and the U.S. military invaded the island, Caribbean writers confronted the reality of entrenched imperialist power in the postcolonial Caribbean. Brand, Collins, Lamming, Purcell, Salkey, and Walcott each made multiple attempts to write about the revolution, searching for new ways to represent the trauma of imperialism and the resistance it inspired. That these writers all made multiple attempts to narrate Grenada shows that the revolution contains many histories and there is no one way to tell its stories, while underscoring that in the end, the Grenada Revolution represented a failure that requires frequent revisiting to unpack all its lessons. For writers working through silence and trauma, repetition is a useful tool. The writers I consider have written about Grenada again and again, often in more than one genre, performing a kind of literary repetition "compulsion."[45] It is as though they were searching for the literary genre best suited to the representation of multiple layers of colonial and revolutionary violence. This form of repetition bears witness to the trauma of the revolution by acknowledging the incompleteness of the political process and the fact that the Caribbean will never know what the full potential of the Grenada Revolution might have looked like. For future generations and those too young to have their own memories, these texts are an important part of the revolution's postmemory. Writing about the impact of the Holocaust on the children and grandchildren of survivors, the literary critic Marianne Hirsch describes how the past can resurface even for those who did not experience it directly or who learned of it only secondhand. These memories arise as "traumatic fragments of events that still defy narrative reconstruction and exceed comprehension."[46] In the literature of the Grenada Revolution, repetition signals the ongoing search for answers to questions such as "What went wrong?" and "Where do we go from here?" These authors use literature to point up the structural violence of Caribbean pasts that ought never to be repeated, mapping a vision of Caribbean futures in literary consciousness.

Evidence of this transgenerational trauma can be found in the repetition of colonial violence and violation. An example is the way Grenadians welcomed the U.S. invasion—what else could that reflect but sustained pressure to accept that they were not capable of managing their own affairs; that another country could best decide what they needed, and should take control of providing (or withholding) those needs? If there was not a deep-seated manipulation involved in that process of stripping a nation of its sovereignty, then the U.S. military would have had no need for the psychological operations—PSYOPS, in military parlance—it deployed to convince Grenadians that the invasion was for their own good. The ambivalence that Grenadians confront in this legacy is also part of the trauma, I would argue—the inability to have complete control of the narratives of their own revolution, the pain of seeing that narrative determined partly by a foreign superpower. The creative literature of Caribbean writers directly addresses these traumas. They wrest the narrative from the hands of the (neo)colonial powers, reclaiming it for Caribbean voices.

In these contexts, trauma accompanies the serial experience of violence. Here trauma is a result not only of colonialism or neocolonialism but also of revolution as the response to colonial oppression. What gets pushed out of consciousness is what members of oppressed populations do to each other during times of revolutionary struggle. The fratricide with which the revolution ended makes it impossible to ignore this aspect of radicalism. A reading of trauma and the Grenada Revolution, however, must extend beyond the revolution's final days. The trauma experienced at the end of the revolution is not simply about its tragic end but also the collective, cumulative experience of repeated tragic endings, this being but one. My intention, therefore, is not to deny the "joyous and creative process" of the revolution but rather to locate its place in a cyclical history of radicalism that is structurally tied to political violence and trauma.[47] In my research, political trauma is explicitly linked to previously silenced voices as they find space to articulate the pain of revolutionary or post-revolutionary violence. Often these instances of violence co-occur with the revolution and are directed at the people fighting for, or at the very least in favor of, the revolution. The agents of this violence are often other revolutionary authorities. This violence curbs the agency of revolutionary subjects and witnesses, threatening their freedom of movement and expression during and in the immediate aftermath of the Grenada Revolution.[48] In Grenada, as in other struggles for decolonization, oppression within the context of revolution frequently has a disproportionate effect on women because of the patriarchal structure of both colonial and postcolonial authority.

The dualism embedded in revolution created a common predicament across the global south as the promise of anticolonialism gave way to postcolonial societies that often replicated forms of oppression initially introduced by the former colonizers. Caribbean revolution is an anticolonial political formation in which this recursion to forms of oppression is evident even as freedom is being sought. After the Haitian Revolution, Henri Christophe sent newly emancipated Haitians to work in backbreaking conditions to build the Citadelle Laferrière in 1805, an imposing fort designed to protect their freedom from the threat of French invasion. The labor conditions were terrible. Despite their initial support of the revolution, many Afro-Cubans continue to face deeply entrenched racism in Cuba, a reality that the Communist Party of Cuba has struggled to address for decades.[49] In some cases, gay men in Cuba have been incarcerated to "protect" the rest of the population from HIV/AIDS.[50] These histories remind us that revolution can simultaneously represent both a radical break from and a return to oppressive sources.

The duality of revolution is undeniably present in the work of the writers I consider in this book. Beginning in 1984, the year after the U.S.

invasion of Grenada, these authors would begin to write the revolution in multiple genres, as if the simultaneous narratability and unnarratability of the Grenada Revolution pushed them into a mode of revision. In form and content, their writings repeatedly represent the revolution as a lost entity that can never be recovered. The anthropologist David Scott has described this ongoing sense of a lack of closure as evidence of "an aftermath without end."[51] The sense of what constitutes an aftermath is different, however, for each of these writers. Some narrate stories of perseverance in the aftermath of the revolution while others are unable to see its end as anything but tragic failure. All are concerned with what forms of sovereignty can exist after 1983.

## Caribbean Radicalism: Revolutions for the Region and Its Diaspora

The Grenada Revolution began optimistically, led by a cadre of young, gifted, and black intellectuals. These revolutionaries were influenced by socialist-inspired movements, including Pan-Africanism, the Cuban Revolution, and the Non-Aligned Movement. They came to power through a coup in the early morning of March 13, 1979, while Grenada's first prime minister, Eric Matthew Gairy, was out of the country. By midday they had seized police stations around the island, and used the radio station to reassure Grenadians that this was a peaceful takeover. The NJM leader, Maurice Bishop, became Grenada's second prime minister through this coup. This was the first self-proclaimed revolution in the anglophone Caribbean. The NJM formed the PRG, which remained in power until October 19, 1983, when Bishop and seven others were assassinated by members of their own armed forces, the PRA. Days later, on October 25, 1983, U.S. Marines invaded the island. The American invasion of Grenada was another first in the anglophone Caribbean.

It is helpful to place the Grenada Revolution in the context of the black radical tradition because this is the way its participants understood themselves—connected to legacies of anticolonial and anti-imperialist resistance across the African diaspora.[52] The temporal relations that surface under the analytic of *tradition* are important not only for understanding how past movements pave the way for future uprisings but also for reevaluating past radical movements based on new information proffered by more recent events. The Caribbean radical tradition, which has included Caribbean people of Asian descent and mixed-race Caribbean people, is closely enmeshed with, and a subset of, the black radical tradition. The NJM meeting minutes from May 1974 note that the party members celebrated African Liberation Day and paid tribute to black nationalist (and Grenadian descendant) Malcolm X.[53] During that same meeting, NJM delegates discussed the Sixth Pan-African Congress, scheduled to take place in Tanzania later that month. The efforts of delegates, including Bishop, to attend the congress were thwarted by the Gairy government working in concert with the United States.[54] African Liberation Day was also celebrated during the revolution, including at one of the PRG's victory rallies in May 1979.[55] Newspaper articles and speeches from during this time cite Grenada's connection to the Haitian Revolution (via Henri Christophe, a former slave and one of Haiti's first monarchs, who is said to have been born in Grenada).[56]

The PRG received support from the People's National Congress and the Working People's Alliance in Guyana, the Workers' Party of Jamaica and the People's National Party in Jamaica, and extensive assistance from the Cuban government throughout the revolution. The PRG was also linked to activist groups from University of the West Indies campuses in Trinidad and Jamaica. This spectrum of support reflects activists from the Black Power movement, the labor movement, and socialists. The revolution responded to uniquely Caribbean concerns while being part of conversations generated throughout the global south but circulating transnationally via diasporic circuits. These conversations were about the intersection of racism and colonialism, and the roles of writers and activists outside the Caribbean. In some ways the dialogue picked up where the West Indies Federation left off in terms of figuring a regional Caribbean identity rooted in a rejection of neoliberal and neocolonial discourse. At the same time, however, many of the players involved were deeply committed to a sense of nationalism, having only recently won independence.

The NJM was eager to flout certain political norms, such as the Westminster system of democracy the country had inherited from Britain, in order to pursue a third way, namely, socialism. The NJM founded the Centre for Popular Education (CPE), whose cornerstone initiative was a literacy campaign that used locally produced texts instead of British primers. These texts presented students with explicitly Caribbean scenarios for learning. The CPE was one of the NJM's various initiatives to promote the revolution that relied on local literature and folk arts.[57] To further their goals, NJM leaders also created the National In-Service Teacher Education Program, designed to boost the skill level and qualifications of the nation's teachers. Grenadian writers such as Christopher DeRiggs, Jacob Ross, Francis Urias Peters, and Merle Collins were part of this new generation. They drew inspiration from the way the PRG promoted the arts. This emphasis on cultural production as part of revolutionary struggle was a part of a diasporic circulation of ideas about how to build black and third world radical movements. Several writers of Caribbean descent who were living in the diaspora were also deeply moved by news they heard of the Grenada Revolution.

"Grenada Revisited: An Interim Report" is the final essay in Audre Lorde's *Sister Outsider* and a striking example of the intersecting agendas of black and Caribbean radical visions. Born in New York City to a Grenadian mother, Lorde took a special interest in Grenada in part because of her familial connections, but also because she saw the Grenada Revolution as a world historical event for African Americans. In "Grenada Revisited," written in the aftermath of the invasion, she reminds her readers of the value of the revolution as a symbol of the cultural and political sovereignty possible, if only fleetingly, when a black nation organizes itself against imperialism. She links a critique of the U.S. invasion and the violence America inflicted on Grenada with a critique of racism and imperialism *within* the United States, writing, "In addition to being a demonstration to the Caribbean community of what will happen to any country that dares to assume responsibility for its own destiny, the invasion of Grenada also serves as a naked warning to thirty million African-americans.

**Figure 3.** Teachers receive pedagogical training as part of the National In-Service Teacher Education Program (NISTEP), St. George's, Grenada. (© Kathy Sloane, courtesy of the photographer)

Watch your step. We did it to them down there and we will not hesitate to do it to you. Internment camps. Interrogation booths. Isolation cells hastily built by U.S. occupation forces. Blindfolded stripped prisoners. House-to-house searches for phantom Cubans. Neighbors pressured to inform against each other. No strange gods before us."[58] Lorde reflects on the imbrication of U.S. foreign policy with third world politics and the systemic devaluation of black lives domestically. In her view, the Grenada Revolution ought to be a key concern for African Americans because the U.S. invasion demonstrated their government's fear of black power and disregard for black life. Her writing on Grenada is part of a broader black internationalist politics that understands revolution as a diasporic formation, distinctly Caribbean and undeniably black. Encoded in this passage is a vision of solidarity—her description of the terror visited on Grenadians is a call to action for African Americans and Caribbean people to collectively reject American racism and imperialism in a postrevolutionary movement. This movement is inspired by women. "I hear my mother's voice," she writes, "'Island women make good wives. Whatever happens, they've seen worse.'" Alongside her mother's maxim, Lorde adds "and they have survived colonizations before."[59] Alluding to prior moments of resistance and survival, she defines revolution as an ongoing project that reinvents itself to respond to shifting iterations of empire across black and Caribbean worlds. Marginalized by both their race and gender, black women, she argues, are uniquely positioned to articulate these reinventions because they are familiar with multiple axes of oppression.

A Marxist sense of revolution—that is, "the violent overthrow of the ruling class and the seizure of power through control of the means of production by a class to whom such control was previously denied"—was very important to the leaders of the NJM.[60] The party was united in its goal to bring sweeping changes to the governance of Grenada. Underlying their activism was a critique of capitalist modes of doing business that were unfavorable to the vast majority of Grenadian workers. They had support from small business owners, who were frustrated with Gairy's self-serving, bullying tactics. This was the situation under which the NJM came to power and enjoyed broad support throughout the nation. Strictly defined, the events of March 13, 1979, when the NJM seized power from Gairy, amounted to an illegal change of government—essentially a coup. But in their vision, youthful audacity, and the popular support they enjoyed from the Grenadian public, the NJM leaders represented a radical shift from what Gairy's two decades in power symbolized. There was an excitement for the public in hearing the word "revolution" used to describe what was taking place in its midst. There was also uncertainty, shock, and silence for those who were apprehensive about the change revolution promised and concerned about the means through which this change was being pursued.

In its commitment to the unfinished business of decolonization, the NJM embodied another definition of revolution: the idea of revolution as a "circular movement" or "cyclical recurrence." Even the NJM leadership spoke of the 1979 revolution as a continuation of the 1950s political project that brought adult suffrage and improved wages for agricultural workers; the leaders simply neglected to mention that the 1950s movement was led by Gairy. This second definition, revolution as repetition, is salient to the study of the Grenada Revolution as part of a radical tradition. While most frequently applied in the fields of astronomy and physics, this definition helps to place events in Grenada in their cultural and historical contexts. These contexts are not simply linear, teleological histories but rather a more complex set of temporal relations that lays the groundwork for thinking through the implications of Grenada in multiple directions. Recognizing revolution as repetition recasts previously accepted conclusions about other revolutionary movements, including Gairy's labor movement, the Cuban and Haitian revolutions, and the Black Power movement, as it repeats and extends the black radical tradition. It signals what is possible for the future. Reading the Grenada Revolution both as a radical break and as an example of cyclical recurrence opens space for an analysis that sees Caribbean revolution not as a linear set of events or as the staging of ideological dichotomies but as a dynamic political formation in pursuit of sovereignty.

Sovereignty for the revolutionaries meant self-determination in the economic, social, political, and cultural matters of the nation. It was the power to create an economic path that rejected the inequities of capitalism and U.S. neocolonialism. Sovereignty meant pride in Grenadian cultural forms—language, music, theater, and dance. It meant the right to adopt democratic socialism as a more equitable alternative for a nation fighting for the right to claim its place on a world stage on its own terms. Sovereignty also included the right to exist in solidarity with other Caribbean nations and formerly colonized nations around the globe that were working toward similar goals. In *Non-Sovereign Futures,* Yarimar Bonilla challenges the relevance of the Westphalian mode of sovereignty for contemporary Caribbean societies. She argues that the Caribbean is home to a set of political histories that highlight the limitations presented by the categories of freedom and sovereignty. Working from the idea of nonsovereignty, Bonilla's study of French Caribbean politics traces the widespread disenchantment with ideas of national independence while uncovering the unexpected ways in which Caribbean labor activists conceptualize their power "within and against the constraints of postcolonial sovereignty."[61] In a corresponding manner, I am interested in how gender affects the ways that sovereignty is imagined and experienced in the literature of the Grenada Revolution. Several decades after its collapse, the Grenada Revolution is critical to conversations about sovereignty in Caribbean studies because it remains a vivid example of the quest for radical political change. The literature that is produced in the wake of this revolution often questions what is left of the idea of sovereignty following the American invasion. For Grenadians and other Caribbean people who supported the Grenada Revolution, the NJM's work represented a moment of reimagining what the fullness of freedom could look like in the region. For some, the end of the revolution threw the promise of the earlier moment into crisis. But for others, the limitations of the freedom promised by the revolution were a given, all but ensuring that the process of defining and redefining one's relationship to sovereignty would necessarily continue past the life span of any particular political movement. Being caught in the crosshairs of Cold War conflict only hastened the transition from one historical moment to the next.

The Cold War undoubtedly influenced the direction the revolution took—both in the agenda of the PRG and in the response of the United States and surrounding Caribbean nations. Yet there are ways to read the revolution (and its representations) that reflect attempts of Caribbean people to opt out of the Cold War and attend to more locally centered concerns. The tensions arising from these contradictory characteristics (newness/cyclicality, commitment to Marxism/commitment to the particularities of Caribbean life elided by Marxist theory) contributed to the successes and failures of the revolution and, ultimately, the trauma it caused the Caribbean psyche. The full range of these experiences is borne out in the literary imaginary. By focusing on this literature I am able to connect the cyclicality of revolution and the effects of repeated experiences of political trauma with the insights that women writers provide into how best to intervene in such cycles to reduce the harm that often occurs as a by-product of revolution.

## "Feminist" Beginnings

Bishop once said that the revolution was about creating a new man and a new woman. His government championed women's rights in a way they had not been championed before. Official policies such as the 1980 Maternity Leave Law promoted women's equality by helping women keep their jobs in between birthing and raising children. By making secondary education more affordable, the PRG also helped support poor families. Women working within the PRG and NJM, including Minister of Education Jacqueline Creft, representative to the Organization of American States Dessima Williams, President of the National Women's Organization (NWO) Phyllis Coard, and NWO executive members Claudette Pitt and Tessa Stroude represented a new generation of women leaders playing a key role in revolutionary politics. Writers such as Brand, Collins, Christine David, and Merle Hodge were more active within literary and political arenas than the women writers and politicians who had come before them.[62] Their work and the work of others like them helped increase the overall visibility of women engaged in political activism in the public sphere. Within the private sphere, however, women continued to struggle with societal expectations around traditional gender roles. Even within the households of the few women who formed part of the NJM leadership, women were expected to do a full load of party work while keeping up with child care and traditional housework.[63]

Grenada's revolution was a response to an incomplete transition from colonial dependence to postcolonial independence, and a rethinking of the principles that guided the independence movement. Women's voices are at the center of the literary response to the Grenada Revolution as gender inequality was a big part of the work left undone during independence. The public recognition of women as political beings was central to the rhetoric of the revolution and the spirit of the times. For example, articles from the *Torchlight,* one of the most widely read newspapers in Grenada during the late seventies, show how pivotal women were to political discourse during the revolution and yet how challenging it was to tease out their perspectives in the public sphere. In June 1979 a women's organization, the St. George's Progressive Women's Association (SGPWA), hosted a National Conference of Women in Grenada. The *Torchlight* published an editorial about the event titled "Local Feminists' Dream" and outlining what the male editor hoped the conference would achieve. The SGPWA was relatively new, having formed two years earlier, and consisted mainly of middle-class women. They had criticized Gairy's government but had also declined to align themselves with the PRG, even as the PRG looked favorably on some of their work.[64] About the women attending the conference, the editor wrote: "Directing the emphasis to our womenfolk in rural areas is particularly refreshing. . . . In spite of a little progress here and there, they [rural women] are not often exposed to serious thinking and progressive ideals. One hundred of them are in attendance as delegates, thus affording the rare opportunity of hearing points of view of prominent and qualified women speakers from Jamaica, Trinidad, Barbados, St. Vincent and our own Grenada. . . . The Conference will then be a learning process helping to raise the level of consciousness of these women to higher stages."[65] The editorial reflects the editor's dim view of rural women and his belief that they had little to offer public discourse. It does not occur to him that rural women, by virtue of their work and life experience, might have worthy contributions to make at a conference for women. He assumes they could participate only as listeners and learners, not as teachers or leaders. He describes the urban women who led the conference as "more developed women, who are themselves actively engaged in the struggle for the improvement of Caribbean women and society."[66] This description indexes the higher socioeconomic status of these "feminist leaders," making their contributions inherently more valuable and visible than those of rural women, in the editor's view. It never occurs to the editor that the learning might move in both directions between women of different classes. The condescension in his response epitomizes the failure of some—both men and women—in positions of cultural and political power to recognize the diversity of women's experiences and the legitimacy of women's concerns across boundaries of class, education, and geography. The editorial also limits the definition of the term "feminist" to exclude rural women.[67] Grenadian women in general were silenced in this editorial penned by a male editor, but the voices of poor women in particular were ignored. The marginalization of these women is normalized in the *Torchlight*'s editorial. The conference organizers may have planned an exchange between women across classes; however, the editorial made it appear as if rural women's voices were not valued. These assumptions reflect a long-standing power imbalance in political organizing and representation whereby a small, educated, or moneyed vanguard is seen as leaders and the lower-class masses are supposed to be followers.

The Grenada Revolution was no different. The vanguard NJM party sought to lead the masses. Even if the masses did not always follow, it is still true that where one patriarchal hierarchy, the neocolonial-style bullying of Eric Gairy, was dismantled, another was erected, the Marxist-Leninist

PRG, led by men educated primarily in the United States and United Kingdom. While the leaders of the NJM were focused on helping the lower class, the government structures they inherited were not particularly friendly to lower-class women. Though espousing the ideals of participatory democracy and socialism, the party leadership was a top-down affair in which the vanguard saw itself as instilling political consciousness in the peasant and working classes. Ironically, to bring a truly democratic form of governance to Grenada, the PRG sometimes had to function in an authoritarian manner. In a situation like this, it can be very difficult for women, and particularly poor women, to seize the political apparatus and shape ideologies. In one sense, the ideology is delivered to the masses ready-made, and their ability to gain status within the party depends on their willingness to adhere to the party line rather than those of poor and rural women. For the most part creative literature on the revolution does not focus on the ministers of government or political leaders who are typically found at the center of historical narratives, pushing readers to consider what is lost when we understand the work of revolution only at the highest levels of political power. Still, it is important to understand at least some of the conventional historical narratives around the Grenada Revolution in order to appreciate the intervention of Caribbean women writers who work to revise these histories.

**Tragic Endings**

The end of the revolution is the part of the history that requires our greatest capacity for entertaining multiple perspectives at once. By the beginning of 1983 an intense fatigue had set in among the PRG and NJM leadership. Despite legislative achievements, the exponential growth of unionized workers, and the formation of workers' and parish councils facilitating grassroots democracy through regular community meetings, the revolution's leadership was still under a tremendous amount of pressure. The leaders faced regional opposition regarding their legitimacy to govern. Other Caribbean Community (CARICOM) governments pressured them to hold elections. Early in the revolution, Bishop had promised that elections would take place soon, but with no elections on the horizon after four years in office, the chance of elections in the near future seemed dim. Among Grenadians the early enthusiasm for community improvement projects in which regular citizens volunteered their time and expertise was waning. While folks would come out in the hundreds to paint and repair schools in 1979, by 1983 it was harder to attract people to these volunteer endeavors. The government faced its greatest economic challenge as aid from foreign governments dipped in response to the global recession. This meant that funds made available for early outreach programs were no longer readily accessible. During September and October 1983 the fatal disintegration of the NJM played out privately at first, before spilling out into the public sphere. Bishop had to confront his own weariness, the exhaustion of the entire party leadership, and its criticism of him, which included charges of lack of discipline, poor organization, and Bishop's alleged womanizing. The NJM's Central Committee called on Bishop to accept an arrangement of joint leadership with then deputy prime minister Bernard Coard. Bishop initially agreed to this arrangement. Though news of the arrangement was not shared openly with the Grenadian public, all members of the party were privy to these changes, and the word spread throughout the nation. On October 8, however, after returning from a trip to Eastern Europe (which included a brief stop in Cuba on the way home), Bishop decided he was no longer in favor of joint leadership. In the following days he felt off-balance enough with the party to suggest to those close to him that his life was under threat, and that Coard and Coard's wife, Phyllis, were planning his death. On October 12 the Central Committee placed Bishop under house arrest. This was meant to censure him for starting the rumor about threats being made against his life. The following day Coard resigned from government.[68] On October 18, several ministers of government who supported Bishop resigned from their positions to express their disagreement with his house arrest.

A large sector of the public was also angered at Bishop's detention. His supporters took to the streets on the morning of October 19, bound for his Mount Wheldale home. A crowd of Grenadians from across the island gathered outside Bishop's home and demanded his release. Among the crowd were high school students who had walked out of class en masse to join the protest for Bishop's release. Overwhelmed by the protesters, and under orders not to resist, the members of the military posted at Bishop's home fired warning shots into the air but did not prevent the throng from surging forward to free Bishop. "We get we leader," the crowd chanted as they brought Bishop out into the street, and impromptu plans were made for him to address the people. At first, they were to convene at the Market Square in the middle of St. George's, but that plan changed suddenly, and Bishop along with an enthusiastic group of supporters switched directions and headed up to Fort Rupert, the army headquarters. At Fort Rupert members of the military confronted Bishop. This was a military installation, they argued, and the crowd was not permitted to enter. He had them disarmed and proceeded to occupy the Operations Room with a group of his supporters. From there he attempted to communicate with the outside world and determine how to address the nation. Present in the Operations Room were soldiers and security forces, schoolchildren, nurses, spouses, and civil servants; civilians and soldiers were also in other parts of the fort. In the meantime, military leaders at nearby Fort Frederick had dispatched soldiers to retake Fort Rupert.

There are at least three versions of what happened next. In one version an armored vehicle was making its way up the hill to recapture Fort Rupert when shots fired from Fort Rupert killed Cadet Conrad Meyers, who was riding on the outside of the vehicle. In another version of the story, as the armored vehicle was making its way up the hill, shots were fired from this vehicle into the fort, and these actions precipitated the gun battle that killed Meyers.[69] In a third version, the shots fired came from the crowd, possibly from planted provocateurs. At stake in the discrepancies of these three versions is the question of who initiated the violence that ensued. Some argue that the minute Bishop decided to head to a military installation as opposed to the Market Square, he set off a deadly chain of events. Others insist that the military should not have turned its guns on the people, no matter the circumstances. What is indisputable is that many people were killed or wounded by gunfire, some falling to their deaths from the steep fort as they tried to avoid the bullets. The military recaptured the fort and released some of the surviving civilians and lower-level government officials, many of whom fled to the hospital for medical attention. Members of the military then forced Bishop to remain at Fort Rupert, along with Fitzroy Bain, Norris Bain, Evelyn Bullen, Jacqueline Creft, Keith Hayling, Evelyn Maitland, and Unison Whiteman. Shortly thereafter they were lined up against a wall and shot dead. Members of the PRA transported the bodies of the prime minister and his comrades to Caliviny, where they were burned and buried in a shallow grave.

In the hours following the assassinations a new organization, the Revolutionary Military Council (RMC), comprising members of the armed forces, announced it was now leading the nation. The RMC placed the island on a round-the-clock, shoot-to-kill curfew. General Hudson Austin was the voice of the RMC, making radio announcements about the curfew. The country was in a state of collective shock and grief. Bishop and others had perished in a gunfight with the military, the RMC announced over the radio. The RMC's statement on the manner of Bishop's death was discredited by word of mouth circulating across the island. This deception complicated even further how the Grenadian people viewed the RMC. How could they trust a new authority that began its tenure by lying about how the beloved prime minister had died? Weren't the RMC people also NJM people? What had happened? The RMC warned the public that an attack by the United States was imminent, that members of the army and the militia should report for duty, and that all citizens should prepare to defend the nation. But the Grenadian military made it very difficult for Grenadians to support them after the assassination of Bishop. Grenadians were caught between two difficult choices—fighting alongside those they deemed responsible for the prime minister's death or allowing the United States to invade without resistance.

In the midst of this chaos, the U.S. military made its move. Acting on President Ronald Reagan's directive, they put in motion Operation Urgent Fury, whose goal was to stamp out the NJM, sending a message to the rest of the Caribbean that alliances with communist Cuba would not be tolerated. Under the dubious public relations cover of an invitation to intervene from neighboring Caribbean governments, as well as the ruse of the State Department's interest in protecting the lives of American medical students at St. George's University, thousands of American soldiers began their descent on Grenada in the early hours of October 25, 1983. In his 2003 memoir, *Survival for Service,* Sir Paul Scoon, who was then the governor-general of Grenada, states that the U.S. government provided him with the letter of invitation authorizing their invasion and that he signed it only after the invasion started.[70] Support for the U.S. invasion came from conservative Caribbean leaders, such as Jamaica's Edward Seaga, and Dominica's Eugenia Charles, who even appeared with Reagan at a press conference.

The fighting lasted four days. The U.S. military dropped bombs on buildings, including the radio station, the prime minister's office at Butler's House, and a hospital for the mentally ill. Grenadian forces fought back from various positions across the island. The United States did not allow any journalists onto the island to cover the invasion until three days into the fighting. Over the course of the four-day assault, and in subsequent weeks, the surviving members of the NJM leadership and others suspected of involvement with the party or the Grenadian military were taken into U.S. custody. The conditions in which they were held were appalling—small wooden boxes kept out in the sun. There are also reports that Grenadians pointed the U.S. forces to the shallow grave where the remains of Bishop and his comrades were buried. A contingent of three hundred soldiers from across the Caribbean (mainly

Jamaica and Barbados) was brought in once most of the fighting was over. It served mainly to provide security across the island after the main fighting had ceased. The UN Security Council decried the invasion and even tried to pass a resolution condemning it; however, this attempt was vetoed by the United States.[71]

In the aftermath of such violence, it is difficult to conjure up an image of revolutionary heroes. In the wake of the violence of October 19, the United States could no longer be characterized simply as the first world bully. Steps taken by the NJM and the Grenadian military in those final weeks of the PRG had laid waste to the idea that the demise of the revolution could ever be pinned solely on American destabilization or interference. Painting Bishop's assassination as the result of a bitter conflict between two opposing political ideologies is tempting; however, those interested in a hagiography of Bishop must also contend with decisions he made to detain others while he was alive, and with the ideological platform he shared with the same people responsible for his death. They agreed with each other more often than they opposed each other. The relative youth and inexperience of the NJM leaders are apparent in this series of fatal missteps. There was no question that the Grenadian people suffered tremendously as the revolution collapsed; however, multiple sources were responsible for that suffering, some much closer to home than others. This history, as far as it can be known, is complex, and should not be reduced to a simple binary. In the uncertainty that followed October 19, many Grenadians welcomed the intervention of the U.S. military, fearing that only American authorities could fix the chaos into which the country had descended; the United States took full advantage of the situation, promoting itself as saving the island from the authoritarian rule of the RMC.

The narrative through-line that defines most journalistic and historical accounts of the Grenada Revolution is the one I have just outlined. It is the narrative that allows us to understand Grenada in a conventional fashion and a linear context; however, it still leaves many questions unanswered and others unasked. The literary works examined in this book defy this convention. While they reference the general contours of this narrative, they also present a people's revolution not easily discernible in traditional archival sources. Turning a literary analytical lens on the political and cultural representation of Grenada ruptures long-standing discourses on Caribbean revolution. These works make apparent visions of revolution with varying senses of narrative and temporality. Here we gain access to the intimate spaces of revolution through personal stories of individual and collective struggle.

## The Structure of This Book

Each of the four chapters (plus conclusion) traces an aspect of the main theme, how the revolution fits into a Caribbean-inflected black radical tradition, while investigating the retraumatizing aspects of that tradition and its limitations in creating conditions of freedom for Caribbean people. Chapter 1, "Generational Ties, Revolutionary Binds: Family as Archive in the Writing of Merle Collins," examines representations of revolution in the novels *Angel*, published in 1987, and *The Colour of Forgetting*, published in 1995. *Angel* explores Grenada's late colonial and early postcolonial history from the vantage point of rural women of modest means, while *Colour* imagines ancestral links between colonial slavery and postcolonial struggles for land ownership. Both novels explore how memories of violent struggle and bloodshed must be passed down for younger generations to successfully navigate current political discord. Collins foregrounds the importance of feminist decolonizing methodologies in achieving Caribbean sovereignty. Her writing, like that of Brand, becomes a critical space for the voices of subaltern women who intervene in Caribbean radicalism but leave little archival trace.

Chapter 2, "After the Invasion: Masculine Authority and the Anxiety of Revolution," examines representations of apprehension about revolutionary ideology and authority in the writing of George Lamming, Derek Walcott, and Andrew Salkey. Lamming's 1982 essay, "The Education of Feeling," and Walcott's 1984 "Good Old Heart of Darkness" capture the anxiety these established writers felt about the new generation of radical men leading the Grenada Revolution. Lamming was a cautious supporter of the revolution, while Walcott was a critic. Salkey's 1995 short story, "After the Counter-Revolution, After the Invasion," set in 1987, envisions a radical future that sees Grenada as host to yet another revolutionary movement, this one led by a working-class family and its allies, but also failing. These writings foreground themes of the survival of Caribbean literary nationalism, the loss of masculine authority, and the (im)possibility of future successful revolts.

Chapter 3, "Comrade, Sister, Lover: Dionne Brand and The Limits of Radical Movements," analyzes the simultaneous experience of sovereignty and nonsovereignty that defines Caribbean postcoloniality in the 1984 poetry collection *Chronicles of the Hostile Sun*, the autobiographical essays in the 1994 *Bread out of Stone,* and the 1996 novel *In Another Place, Not Here*. Brand creates liminal spaces in her writing to account for the messiness of a revolution that was both a success and a failure.

Her oeuvre confirms that any account of the revolution must be told from multiple perspectives. Brand's writing refracts historical events through creative literature in order to invent narratives that center the lives of black women, especially black queer women, whose radicalism may not fit within traditional definitions of Caribbean revolution. She emphasizes the importance of possibility in the experience of transnational black radicalism. Through her writing we can reconceptualize revolution as a series of movements, as opposed to a marked arrival at a single place or ideology. This new formulation sees Caribbean revolution as a dynamic political formation that is both personal and national. In some cases the women she writes about, such as Elizete in *In Another Place,* reject the idea of national politics altogether.

Chapter 4, "Legacies of Mercy: Neoliberalism and the Disavowal of Revolution," analyzes *Memoirs of a Woman in Politics: Spiritual Struggle,* published in 2009 by the Grenadian politician Joan Purcell. An evangelical Christian, Purcell was skeptical of the PRG's politics. After the U.S. invasion she was appointed to a post with the interim government and was charged with making the decision to commute or carry out the death sentences of those found guilty of the assassination of Prime Minister Bishop. Purcell is a contradictory figure whose life and career reveal the limits of and possibilities for radical politics in postrevolutionary Grenada.

A common theme in these works is that revolution is about diasporic kinship and inheritance, about tensions between autochthonous and global influences and between political and spiritual ways of knowing. The questions motivating this project involve the relationship between revolution and nationalism in the anglophone Caribbean, how the project of nation-building changes from the late 1960s and 1970s to the early 1980s, and the shifting importance of a black internationalist vision of Caribbean sovereignty during this time. I analyze how visions of nationalism and internationalism were often situated uncomfortably alongside each other as Grenada moved through various forms of revolution and resistance. Underlying these questions is my investment in bringing Caribbean feminist perspectives to the challenges raised by the Grenada Revolution because these perspectives are uniquely positioned to critique and reread the hegemonic narrative as well as the radical, anti-imperial counternarrative. Both are problematic in their exclusion of women, and when this blind spot is addressed, new ways of thinking about revolution come to the fore. These are ways that see the black radical tradition and Caribbean radical tradition as truly working across generations and genders to secure the well-being of people throughout the diaspora.

# 1 Generational Ties, Revolutionary Binds

Family as Archive in the Writing of Merle Collins

IN A scene from Merle Collins's *Angel*, first published in 1987 (a revised edition was published in 2011), a group of Grenadians are engaged in a parish council meeting, a participatory democracy style of governance promoted by the New Jewel Movement (NJM) whereby government officers were directly responsible to the people within their districts. At this political gathering, however, before a word is spoken about the construction of new roads or access to running water, the meeting chair announces a skit by a women's group and the reading of two poems by members of the community. A woman by the name of Sister Miona Spencer comes to the stage. Collins describes her as middle-aged, dressed in the red and black colors of the revolution, and as a participant in a literacy program, where she has been learning to read.[1] Sister Miona is a rural woman who exhibits a natural affinity for politics. She recites a poem about the 1951 protests led by Leader, and how these events served as a precursor to the 1979 movement led by the Horizon political party. Collins uses the pseudonym "Leader" for Grenada's first prime minister, Eric Gairy, and "Chief" for Maurice Bishop, Grenada's second prime minister and revolutionary leader. "Horizon" is the fictionalization she chooses for the NJM, Bishop's political party. Using rhetoric to move the crowd with the ease of a seasoned politician, Sister Miona begins with a description of Leader's 1951 efforts, alludes to his downfall, and then describes the rise of Horizon and the changes they have brought to her life and the nation as a whole:

> Ay! Well we try it in '51!
> We say come Pa come
> Ting bad for so
> Take up we burden
> We go help you go![2]

In Collins's description of the scene, cheers from the crowd punctuate Sister Miona's performance. Sister Miona's praise poem for the revolution encapsulates a brief history of Leader's radical political movement in the 1950s, when he fought for universal adult suffrage for Grenadians and increased wages for rural laborers. Initially the rural masses supported Leader and he championed their cause. When he dropped their "burden" in order to fatten his own purse, however, they "cant im over." This "canting over" of Leader clears the way for Horizon to seize power and bring opportunities such as free education to Grenadians across generations, including Sister Miona and her grandchildren. The poem establishes a local genealogy for the Grenada Revolution as a radical process that follows, and in some ways grows out of, Leader's previous politics. Sister Miona legitimizes the revolution through her description of the ousting of Leader as a collective endeavor. "*We* cant im over," she insists.

What is critical in Miona's narration is her attention to the trajectory of radicalism and political leadership in Grenada, from Leader's attempt to lead the people in the anticolonial struggle to the ascent of Horizon in the public sphere and Leader's eventual descent:

> De Horizon come up
> Pa star go down!
> An we watchin de Horizon
> Like is really a dream

Sister Miona's status as an elder allows her to hold this double vision of radicalism in Grenada. She has been a participant in both movements and can therefore offer an account of them both. Her poem thus functions as an oral history while at the same time offering her audience some philosophical insight into the shape of Grenada's radical histories. In this poem and in the novel more broadly, Leader's radical movement of the 1950s makes the Grenada Revolution itself legible.

I begin with a reading of this poem embedded in the novel because it is exemplary of the structure of *Angel* and Collins's second novel, *The Colour of Forgetting*, which came out in 1995. In both novels Collins conceptualizes the Grenada Revolution as in a long genealogy of conflict and radical politics. I read *Angel* for its fictionalized representation of the 1979 NJM-led revolution as a response to and a legacy of the 1950s anticolonial struggles, led by Eric Gairy; and *The Colour of Forgetting* for its staging of centuries of conflict from the earliest encounters between the Caribs, the early indigenous island inhabitants, and the French colonizers in the seventeenth century to the revolution in the 1970s. I link the themes of radicalism and repetition by arguing that Collins's novels trace cycles of radicalism in Grenada between the multiple political eras. By narrating the revolution as part of a genealogy in her poem, Sister Miona naturalizes the work of Horizon in a Grenadian political history spanning nearly three decades. Collins does similar work in *Angel* and *Colour,* where she represents revolution as a cyclical construct, emphasizing the Grenada Revolution as part of multigenerational efforts to thwart empire. In both novels Collins's linking of different periods of radicalism is an effort to work out the patterns of colonial resistance in Grenada and the instances of violent trauma that these patterns produce. By the end of each work she arrives at a vision for revising revolution that moves beyond the sense of tragedy that characterizes the final days of October 1983.

Collins refuses to narrate revolution as romance, tragedy, or epic—all genres relying on tropes of masculine heroics that her work rejects.[3] Instead her writing is a disarticulation of these genres as she imagines revolution as a complex series of multigenerational experiences among women, the working class, and the peasantry. Alongside the emphasis on multigenerational struggle, her novels and the poetry of the 2003 *Lady in a Boat* explore the impact of women in particular in predicting and trying to guard against the repetition of tragic errors in anticolonial efforts. When their perspectives are sidelined, women are left to reconcile the aftermath of revolutionary struggle by finding ways of healing and moving on. I read Collins's oeuvre on Grenada as comprising feminist, decolonizing texts that disrupt imperialist epistemologies of linear history and time. Her work functions as an alternative archive, expanding the temporal contexts of the revolution and narrating Grenada's radical history from the points of view of figures that often fall out of conventional archives, which focus on institutions and the powerful men who run them. Her novels set up the problem of thinking revolution and revolt in cyclical time, and her poetry works through ways of reconciling the trauma and shame that accumulate over several generations of political violence. Reading this literature as a historical source, it is possible to see how Collins presents different voices working through colonialism and radicalism, using ancestral knowledge to address the violence and trauma produced by these processes.

## The Doubling of Radical Politics and Violence

Collins wrote her first novel, *Angel,* while she was conducting research in British colonial archives for her dissertation on Caribbean governments.[4]

The novel details Angel's upbringing in rural Grenada, her undergraduate years at the University of the West Indies (UWI), and her return to Grenada as a young teacher. During this time we see the rise and fall of Chief and the building of the Horizon political party with the support of younger Grenadians such as Angel and her brothers. Though much of the novel is dedicated to narrating Angel's coming of age contemporaneously with that of the nation, the novel cannot be accurately described as a *Bildungsroman* because Collins begins with the perspective of Doodsie, Angel's mother. The prominence of Doodsie's voice signals Collins's investment in a multigenerational story. We see Doodsie's own social and political views influencing those of Angel. This idea is echoed in the novel's representation of the similarities between the politics of 1950s colonial Grenada and those of 1970s postcolonial Grenada. Here Collins pushes the beginning of the Grenada Revolution beyond the neat historical time point of March 13, 1979, and into the longer temporal frame of radicalism on the island. In *Omens of Adversity*, the anthropologist David Scott discusses the representation of cycles and generational time in Collins's work on the Grenada Revolution. Analyzing the "allegorical economy" of *Colour*, Scott writes: "The collapse of the Grenada Revolution is conceived not as the catastrophic end of a teleological history of continuous progress but, rather, as merely one significant *episode* in a larger story of generations of conflict in what is now imagined and represented as the cyclical pattern of a general history whose generative logic is catastrophic."[5] The cyclical pattern that Scott identifies in *Colour* is also present in *Angel*, even though I do not read the generative logic of the histories in *Angel* as catastrophic but rather think of Collins's work as focused on the constant need for political struggle and thoughtful dialogue with history. Both novels use the conceit of the familial generation as the primary measure of time while highlighting relationships between characters of different generations in order to narrate local history. For the reader who expects *Angel* to be about the revolution, the novel begins with what feels like a prequel. To see Chief, we must also see Leader, and to understand Angel, we must also understand her mother, Doodsie. Revolutionary time in *Angel* is cyclical. It is a temporal double consciousness that evokes a radical past in order to assert a radical present. In these assertions, however, the voices of women characters often serve to interrupt the cyclical movement by articulating a dis-ease with the present political choices. By articulating their dis-ease, they open up the possibility of imagining other ways forward.

In the novel's opening scene, rural workers watch a local estate burn to the ground.[6] The year is 1951, a period in Grenadian history known as "Sky Red." During that time Eric Gairy, then a union leader and activist, began organizing Grenadian estate workers to demand better wages and improved working conditions. Large segments of Grenada's rural working-class population joined him in strikes and protests before the Grenadian legislature. The protests also involved more clandestine action, such as arson and methods of resistance that can be traced to slavery.[7] In the novel, the opening scene is populated by workers and their families, including Doodsie, and Angel, who is a toddler at the time. Before children like Angel are able to truly process what they are seeing, they are already witnesses to the anticolonial struggle that defines the experiences of their parents. These events will have an impact on their own anti-imperialist struggles in the future. Whether the reader knows, if only vaguely, what is to come, or even has no previous knowledge of Grenada's history, by the end of the novel Collins forces us to hold two moments of political rupture simultaneously, Leader's era overlapping with Chief's, Doodsie's political experiences overlapping with Angel's, as two generations experience radical movements that mirror each other.

By presenting a dual view of history, Collins sets up readers to understand that the end of the Grenada Revolution was not the first instance of the intermingling of radical politics and violence in Grenada. The challenge for Collins, and for readers, is to acknowledge that the benefits of resistance tend to be coupled with elements that are violent and potentially traumatic, even for the beneficiaries of that resistance. Doodsie's mother, Ma Ettie, serves as a reminder of this during this opening scene. Ma Ettie observes Doodsie and Angel that evening, noticing the "strange mixture of fear and acceptance" on Doodsie's face as the estate house burns to the ground. She then utters a prayer as she, Doodsie, and Angel—three generations—enter their home for the night. "Let not our enemies triumph over these your children, Lord. Take a thought to the life and salvation of the little children in that burning house, Lord, and to all your children of this world." Collins is careful not to represent this moment of resistance as one of uncomplicated victory for the workers. As the estate house burns, Ma Ettie's prayer is motivated by concern, mirroring the look on Doodsie's face. The precise enemies and tribulations from which she seeks protection are not named, but it is clear that she has reason to be frightened of both the prevailing colonial elite and those from within the collective of workers resisting that elite, who decided to set the fire. Ma

Ettie and Doodsie are concerned about not being able to make ends meet because of the meager wages their family earns, but they are also troubled by what the burning of the estate house portends. The disregard for life is at the front of Ma Ettie's mind. The children in her prayer are both her fellow workers—children in God's eyes—and the young offspring of the estate owners, children who were likely Ma Ettie's charges when she worked as a housekeeper on the estate. She is disturbed by the violence of political resistance. Other workers depicted in this opening scene appear ambivalent about the burning of the estate house as a mode of resistance. Their silence and apparent discomfort around the fire betray certain misgivings about what implications this anticolonial resistance might have for their society and their concerns about violence.

Another important intergenerational scene of violence and witnessing takes place much later in the novel. The time is October 1983, and the government that led the Grenada Revolution is on the verge of collapse. Reflecting historical events from 1983, the novel depicts the prime minister, Chief, being freed from house arrest by a crowd of spectators, including schoolchildren. At odds with Horizon, his own party, Chief finds he still has the support of the general public. After freeing Chief, a group of civilians carries him to the military installation on a nearby fort. Before long, however, several army tanks approach the fort, and a gunfight ensues between Chief's supporters and the soldiers on the tanks, who support Horizon's Central Committee. The civilians caught up in the chaos are stunned: "The people hadn't moved until the very end. They knew for sure that the soldiers wouldn't shoot them. Until the shots came, . . . On the road below, people rushed by, screaming, hurtling along the road, bending forward, glancing back, mouths parted, eyes wide in faces frozen into silent masks of unbelieving terror."[8] The faces frozen into silent masks represent voices that are violated during this moment of political violence. Most people were in disbelief that the soldiers would turn their weapons against the people. Those witnessing it include schoolchildren, the leaders of the revolution, and the older generation, who would have remembered scenes of violence from the 1950s under Leader.

I juxtapose the 1951 estate burning and the 1983 massacre at the fort to highlight the dialogue Collins sets up in *Angel* among multiple generations experiencing radical violence. Collins represents violence in all its complexity in these scenes. It is a tool used in anticolonial resistance, but it is also available to the political and military leadership to discipline and control the general population. A feeling of discomfort undergirds the estate-burning scene: the people witnessing the burning of the buildings are torn between their desire to be free of the oppression that the estate (ostensibly a modern-day plantocracy) represents and a troubling sense that the destruction of those buildings will not produce their freedom.

I am interested in how Collins represents the history of violence that accompanies Grenada's history of radicalism. In the estate scene the people in the crowd know they must accept this violence to gain certain freedoms and make progress in their efforts to shape a more just society, but they still find it distressing. Their concern is borne out in the legacies of 1951. When Gairy first came to power in the 1950s he was a beacon of racial progress, a dark-skinned Grenadian from humble roots with no connection to the entrenched planter class. As he rose to greater power throughout the 1960s and 1970s, however, he oversaw legal and extra-legal forms of state violence, including the use of the police force and the secret force known as the Mongoose Gang to terrorize his opponents. This is exactly how Collins represents the character Leader in *Angel*. He begins as a union organizer, agitating on behalf of the black rural working classes for adult suffrage and fair wages. He stands up to the white and fair-skinned upper classes. Once he achieves state power, however, he abuses this power for personal gain and inflicts violence on his detractors. Grenadians are betrayed and physically attacked, then, by someone who was once their champion; and this betrayal results in a trauma that is related to but different from the trauma of colonialism. Whereas trauma inflicted by the colonizer functioned to highlight the otherness of the colonized, the trauma inflicted by local political leaders whom Grenadians had come to trust represents a deeper, more troubling violation because it suggests limited pathways to real freedom.

What Collins reveals in her depiction of the 1950s and again of the 1970s and 1980s is that in the course of pursuing radical, liberatory politics, the people of Grenada both employed and witnessed violence to various degrees. The experience of this violence generated feelings ranging from mild discomfort to unqualified horror. Throughout *Angel*, with Leader and then Chief successively at the helm of power, Grenadians are forced to accept violence as the price to be paid for anticolonial and anti-imperialist resistance. According to the theorist Frantz Fanon, they are socialized to accept that "decolonization is always a violent event."[9] Fanon's analysis does not sufficiently address, however, the effect of repeated instances, over multiple generations, of anticolonial violence inflicted on the formerly colonized. Nowhere in the Caribbean is decolonization a single event. The serial experiences of violence waged in the name of radical politics leave residual wounds as their mark, making apparent the ongoing trauma of colonialism *and* revolution as a response to colonialism. Taking gender into consideration means having to track even further differentials in the experience of violent trauma in the course of the decolonizing struggle.

## Follow the Leader: Charisma and Corrupting Political Power

In *Angel,* the years during which Leader controls the nation's politics are fraught with tension for multiple generations of Grenadians. In the first half of the novel, Collins represents some of the scenes of conflict spurred by Leader's actions. This conflict tends to take place between Regal, Angel's uncle and a staunch supporter of Leader, and Doodsie and Ma Ettie, with Doodsie in particular remaining distrustful of Leader and trying to warn her brother about getting tangled up in Leader's organization. Later in the novel, when Angel returns home from college, she clashes with her father, Allan, over Leader's corruption and the socialist alternative being offered by Horizon. Allan loves what Leader achieved for rural Grenadians. There are parallels between Doodsie and Angel as women trying to warn men against corrupt leaders. These parallels allow us to understand popular support for radical leaders through the eyes of women and youth. Through the figures of Ma Ettie, Doodsie, and Allan, Collins offers the perspective of an older generation responding to the idealism of the younger folks. This type of conflict is a major theme for Collins and allows her to explore the production of revolutionary time around cycles of radical politics. She uses Doodsie as a moral center connecting all three generations.[10] Doodsie's political views transcend generational or ideological boundaries, and she is able to cut to the character of politicians and politics with more clarity than the others. Her speech directs our attention to some of the pitfalls that accompany cycles of radicalism. Through her eyes we understand how political leaders often put their supporters in compromising positions.

In 1951, Regal becomes one of Leader's "top men," aiding in the organization of the estate workers and strategizing against the landowners.[11] When Doodsie warns Regal about getting too close to Leader, she cites her experience observing Leader as a union boss in Aruba, where they were part of a community of migrant workers. Leader's flashiness and the extravagant wedding he held there—one so grand that the locals in Aruba made up a rhyme about him—did not escape Doodsie's notice. Even after Doodsie hints that Leader may have been abusing union monies in Aruba to finance his expensive tastes, Regal is not willing to accept this information as sufficient reason to keep his distance. When Leader organizes an islandwide strike for all estate laborers across Grenada, Regal helps coordinate groups that go into "the cocoa" (the farming areas) to stop any workers who break the strike. When they find a worker, Mano, in the fields, Regal's co-conspirators at first try to reason with him in order to convince him not to break the strike. They explain how and why they need to work together to improve conditions for all laborers. Regal, however, insists that he is not there to "have conference wid Mano" and proceeds to "planass he ass," using the flat side of a machete to strike him repeatedly. Once Regal begins the beating, others join him, kicking and planassing Mano until they draw blood as he begs for mercy.

While the strike itself is mainly an effective practice, that Leader commissions groups of his followers to use violence to coerce participation from estate workers demonstrates the extent to which he is motivated by a desire for absolute power. It also shows the difficult choices workers such as Mano face with regard to joining protests. This kind of intimidation foreshadows the more extreme forms of violence Leader will later sanction when he faces organized opposition from Horizon in the 1970s, when Horizon and its supporters organize strikes to protest Leader.[12] It also portends the future circumstances under which Horizon and the military will clash later in the novel.

The climax of the 1950s workers strike is a large rally at which Leader plans to address the people.[13] Leader appears on stage dressed all in white, a sartorial choice intended to play into the public image of him as a savior. Using the balcony of a government building as an impromptu stage, he presents himself as both challenging and occupying state power. As Collins describes it, Leader is a charismatic politician able to control the crowd by modulating his voice and through the use of call and response to engage the audience. His subsequent arrest by colonial authorities only serves to increase the support he experiences among the masses. While Leader is imprisoned, his supporters continue to burn buildings and kill and maim farm animals until the governor agrees to release him.

Collins uses the occasion of revolt to stage a conversation between Regal and Ma Ettie about Regal's radical politics. The tense conversation between parents and adult children around political resistance is a technique Collins employs throughout *Angel* and *The Colour of Forgetting*. Regal defends his politics, explaining to Ma Ettie that those who support Leader are fighting against a system designed to benefit the plantocracy at the expense of the descendants of the formerly enslaved and landless. "Mammie, lissen. Is not covetous I covetous. The lan couldn't be mine because I too black for one, an is white people that own lan because is them that did have slave in this country." Regal has a clear understanding of how the island's history of slavery and colonialism has led to class and color divisions in Grenada. The descendants of the plantocracy benefited from advantages related to their economic status and from their proximity to whiteness. Regal's explanation to Ma Ettie reveals just how important Leader's blackness is to his ability to mobilize the people. The predominantly African-descent rural workers see Leader as one of their own and one of the earliest black leaders from a rural background. When Leader is released from prison, however, he calls for an end to the strike, even though the estate owners have met only some of the workers' demands. Collins uses the section subtitle "Something in de mortar besides de pestle!" to suggest that there is more to the relationship between Leader and the estate owners than is apparent: he conceded to fulfilling only some of the demands of the people in exchange for personal power.[14] This betrayal is itself a form of political violence as it limits the ability of the people to be recognized by the colonial government and it violates the trust they put in Leader to represent them. As Collins explores anticolonial resistance in 1950s Grenada, she depicts both the promise and the pitfalls that arise from Leader's activism. Despite his radical politics, Leader was willing to compromise with the colonial administration and plantocracy, to the limited benefit of his constituents. As a result, Angel's family, representative of lower-class laborers, benefit only marginally from Leader's efforts and the push for decolonization.

The story of Leader is exemplary of the anticolonial struggle of small island nations such as Grenada. The postcolonial period brought a change in leadership and important strides in racial pride; however, the appearance of these new, black leaders did not necessarily coincide with radical social or economic change in the burgeoning nation, especially for black and lower-class laborers. In the Caribbean, the transition from colony to independent state typically meant the transfer of power from the colonial administration to a local elite or local grassroots leaders, who rose to power and then got caught up in their newfound privilege. Caribbean populations thus found themselves independent in name and little else. Their social and economic status, and the conditions under which they labored, remained dreary.[15]

In the final third of the novel Collins begins to explore tensions between Angel's generation and that of her parents. The setting is Grenada in the 1970s. Leader has now been in power for two decades. The tensions in this period come about as a result of the antagonism between Leader and the burgeoning revolutionary movement led by Chief and Horizon. Angel's transition to womanhood occurs just as she discovers her ability to grasp issues surrounding race, politics, and power and how these issues matter in Grenada, the Caribbean, and the African diaspora. She attends UWI in Mona, Jamaica, and begins to explore Black Power politics with her colleagues from other islands. Upon her return to Grenada she takes up a teaching post and tries out her newfound political identity in different ways. In a scene involving Angel and her father, Allan, we learn that Allan has kept a framed picture of Leader on the living room wall in the family home. He returns home one evening to find that the picture is missing. Allan questions Angel as to the picture's whereabouts, and she says that the picture is broken and that she has placed it under Allan's bed. The gesture is highly symbolic, simultaneously displacing Leader as a father figure in Grenadian politics and challenging Allan's authority as the head of the household. As they argue, Angel reveals that the picture of Leader is a source of embarrassment and anxiety for her. "Daddy, that picture on the wall will make me feel ashamed. I could never bring no friends here," she says. When Allan probes further, she continues, "A man who have the country in such a mess, we have him up on the wall like a hero. They would think everybody in this house stupid."[16]

The friction between father and daughter is illustrative of the generational and ideological gap between the majority of the older people, who support Leader, and the younger set, who support Chief and Horizon. Angel is too young to fully grasp the good that Leader achieved in the 1950s, nor does she interpret his leadership as a symbol of black power. For Angel's generation, Leader's blackness is not enough to legitimize his authority or prove his commitment to the nation. Allan's response to Angel is similar to the response Gairy cheekily offered to young Black Power radicals in Grenada during the early 1970s: If you believe in black power, then why not support a black man representing a majority-black population? Allan chastises his daughter's seeming hypocrisy: "You and you friends, I don understan youall. Talkin about black people havin power and a whole lot of nonsense. An when black people really have the power now, you still looking for high brown people who still don have you interest at heart to give the power to." Allan's perspective suggests that the gains Leader brought to the peasant class during the colonial period still held sway in the minds of some Grenadians of Allan's generation, even in the face of Leader's later corruption. For these older folks, Leader was the first black politician to stand up to the large landowners and bourgeoisie, who were mainly white or mixed race. Leader's ability to claim power represented a resounding defeat of the nation's high brown elite, which never recovered political power.

As with Regal's earlier exchange with Ma Ettie, Leader's complexion is referenced as proof of his fidelity to the people. Allan's mention of "high brown people," on the other hand, can be read as an allusion to an elite class of Grenadians and to several leftist Caribbean political leaders from this time who happened to be "brown" or mixed race, including Maurice Bishop and Unison Whiteman in Grenada and Michael Manley in Jamaica.[17] Manley's leftist politics are part of what Allan criticizes when he tells Angel she has learned "so much stupidness in Jamaica." Indeed, when Angel tries to argue that distinguishing between "high brown" and "black" is pointless since they are all black and fighting for a better quality of life for the poor, Allan retorts, "That is what you think, that is the communist nonsense they telling you." Allan thinks of communism as an objectionable ideology causing the younger generation to forget their roots, leading them to be unnecessarily drawn into international political conflicts. He prefers Leader's more locally grounded vision.

This moment provides an opportunity to understand how many Grenadians wanted to opt out of the Cold War and chose not to understand Grenada's decolonization process as part of a global, diasporic project of liberation. During the 1960s and 1970s, many leftist political movements in the Caribbean, particularly those associated with the Non-Aligned Movement (as Grenada was), were labeled "communist" by the more right-leaning leaders, even if they did not identify as such. This was an attempt to discredit the Left by burdening the term communism with negative connotations.[18] In the novel the political party Horizon envisions itself as a part of a cadre of third world revolutions, and as such it is dismissed as a mere communist organization by Allan, who, in his resistance to Marxism-Leninism, is representative of many in his generation. But these young, leftist leaders were not deterred by their detractors. They sought a united Caribbean region, like the one that was sought but then dismantled in the short-lived federation project of the 1950s. For them, too much emphasis on nationalism was part of what led their elders to the failure of federation. Angel's generation sees communism, Marxism-Leninism, Maoism, and African socialism as real alternatives to capitalism, which they recognize as the centerpiece of the colonial apparatus. They were actively engaged in interpreting these ideologies for Caribbean contexts. Angel rejects Allan's view of nationalism and his critique of communism. Instead she takes a stand for regional solidarity across linguistic borders by evoking Fidel Castro and Cuba: "All you life you hear that communism bad. Years ago, you, me too in the convent [Angel's high school], all of us, say endless prayers for merciful God to kill Castro and leave Cuba in the hands of beautiful America. But explain to me in detail what you know communism is."[19] The capitalism/communism binary animates their discussion, but Allan does not have a robust response for his daughter. Angel exposes the way American and English news sources have shaped her father's viewpoint. Since Allan has no concrete critique of communism or how it might work in the Caribbean, Angel is not ready to acknowledge the validity of some of his concerns. The good that Leader achieved in the 1950s is of no interest to her, just as the possibilities presented by communism are of no interest to Allan. In some ways they were each influenced by the leaders they most identified with, each carrying different messages about Caribbean identity and freedom.

## Searching for a Third Way

While Allan and Angel represent generational and ideological divisions, Collins uses Doodsie to mediate between the two and to present more complex views of leadership. Through Doodsie she explores the idea of a revolutionary consciousness untethered to either communist or capitalist ideology. Doodise is in favor of Chief, Horizon, and the revolution. She puts an end to the argument between Angel and Allan by exclaiming: "De communism oh, de what ism, who want to know, all we want is for ting to go good."[20] Doodsie is not interested in aligning herself with a particular ideology; instead, she favors a commonsense approach where things will "go good." For her it means supporting political practices that are not necessarily linked to theory or book learning. Her education is mainly informal; therefore, she evaluates these practices through observation and in light of her own experiences. Doodsie has always been suspicious of Leader, and as local support for him dwindles and Chief becomes more popular, she listens carefully to what Chief and Horizon are proposing for Grenada. Her support for them is never presented as a shift toward communism. Instead she focuses on what she understands to be the value of Horizon's proposals for the community versus the abuse of power she sees in Leader's behavior.[21]

I read Doodsie's support for Horizon, coupled with her rejection of a named ideology, as a desire to approach revolution cautiously. Doodsie behaves as if this caution might somehow save her from the potential violence and trauma she already knows the political process entails. Her circumspection is not simply support for Horizon that does not want to be named but also support for particular principles of revolution that may fall outside the version sanctioned by the political party itself. Doodsie represents an attempt to redefine the revolutionary process from below. She is a bridge between her own generation and that of Angel. This is not only about finding a middle ground but also about Doodsie's freedom to shape revolutionary possibility according to her own vision.

Melda, one of Angel's neighbors, is another character of Doodsie's generation through whom we see resistance to established ideologies of revolution. Late in the novel, after Horizon has been in power for several years, Angel's community grapples with rumors that an internal power struggle has taken over Horizon and that the party has put Chief under house arrest—a fictionalization of the final days of the NJM in October 1983. Melda insists that the party is wrong, regardless of party rules, to put Chief under house arrest since the will of the people trumps the will of the party. The people support Chief, she rightly points out. As Doodsie tries to explain the situation to Melda, Melda interrupts her in frustration: "Dey jokin! Arres Chief! Dey sayin is Party business! To hell wid dem an dey Party!"[22] Through Melda and Doodsie, Collins disarticulates the vision of revolution promoted by Horizon. These women characters exemplify how the masses took ownership of the revolution and, near the end, came to resent the party politics that interrupted a process to which they felt closely connected. In this way the end of the revolution is a struggle within the party, but also between the party and the people.

For Melda, unless the party is dedicated to realizing the will of the people, it becomes irrelevant. Her ideas of the revolution are mediated through her conception of Chief as the nation's most important leader. Whatever Chief's faults, he established a certain connection with the people, he could translate the party's goals to them, and they believed he had their best interests at heart. Melda and Doodsie share the perspective that the masses mobilized the revolution with Chief and there is now no need to detour through the party, Marxism, or any ideology to advance the goal of improving living conditions for Grenadians. This is important because it emphasizes again how Grenadians plotted their own course for the revolution. They were not going to be cajoled by the party into taking positions they did not support. The gulf between the aspirations of the people and the aims of the party is similar to the divergence that crops up between Leader and members of his political base after he was in office too long—another instance of repetition in Collins's reconstruction of events between these two periods of political change. Collins is again underlining the way politicians' mishandling of power causes the politics of the nation to shift in directions that hurt many Grenadians. In such instances revolution becomes a source of violence and trauma because in this fatal shift during the revolution's final weeks, members of the People's Revolutionary Army assassinate Chief and his comrades.

The assassination of Chief is not represented in the novel. However, the time immediately after his death is described as a time of nationwide fear and confusion. Once news of Chief's death reaches the public, it is understood that a U.S. military invasion is not far behind. Collins uses the pseudonym Interim Army Council for the Revolutionary Military Council that took over after Bishop's assassination. The council calls on Grenadians to join it in armed resistance against the invasion, but it is difficult for the people to side with those responsible for Chief's death, even to defend national sovereignty. Collins keeps the focus on Angel's and her family's experience of these events. Angel and one of her brothers, Rupert, argue over whether it is more important to resist American imperialism or to resist the council. Through this conversation Collins exposes readers to the difficult position Grenadians were put in as a result of conflict between Bishop and the party. Rupert thinks that Horizon is at fault for the violence and refuses to support the party and the council any further. He was at the fort and witnessed the confusion there just before the army killed Chief.[23] Angel, like her mother, tries to maintain a balanced view, not siding with the party or with Chief. Rupert excoriates her for vacillating, and she decides to join the council in resisting the U.S. invasion. It is not an easy decision for Angel, given her devastation at Chief's death and Rupert's stance, but she finds it more important to take a stand against imperialism. In conversation with her family, Angel compares this critical moment of anti-imperialist struggle to the 1951 anticolonial struggle. It takes a tragedy for her to finally see a connection between the two periods. She says, "We go get out o it, Daddy. We get outa Leader. People march to get Chief free. We did fight for weself in '51! Dese same people dat comin to *save* us now did only too anxious to kill us yesterday! They don like us! They don like Chief! They just tryin to control us. But slavery days done!"[24]

Angel is in shock. Angry at the collapse of a revolution in which she had invested so much, she searches for hope in a moment of hopelessness. She conflates multiple instances of radical resistance in Grenada's history. The lack of chronology in her recounting of Grenadian history is significant as it represents these different instances as a single trauma repeating itself in the national consciousness. She references the 1970s protests to remove Leader from office, the protests of just a few days earlier to release Chief from house arrest, the 1951 Sky Red protests of her early life, and even slavery. Most striking in Angel's retelling of these histories of resistance in Grenada is that she does not associate the struggle of 1951 with Leader; she only references it as the people's struggle. Angel's omission is symptomatic of a desire to push out of consciousness the problematic aspects of Leader's practices during 1951 in order to promote armed resistance against the United States in 1983. Resistance to the United States is part of a legacy of resistance to empire in Grenada, she is arguing. She names these histories using the first person plural pronoun "we" in order to legitimate continued armed resistance, but her process involves a selective reconstruction of Grenada's radical histories. Doodsie and Allan sympathize with Angel but do not buy her argument.[25] Angel's speech is typical of the compulsion to narrate revolution and radicalism in victorious terms. This, I propose, is how radical movements in the Caribbean secure support and legitimacy for their agendas during times of contested political transition—by claiming connection to a triumphant legacy. Angel's inability to convince her parents of the legitimacy of the Interim Army Council and the illegitimacy of the U.S. invasion, however, represents a break in this cycle of narrating revolution as vanquishing imperialism. The reality is more complex, with anticolonial revolution absorbing some colonial relations.

The fratricidal assassinations that mark the end of the Grenada Revolution brought a mixture of shame, fear, confusion, guilt, and trauma to the Grenadian public and to the narrative of revolution. In Collins's writing, therefore, we find a questioning of revolution as a response to colonial empire via a working through of the complicated history of radicalism in the nation. When Angel persists in her argument that white neocolonialists should not be allowed to control black lives in Grenada, Doodsie responds, "But, Angel, chile, the way ting happen."[26] Collins simply allows Doodsie's voice to trail off. The violence of October 19 is unspeakable for her. The trauma brought about as a result of this bloodshed mutes further calls for resistance, rendering those calls inseparable from the spectacle of violence that the nation was subjected to with Bishop's house arrest, the shootings and assassinations at the fort, and the shoot-to-kill curfew. Under these circumstances, Doodsie, like her son Rupert, simply cannot side with the council, even if failure to do so means yet another violation of Caribbean sovereignty at the hands of the American empire. The brutal violations committed in the name of revolution are finally so deeply felt that they can no longer be ignored.

## Blindness and Insight

*Angel* is Collins's initial attempt at understanding the cyclical history of revolution and violence in Grenada and a working through of ways to both recognize and break free of this cycle while still valuing revolution as a critical part of Caribbean struggles for sovereignty. At the novel's close Angel has suffered the loss of an eye while fighting U.S. forces. Ironically, she is sent to the United States for treatment, where she is cared for by family friends until she is well enough to return home. In the novel's final scene Angel is back in Grenada and walking alone to the river by the Delicia Estate, a place with a "reputation for spirits," to perform a water ritual for cleansing. She lights a candle while silently rehearsing a song she recalls from wakes—the words "Chandinel kléwé-é-é! / O cièl!" (Light the way for us, O Heavens!) are a cry for insight from the ancestral world. She waits for a response from the spirits she believes are present in the land. Even as she performs this small, personal ritual she is deeply uncomfortable with what it says about her. "She looked around quickly, guiltily," Collins writes, "feeling a little bit stupid about what she was about to do." And yet for Angel, it seems there is no other recourse.

Just before the invasion Angel had a dream that a woman in a "long, flowing white gown" came up from the river and into Angel's yard to bring her some message that Angel could not hear.[27] In the dream the woman is joined by more people, most of whom appear to be rural workers. They all gather on a boat, as if leaving Angel and the island behind.[28] In this final scene Angel exhibits faith not in the Christian god she was raised to honor but in the land and its people. It is a faith that had been missing from the political movements she lived through with Leader and Chief. By having Angel assume a position of listening, seeking ancestral knowledge from the land scorched by American bombs just a few months earlier, Collins closes the novel by attending to a different kind of cyclical pattern, one evident in nature. Nature does not provide a solution to the problem of political violence, but it does offer a way of understanding violent cycles by bearing witness to those who have inhabited the land before.

Collins refers to the potential violence of nature in the epigraph to the novel, which is a poem about a river. By opening and closing the novel with images of a river, Collins introduces yet another form of doubling. The epigraph foreshadows the novel's subject matter, describing patterns of violence within the Grenadian landscape:

> Violence
> comes in gentle form sometimes
>
> The river looks calm until rain falls
> Then
> it vomits old pans, old cans, sticks and stones
> a tumbling mass of mud
> everything swallowed for years gone by
>
> Sometimes
> violence comes in gentle form[29]

In this poem, the heavy rainfall causes a river to breach its banks. A muddy mess erupts and brings to the surface of the river a mix of objects, both natural and man-made, that had been buried underwater. The river "vomits" objects from an earlier moment in its history, forcing these objects into view and giving them a renewed life. Much as the gentle river transforms into a violent torrent once the rain falls, so the violence of the Grenada Revolution (in particular its final days) and the American invasion come as a flood providing the momentum that drives the novel to its end. The "old pans, old cans, sticks and stones" that reemerge symbolize the resurfacing during the revolution of many of the same issues that Grenadians had faced during Gairy's radical period in the 1950s. In *Angel* these issues include the disconnect between a government and its constituents, the use of violence in confrontations between the people and the political authorities, and the fall of a popular leader—all issues that punctuate the careers of both Leader and Chief. Collins introduces this violence as "gently" as possible in *Angel* through her use of repetition. Readers experience the violent end of the Grenada Revolution in the final third of the novel, but only after they have already witnessed Angel and her family survive the rise and fall of Leader. Beginning at a point other than the end of the revolution also gives the author the opportunity to create a more balanced vision of the revolution, one tinged by the good intentions and initiatives with which the entire process started. "Everything swallowed for years gone by," Collins writes, but these swallowed objects come to the fore again between 1979 and 1983. The key to grappling with the violence of the revolution's collapse may lie in one's ability to draw on the challenges of the past in order to recognize political patterns and solve current problems, the epigraph suggests. The poem structures this repetition formally in Collins's choice to bookend the epigraph with the following antimetabole: "Violence/comes in gentle form sometimes. . . ./Sometimes/violence comes in gentle form." By beginning and ending the poem with two lines that mirror each other (repeating them in reverse grammatical order), she emphasizes the cyclical nature of violence and recovery in the natural world and suggests the possibility of nature serving as a metaphor for violence in social and political spheres.

By approaching the river with the intention of simply observing—of listening and watching—Angel demonstrates the ability to do precisely what the nation's political leaders could not: she listens to hear what wisdom the ancestors might have to offer in the present. When the candle's flame remains lit, she determines that the spirits are "either gone, or they sympathetic. Nothing to fraid."[30] It is not clear what, if anything, she learns from that experience, except that the ritual is available to her when all else has failed. The final image Collins offers readers is that of the river, "so calm before the rains, rushing down now to rid itself of the tumbling dirt."[31] The line runs parallel to the epigraph, as the novel returns to its own poetic source. In a similar way Angel and her family are left to determine what insight can be gained from this latest episode in the nation's quest for sovereignty. They have come full circle since the novel's beginning in 1951. They are still in imperialism's shadow. And they have survived.

In her second novel, *The Colour of Forgetting,* Collins remains attached to the project of representing the revolution through the stories of women and rural families. *Colour* picks up the themes of ancestral knowledge and tension between the ideology of the revolution's leaders versus that of the people. The novel, however, insists more directly on the responsibility of a younger generation to intervene in cycles of political violence.

## Generational Ties in *The Colour of Forgetting*

*The Colour of Forgetting* was published in 1995, eight years after *Angel.* Set on the fictional island of Paz, the story follows successive daughters, each named Carib, over multiple generations. It also details the lives of two intertwined families that can trace their roots back to an enslaved African named John Bull and his murderer, a white man named Malheureuse. Tracking these characters, it features a history of conflict on Paz figured both in major historical moments (a fatal seventeenth-century encounter between the indigenous Caribs and French colonizers, World

War II, and the 1979 revolution) and in the microhistory of a rural family (land theft by relatives, marital strife, political tensions between parents and children). *Colour* thus is constructed as a series of family histories that build on each other and provide a way of understanding national history: "Mixture in the blood of the story," Carib explains.[32]

Thematically and structurally, the novel has much in common with *Angel*. It insists on placing the Grenada Revolution in a broader historical context that expands the way Caribbean radicalism is conceptualized. The feminist impulse of the novel is relayed in several ways, such as in the prominence of women's voices and the absence of a heroic protagonist. Instead, multiple voices and lives are featured. *Colour* could be read as a peasant novel, in the vein of Jacques Roumain's 1944 *Masters of the Dew* or Alejo Carpentier's 1949 *The Kingdom of This World*; however, Collins rewrites the genre by making women's voices central to her narrative. The multiple characters named Carib are "warner" women for their generation. They walk the island wailing about the violence and pain of the island's past, present, and future. Time is multidirectional and dynamic for Carib, continuously repeating itself. History, myth, and prophecy are the languages she speaks. There is no new trouble or trauma for the women in this novel. Everything that happens is something they have seen before or understand through their connection to the stories of their ancestors. Ancestral knowledge equips them to intervene in the circumstances of their lives to avoid certain difficulties or to share ancestral knowledge with younger generations to help them avoid or deal with conflict. This vision gives the women a sense of their own resilience. They survive all manner of adversity, not in heroic form but through gestures (often intimate) of love and care. In Collins's work, relationships and shared histories enacted at the level of family and community are an important expression of decolonial love.[33]

There is also something uniquely feminist about the representation of Thunder, a male character who comes of age just as the revolution begins. Much like Angel, Thunder is deeply invested in the revolution, inspired by its promise of a better life for the struggling poor. Collins paints a picture of him as a sensitive child, whose nickname comes from his fear of thunder. As he matures, he maintains this sensitivity, eschewing the stereotypical masculine bravado of adolescence in order to seek a more open and communicative relationship with his father. Thunder's masculinity is shaped by the women in his life, his mother, Willive, and his great-aunt Mamag, who together ensure that he carries the family history with him. Thunder's parents are poor and landless, having been forced off the family property; their stories are his only inheritance. This is critical for him to understand the community from which they come and particularly the land that has sustained the family over multiple generations. Throughout the novel the struggle for land is at the center of the violent conflict and is the cause of the revolution's end. Through Collins's representation of Thunder and his family, *Colour* is a novel about how society deals with successive encounters of violence, violation, and oppression and the sense of ongoing, collective trauma.

The primal scene of violence in the text is the murder of enslaved African John Bull at the hands of the white carpenter Malheureuse. The murder, which took place very publicly in the market square, represents a gendered form of violence, figured as masculine aggression. Malheureuse's motivation seems to have been his anger at his status as a lower-class white man, which nonetheless allowed him to exhibit physical dominance over a black man. Legend has it that heavy rains began to fall as Malheureuse beat Bull to death with a stick. Instead of washing away Bull's blood, however, the rain made the blood thicker until it stained the earth on which his body lay. As a poor white man in the West Indian colonies, Malheureuse would have had limited means for improving his social status; however, his race would have been key to any possible mobility. In an economy driven by slavery, he performed his racial superiority by killing a slave. Whiteness grants Malheureuse immunity from criminal prosecution for Bull's death. In subsequent generations, the narrator reports, one of Malheureuse's descendants rises among the ranks of whites on the island to become a planter, the pinnacle of power in a Caribbean slave economy, suggesting that physical brutality toward enslaved people was a stepping stone to upward mobility. The Malheureuse of a later generation extends the exploitative behavior of his ancestor, having sexual relations with enslaved women, including the descendants of John Bull. In this sense the men cross paths again, their blood mixing through the sexual violence of subsequent generations.[34] Collins thus links these different forms of racial and sexual violence, which contribute to the plantation complex and the development of a colonized, patriarchal, and creolized society on Paz.[35]

Blood is a motif throughout the novel. Initially blood symbolizes the history of slavery and violence. Later the idea of "bad blood" makes its appearance as an uncle, Son-Son, betrays his nephews, Ti-Moun (Thunder's matrilineal grandfather) and Cosmos, by robbing them of their land. Though Ti-Moun and Cosmos are the sons of Son-Son's brother, Son-Son claims they are illegitimate heirs because their parents did not marry each other until years after the boys were born. Ti-Moun continues to work the land because it is his only means of earning a livelihood, and Son-Son sends goons to beat him and chase him off.[36] Mamag, Son-Son's sister, escaped her brother's scheming because she sold her piece of family land and purchased another piece of land for herself independent of the family plot. It is Mamag's commitment to blood relations that keeps Ti-Moun and his family afloat after this catastrophe. She leads the community in a "maroon," days of collective work, during which they move Ti-Moun's home to a plot on Mamag's land. The community interprets this intrafamily violence as the fulfillment of the "land confusion and blood to come" that they have heard Carib proclaiming on her walks.[37] Mamag's sacrifice ensures that Ti-Moun's daughter, Willive, is taken care of after Ti-Moun dies. Willive grows up to marry Ned, with whom she raises a son, Thunder. In this sense, Mamag is the protector of bloodlines and histories. Both are vital to the family's survival.

The conflict between Ti-Moun and Son-Son foreshadows a larger national land conflict. As the novel moves forward to the late 1970s and early 1980s, Collins again uses the market square as the setting for a watershed moment of violence when a meeting of village representatives, called by the national Land Commission, ends in gunfire. This scene is a more heavily fictionalized representation of October 19, 1983, than Collins wrote in *Angel,* with fewer details about the national context that led to the revolution's rise. In *Colour* even less is said about the government leadership, while Collins gives prominence to the family life of Thunder, Willive, and Ned. The main policy introduced by the revolution is a land reform proposal that would prevent citizens from purchasing parcels of land smaller than five acres.[38] The logic behind the proposal is that to grow the economy, larger pieces of land must be farmed collectively to increase the export of agricultural produce. The new government deems small-scale, subsistence farming "uneconomic." Ned and Willive are dismayed by this proposal as they were hoping to purchase a three-acre plot of land in "the Dip," the area where Ti-Moun was disinherited by Son-Son in years past. Willive is particularly vocal in her critique of this proposal. She writes to Thunder, asking him to "stand security for her" so she can afford the loan. Willive's desire for land is directly linked to the "family story" of the tradition of subsistence farming that she grew up with.

The scenes where confusion over land becomes a national concern demonstrate the revolutionary government's inability to understand the needs and concerns of the rural people—their basic need for land—and the rural folks' disconnect from the revolution's policies. When the government labels traditional subsistence farming "uneconomic," it inadvertently insults the intelligence of the rural working class and displays a lack of understanding (at worst) or underestimation (at best) of how the consequences of slavery have continued to influence rural communities, for whom land to own, farm, and pass down to their offspring is important, regardless of how small the plot. The town versus country and class divides between the revolution's leaders and their constituents are also evident in the response of some of the poorer rural characters: "Them, they all right, yes. They could sit down there and talk through their ass. What they know bout land? If they never had land and get chance to have a acre, they would know about uneconomic. Them? They happy, *wi.*" The people's critique is that those in government have no experience with the lifestyles of working-class country people such as those from Thunder's community, Atta Seat. The vanguard party tries to lead, but the novel issues a clear warning that political leaders need more humility in their approach to governance. The conflict foregrounds the complexity of revolutionary struggle. It is not simply about people who are for or against the policies of the revolution but rather how people negotiate revolution's various aspects as they relate to, and at times deviate from, the public's own sense of sovereignty.

Thunder supported the revolutionary government even as its admirable goals were not in sync with the people's needs. In the end he is accountable to his family because he understands the importance of their past to his own future. When the public meeting becomes dangerous as shots are fired in the market square, several people in the crowd jump into the sea to escape bullets, repeating the actions of the early Carib inhabitants, who jumped into the ocean to avoid capture by the French colonists in the seventeenth century. Several members of the public are killed or wounded, along with some government officials. After this violence, an unnamed first world country intervenes to restore order and bring aid to the citizens of Paz. Collins's description of the intervention is brief, her formal choice indicating that certain events are too painful to revisit in detail. The trauma is suggested in the gaps, in what she does not write. This fragmented or partial view of the revolution's end might also signal Collins's expectation of a readership already familiar with the basic contours of Grenada's history. For this readership a reference to political violence alone is sufficient to conjure up a series of vivid, painful memories. The narrative remains focused on the familial relationships of Thunder's family, otherwise anonymous citizens of Paz. The cycles of colonial oppression play out in both intimate and national contexts, but the emphasis on the intimate sphere is what draws the novel back to women's voices at regular intervals.

Collins gives an elevated status to family histories. In the middle of the market square debate over small plots of land, Thunder's parents question whose side he is on, theirs or the government's. They are not satisfied when he claims to be on everyone's side. Willive is calmed only when Thunder reassures her that he understands their views because he "know about the land story." Collins's choice of "story" rather than "history" to describe Thunder's relationship to his family's past indicates the secondary status of family history relative to larger-scale national histories. But it also reflects the family's comfort with its modest view of its place in the world. The smallness, yet centrality, of the family stories is echoed in the modest size of the family's plots of land. "We small! We well small! So is small potatoes we dealing with," one woman declares in the midst of the land debate. Not only is she proud of the small size of the nation, she is also arguing that nations, communities, and families that are relatively small need to deal with their unique challenges on their own terms instead of trying to adopt solutions and practices better suited to larger nations. Collins puts this intervention in the mouth of a woman who is nameless in the novel, referred to only as a "vendor who usually sold sive and thyme in the market," again making readers aware of the importance of otherwise anonymous voices. This is another way of pointing out how the nation's anonymous masses are ready and willing to provide insight into what is best for the country, in their view. They draw on their practical experience because the challenges of postcolonialism are not entirely different from those of colonialism. Armed with their stories, the older folk (and some rare youngsters, like Carib and Thunder) are equipped to recognize the patterns of imperialism. The difficulty they encounter is in finding people in power who will listen to them.

Collins reframes the revolution as a magnification of smaller-scale strife, with the family struggle serving as a metaphor for national conflict. The broader question of how to build a postcolonial revolution is refracted through the more intimate challenge of how to live among one's neighbors and kin in ways that are fair. How does one prevent one's family life from being disrupted because of the greed and selfishness of another? Viewed in this light, the crux of postcolonial revolution—to identify and dismantle systems of oppression and replace them with new systems that encourage a sense of collective labor, and that distribute the fruits of that labor in ways that are equitable and just—becomes a philosophical question about what is good and how to teach certain values within a community, and then ensure that these values are transmitted from one generation to the next.

## Return to the Source: Postmemory Warner Women

Throughout the novel, women characters are represented as the carriers of ancestral knowledge passed down through prophecy and stories. The Carib characters carry ancestral knowledge for the nation, and at the level of family, Willive and Mamag do their part to pass along their stories to Thunder. These stories are often painful, but they are part of the community and family identities. Male characters, such as Ned, have access to this knowledge but are seen as reluctant to talk about their past. Indeed, the silence that passes between Ned and Thunder is one of the novel's ongoing tensions. Willive constantly pushes Ned to develop his relationship with Thunder by discussing his family history. Finally, as Thunder reaches young adulthood, he and his father have a few key moments of sharing. When Thunder becomes the recipient of these histories, the novel's gender dynamics shift. The passing down of histories and the equally important use of these histories to make sense of contemporary challenges is feminist but not necessarily female.

Carib is a carrier of postmemory; her utterances are as much about past massacres—events neither she nor the people of Paz remember except through inherited stories passed down through many generations—as they are prophecies of trauma to come. Carib calls her nation to understand present and future violence in relation to the past. While the novel represents Carib as a marginalized figure in Paz's society, she is central to the narrative workings of the text. Collins opens the novel with Carib's voice, so that the novel itself becomes a textual iteration of what poet and literary critic Edward Baugh calls the "bell-mouthed and biblical" force of the warner woman.[39] "Blood in the north, blood to come in the south, and the blue crying red in between," Carib trumpets.[40] This is the central rallying cry of the novel and a refrain that serves both as further warning of future danger and as a funeral dirge for a lost past.

Carib lives near Leaper's Hill, the site from which the original indigenous inhabitants of Paz leapt to their deaths. Leaper's Hill is, therefore, a primal site of death and resistance, and it represents the act of leaping not only as fatal but also as a way of moving into future possibilities and as an alternative to captivity. Carib is rooted in the physical space of resistance. For many years, however, Carib's message remains opaque to her fellow citizens. Her word is often offered simultaneously in past and present tense ("Forgotten and consoled. Forgotten and drownded. And the blue crying red in between"), making it difficult for the people of Paz to decipher the time period she is referencing. When the revolution begins, people around Paz think, "This is the blood that Carib been preaching about all the time."[41] At last, she and her foremothers begin to get some recognition for the word they have been preaching in fragments over the years. The narrator describes the "general support" the revolution received from the public, but tension in the novel continues to build as Carib does not stop preaching. Even as the people of Paz connect her words to the revolution, they are still apprehensive about how precisely to interpret Carib's continued preaching.

The novel ends on an ominous note, with Carib on the *Huddersfield*, a boat traveling to Paz from Eden, a neighboring island. To make the trip on the *Huddersfield,* one must travel over Kick-em-Ginny, an active underwater volcano. Kick-em-Ginny can churn the sea violently when it erupts. As the final chapter begins, the narrator explains that passengers are no longer wary of Kick-em-Ginny because advances in boat-building technology have made for a much smoother ride. Still, out of habit, some of the older folks tense up on this part of the journey, while the younger people begin to question the existence of Kick-em-Ginny since they have no lived experienced of the volcano's violence. For them the volcano is more myth than reality. They refuse to believe. "And come again forgetting," Collins writes, "Kick-em-Ginny disappears."[42] This volcano provides a metaphor for Paz's violent history, always churning just below the surface, a looming threat to the order and daily hustle of island life. Forgotten but not gone. This forgetfulness is dangerous, the ship's skipper insists, warning the passengers that their disbelief may tempt the "spirit of the water." They in turn accuse him of being superstitious.

Shortly after this exchange a baby onboard begins to wail. The sea becomes agitated, and the ocean violently pitches the *Huddersfield* and its passengers about. Just as the skipper predicted, the passengers' flagging belief in the power of the sea and history seems to provoke the wrath of the restless ancestors whose spirits lie uneasily below the ocean's surface. The underwater volcano erupts briefly, a metaphor for the resurfacing of violence, similar to the overflowing river in the poetic epigraph to *Angel* and evocative of the Middle Passage. When the sea settles just as quickly as it had risen, all the passengers turn their attention to Carib as she wails and points to the fort on Paz, claiming to see "red." A new element is added to her prophecy this time, however, when she insists "Is the children to know and to stop it." But just as she gives this responsibility over to the next generation, the baby that was wailing earlier dies suddenly in its mother's arms. The new generation is cut down before it has a chance to mature because its guardians did not have the "right" historical sense—sense, that is, to acknowledge the deadly volcano and watery grave under the ocean's surface.

Carib offers her final prophecy of the novel by suggesting that there is still reason to hope: "Is all right as long as we see and we know and we remember. Is young blood. Is the young people to stop the blue from crying red in between. And it going to be all right." This child's death is but a warning and a call to action. Read allegorically, the loss of the young people during the market massacre can also be understood as a warning. Carib refuses to see the deaths exclusively as tragedy, however, and instead signals another way. By sharing her prophecies and inviting others to listen, she offers a corrective to the violence and loss. In Collins's hands the novel itself functions in a similar way, as a vessel for understanding history, for working through and beyond tragedy and toward renewal, and even hope. It is left for the reader to imagine what "all right" looks like in the world of the novel.

Collins's narrative vision in this text is about the three-dimensionality of time—past, present, and future—and a call to live with history. Disasters and trauma cannot be prevented; however, one can learn how better to handle adversity by reaping knowledge from the ancestors and their traditions. The final scene on the boat drives home one of Collins's central themes: the citizens of Paz ignore history at their own risk, for history anchors all that they do. At the beginning of *Colour* the narrator recounts the legend tale that the sea near Leaper's Hill often "churned up with remembering."[43] This remembering is angry, Collins writes, and especially dangerous for the people who live around the sea but choose not to remember. If, as Derek Walcott writes, "the sea is history," then Collins extends this idea by showing how history, like the sea, is constantly changing, and the *meaning* of history is different for each subsequent generation.[44] Like *Angel*, *Colour* ends with loss, but also with the sense that peaceful resolve is possible when the characters can exhibit sufficient historical awareness. For Collins, the Grenada Revolution continues to give meaning to Grenada's present, and part of this meaning must redirect the gaze of those paying attention to areas where the histories, like the revolution, happened long before 1979.

**Laying the Ghosts to Rest: Poetry and Reconciliation**

Collins's 2003 poetry collection, *Lady in a Boat,* deals primarily with themes of mourning and loss, extending the vision of *Angel* and *Colour* to imagine in more detail how healing is possible. The poems are steeped in memories of missed or misspent opportunities. A section titled "Se Mwe, Nutmeg (Is Me, Nutmeg)" includes several poems that address the end of the revolution from a variety of perspectives. Collins translates the creole "se mwe" as "is me" in Grenadian English. In Standard English it would be "it is me." "Se Mwe, Nutmeg" is the answer to the riddle posed by the book's title: Who is the lady in a boat with a red petticoat? It is the nutmeg plant. The nutmeg riddle also refers to Grenada's moniker as the "Isle of Spice," earned through the island's producing one-third of the world's nutmeg. The nutmeg is important enough to Grenada that it is featured on the nation's flag. It also provides a livelihood for the many Grenadians involved in its cultivation and processing for export, as was the case for Willive in *Colour.* In her choice to name the section of *Lady in a Boat* dealing primarily with the aftermath of the revolution "Se Mwe, Nutmeg," Collins affirms its continued importance in a definitive period in Grenada's history. The subtitle can be read as the personified nutmeg claiming these poems of revolution as part of herself. This moment of self-identification, I propose, also points to the need for Grenadians to accept as part of themselves the history of the revolution, even (and perhaps especially) the traumatic parts.

The poem "Dream Mourning" is about dreams that invite divination but that remain obscure because the dreamers, young radicals, cannot recognize the dream as a form of knowledge. The poem represents a generational knowledge gap between the young revolutionaries and the older people, a gap so wide it prevented the young revolutionaries from seeing that the path they were headed down was fatal. While the young people were concerned with generating greater knowledge about class struggle, in line with certain forms of scientific Marxism, the older heads understood the importance of epistemologies grounded in local, spiritual practices and folklore. In this poem the ability to understand dreams is part of a locally grounded knowledge. The poet-speaker in "Dream Mourning" claims that those more attuned to these alternative epistemologies through dreams and the natural world were aware that

**Figure 4.** Woman sweeping nutmeg-processing station, Gouyave, St. John's, Grenada. (© Kathy Sloane, courtesy of the photographer)

something terrible was about to happen before the revolution's end. The poem presents the idea that the dream itself is not necessarily an opaque genre; rather, those who received the dreams had abandoned the ancestral epistemology that they ought to have inherited from the older generation. This epistemology would have allowed them to accept the dream as a warning and understand its meaning. As in her fiction, in Collins's poetry knowledge—political and otherwise—is shared between generations.

"Dream Mourning" appears on the page as an incantation. It describes the seven-month period during which the poet-speaker is visited by ghostly figures predicting a time of mourning and trouble:[45]

> For seven months, and seven
> days, they trudged every night
> across the yard. Tell me you
>
> didn't see the long white gown
> for death, for mourning, for bit-
> ter endings, for more dread be-
>
> ginnings. Seven months, seven lingering
> days, thirteenth March to nineteenth October,
> they drift down from mountain

The dates and numbers are important to Collins. The numbers seven and three are central to the formal structure of the poem as each stanza except for the last one is composed of three lines. Most of the lines contain seven syllables. She breaks her seven-syllable pattern to include dates in the third stanza. These dates indicate that the poet-speaker is describing the experience of being visited in her sleep by ghosts of death from March 13, 1983 (the fourth anniversary of the revolution), until October 19, 1983, when the revolution imploded and Bishop was assassinated. The history is thus embedded in both form and content.

Throughout the poem the speaker is addressing a complicit reader, one who ought to have witnessed the same premonition but failed to do so or refused to acknowledge the vision. The dream is a collective vision that the older people have experienced and the younger people have not: "Tell me you/didn't see the long white gown/for death." "Tell me you didn't see" is repeated twice more, in lines 20 and 32–33, and at the end of the poem the speaker suggests that the reader refused to "see" because the premonitions constituted the folk knowledge of the older generation. According to the speaker, the "young dreamers" were intoxicated by a "new knowledge" that could not accept ghosts or ancestral epistemologies. The speaker claims that these ghosts "come with the shape of things" as a reminder to the reader. That the warnings are a reminder implies that the reader already has access to this kind of information, that it springs from a previously embedded knowledge that the reader has forgotten or suppressed. The knowledge contained in the dreams is obscured to the poem's addressees because they are preoccupied with a revolutionary knowledge and rhetoric that are not connected to the land or to stories from their ancestors.

Collins writes that the ghosts appear in particular shapes, all of which are garden implements or objects used by people who work the land:

> Pickaxe, hoe,
> cocoa knife, fork, rod, cutlass,
> cane stalk, basket, straw hat, boots,
>
> banana on *kata*, spade

She follows this litany of objects with the question "How else to tell you?" While the ghosts' appearance as farm tools assumes a connection between the natural and ancestral realm, the question also connects these two realms to the political. The poem suggests that there are genuine connections between revolutionary politics and ancestral epistemologies because those who recognized the validity of the elders' perspectives were indeed able to foresee the collapse of the revolution. Picking up on themes Collins first raised in her depiction of TiMoun and his descendants in *Colour*, the logic undergirding the poem points up the limitations of revolutionary politics in that it did not make enough space for the recognition of strategies of survival passed down by ancestors. Resistance to this knowledge blinds TiMoun and his descendants to the connection between ancestral, sacred, and natural worlds.

The poem does not suggest, however, that the violent end of the revolution could have been prevented, even with ancestral knowledge. When the ghosts appear they are already in mourning:

> the long white gown
> for death, for mourning, for bit-
> ter endings, for more dread be-
>
> ginnings

The appearance of ghosts, in what Collins calls "night after prophetic night," is simply prophecy, echoing the role played by Carib in *Colour*. While the dream is described in ephemeral terms, as "smoke," the violent events of October 19, by contrast, are described starkly—in language naming rage, a splash of blood, pounding feet:

> Then come rage, come
>
> splash of blood, come pounding feet
> come horror of the past be-
> come future crucifixion

The image of the crucifixion anticipates the martyrdom that Bishop and his allies achieve in the afterlife. This image has persisted in part because their bodies have never been recovered. The enjambment within and between stanzas echoes formally the fragmentation of people from the government in the revolution's final months, as well as the fissures between the generations. The poem closes with a series of questions:

> What this mean? That
> man more human than he know?
> That woman need to let her
>
> misgivings show? That young dream-
> ers get drunk on the newness
> of knowledge and turn from the
>
> wisdom of old?

The reference to women's misgivings implies both the concerns that were raised by women who were troubled by the militarization of the revolution and questions about the involvement of high school students in the Revolutionary Militia. It can also be read as an allusion to the marginalization of women within the party's highest ranks. This reference to women and the previous reference to agricultural tools together create the sense that those best suited to foretell the tragic ending of the revolution were those with the least amount of political representation—women and rural workers. After the accusatory tone of the earlier parts of the poem it is difficult not to read the final question as a statement diagnosing the circumstances around which the revolution failed: the young dreamers were drunk on its newness and turned away from the wisdom of old. The reliance on revolutionary theory and rhetoric caused them to ignore the historical, political, and sacred particularities of the local context in favor of a more uniform approach to anti-imperialism. Collins suggests that local perspectives rooted in ancestral knowledge were required along with revolutionary theory for the government to create a truly liberatory praxis.

In the following poem, "Morning Glory," Collins works with a similar theme of divination.[46] This poem also mentions ancestors visiting people in their dreams, but most of the imagery focuses on warnings revealed through flora, fauna, and changes in the island's landscape. The poet-speaker picks out dogs howling at the moon, the smell of blood in the air, trees crashing to the ground, and healthy plants suddenly turning up dead. The older folks all understand these happenings as signs that bear particular meanings or warnings. The central image, from which the poem derives its title, is that of the morning glory flower. Here the flower defies its nature, opening its petals at dusk instead of dawn, a clear sign something is amiss. Many of the staple crops for Grenada's farmers are described as failing—pawpaw (papaya), callaloo, and nutmeg: "They say the land upset, sea/*bazoodee* and every fruit,/every flower in distress." The picture is one of chaos in the natural world, a metaphor for the chaos within the NJM leading up to the U.S. invasion.

Like "Dream Mourning," "Morning Glory" carries an air of uncertainty around the sources providing the poet-speaker with this information. The poem begins, "People say since that year be-/gin, the spirit world was rest-/less." The phrase "They say," is repeated several times throughout, as if to remind the reader that the poet-speaker makes no claims to truth and is only repeating information that has already been circulating through the rumor mill, or "bushgram," as Collins calls this kind of hearsay elsewhere.[47] In the sixth stanza the poet-speaker explains, "How I/buy these things, so I sell them./I make not a cent profit." The poet-speaker wants to present herself as a reporter, then, not adding any interpretation to what people say they observed. Yet the idea of interpretation and meaning is raised with a question that also appeared in "Dream Mourning": ". . . what this mean? What change/the balance of things?" the poet-speaker asks. The question is never answered. The role of the poem here is to validate these forms of knowledge, which include spiritual, ancestral, and agricultural knowledge. The questions are followed by the brief description of hearsay of more dreams visited by ancestors. This last proof of trouble brewing is placed in italics, perhaps because the source is identified as "some who/could see," at first suggesting a different population, one with access to the world of the ancestors through dreams and visions or prophecy, like Carib. The poet-speaker uses the plural possessive pronoun "our" to describe the sleep and dreams. Again, the reader is implicated:

> *The ancestors*
> *creep into our sleep, cry in*
>
> *our dreams and leave us feeling*
> *toodie in daylight.*

The dreams and sleep are collective. Like the morning glory flowers that no longer know how to respond properly to dawn, the people of the poem are left feeling "toodie"—Grenadian Creole for having been stunned or made dizzy by the dreams. They can only "see" the dreams by night, not by day, just as the morning glory flower blooms after dark and not in the light. This strange response to light is ironic in the context of the "bright new dawn" the revolution had promised, an image first featured in Bishop's address to the nation on the morning of March 13, 1979.[48] The image of a redemptive morning is also featured in the title of Collins's first poetry collection, *Because the Dawn Breaks*. Here a double reading is possible as dawn breaking evokes the hopeful coming of light, but it also points to the destruction of this hopeful moment—dawn being *broken* by the end of the revolution. "Morning Glory," like "Dream Mourning," ends on unsettling terms with another question: "Which direction to turn/for some warmth from a rising/sun?" Read together, the two poems present a play on the homonyms *morning* and *mourning*. There is a sense that the dawn cannot come during this extended period of mourning while the memory of the revolution's end continues to haunt the Grenadian people. The meaning of dawn has shifted as a result of the revolution's collapse, and the connotation of a dawn that promises a new beginning accompanied by a sense of optimism is now absent. Here we have the retrospective rereading of the initial promise of the revolution. In the aftermath of October 1983, the lost dream is heartbreaking.

### Hurricane Blues

While flora are important to the assemblage of metaphors Collins employs to represent revolutionary violence while also holding on to the possibility of renewal, in another set of poems she draws on hurricane imagery, for the people of the region are as familiar with the seasonal return of these destructive cyclones as they are with political trauma. In Collins's postrevolution oeuvre she turns to this concept to evoke the sense of catastrophe that the end of the revolution brings. The image of the hurricane is one that has endured in Caribbean writing over time. Brathwaite's pronouncement that the hurricane does not roar in pentameter is perhaps the most famous use of hurricane imagery in Caribbean poetics.[49] Ironically, the image of the hurricane also works to illustrate renewal and rejuvenation. Hurricane season is an annual occurrence in the Caribbean. Every few years there is a terrible one that leaves total destruction in its wake, yet life goes on. People rebuild as best they can, but they do not forget, and stories of hurricanes are retold until they assume legendary status. In the image of the hurricane Collins finds a useful parallel for political upheaval and reconciliation in Grenada. Political change comes in cycles, and total destruction might ensue, but the nation repairs itself. As is evident in *The Colour of Forgetting,* part of the reparative process is the telling of stories. In some of her poems Collins stresses the ability to tell stories of political catastrophe as a survival mechanism. For Collins, the ability to narrate the island's history is intrinsic to the collective recovery process after any disaster. The challenge for Grenadians is to learn how to tell stories about the revolution. For many, this also means learning how to put their most painful experiences into narrative form.

In the poem "October, All Over" Collins uses a folk rhyme about hurricane season as a way to remember the end of the revolution.[50] The poem is concerned with political upheaval *and* with how the nation prepares for a hurricane. As Collins stages this comparison between political disaster (the revolution imploding) and natural disaster (the arrival of hurricanes in the region), she is implicitly reminding readers that what happened in Grenada in October 1983 was not at all "natural." The turn to natural catastrophe is not an essentializing gesture meant to equate all forms of disaster but rather an invitation to borrow methods of mourning and recovery from disasters (natural and man-made) of years past. The poem has a separate lyric embedded within it, a rhyme designed to help the listener remember when to expect hurricane season. The citation of a lyric within the poem itself implies the centrality of poetry to the recovery and remembrance process and the possibility of the word, written and oral, to create a fabric of healing within the collective consciousness of the nation:

> June, too soon;
> July, stand by;
> August look out, you must;
> September, remember;
> October, all over

This embedded lyric, like the poem it is framed by, is about rhythm, waiting, and anticipation, but it is also about foresight and divination. Hurricane season is an inevitable risk that Grenadians prepare for every year between July and October. The underlying tension throughout the poem marks the difference between political catastrophe and natural catastrophe. This reminds readers of the difficulty of predicting political violence.[51] The essential differences between the two kinds of violence are located in the ideas of agency and temporality. Collins both evades and draws attention to the problem of agency by drawing a parallel between the two modes of destruction. In situations of political violence, it is tempting to try to identify perpetrators and victims. Especially in a place such as Grenada, much of whose history is rooted in struggles for decolonization, the hurricane becomes an uneasy placeholder to represent political upheaval such as the revolution. Hurricanes often grow out of Harmattan windstorms that develop over the Sahara in Africa and move across the Atlantic into the Caribbean. That is, the hurricane that wreaks havoc in the Caribbean has a past, a trajectory that can be traced backward in time and space. It is an echo of the diasporic movement that created the Caribbean as a mélange of Atlantic societies and global flows. In Collins's writing, political catastrophes have a similar trajectory shaped by time and space. Both poems depend on a multifaceted sense of time to produce their knowledge. The frame poem is grounded in the present, the time of the aftermath of the revolution when the political process might be evaluated, and the embedded poem informed by hurricanes past in order to anticipate future storms. She consistently links the Grenada Revolution to other historical moments, emphasizing that politics in Grenada does not occur in a sociopolitical or cultural vacuum. The politics of decolonization is not only local. It is also part of the social and cultural fabric of the wider diaspora.

Collins uses the homograph *wind*, meaning both force of air and spiral direction of movement, to describe the hurricane's movement as a metaphor for the winding motion of history:

> Caribbean
> hurricane season and wind,
> raging, could just wind down on
>
> rooftop, grab it, lift it up,
> swing it high, fling it free, move
> it with a rhythm and a
>
> rhyme there from time.

The rhythm and rhyme "there from time" suggests that the explanation for the trauma of the revolution can be located in the internal logic that forms the Caribbean. Like the coming of hurricane season each year, so too is the region host to a winding or spiraling cycle of political tragedy and renewal.[52] In a similar way the last phrase of the rhyme, "all over," must be read for its multiple connotations: everywhere, or finished, or anticipating repetition, as in "all over again." As a signature to the events of 1983, "October, all over" marks a year when the island was safe from meteorological hurricane and instead faced political violence—a hurricane in the form of social and cultural destruction.

As in "Dream Mourning" and "Morning Glory," the poet-speaker in "October, All Over" is concerned with methods of reading the signs in nature to predict approaching trouble. In the previous two poems there were visible signs. But the younger generation did not pay attention, and those who could read the signs did not speak up or were not deemed reliable sources. In "October, All Over," however, nature itself is misleading because the signs of hurricane are absent during the height of hurricane season itself: "that hurricane sea-/son was cool as cucumber." The months before October 1983 showed no signs of the impending trauma: "Sky blue, no warning from ra-/dio, days sticky like wet co-/coa, sweating, turning slow." Nature's calm was setting the stage for a different kind of story: instead of striking at the climax of the season, the hurricane blows through unexpectedly at the end of the season, when the nation has let its guard down, thinking it had been spared:

> But sudden so
>
> one day in October ra-
> dio shouting bout rumours
> of wind. Some say, cho, some say,
>
> chupes, is October, all over
> already, man.

The initial signs are misunderstood and taken as false warnings; they are dismissed as "cho" and "chupes." Perhaps Grenadians were complacent because they were accustomed to knowing what was going on in their nation's politics, whether reported in the media or by bushgram. In small places news spreads by word of mouth and can circulate through the entire country fairly quickly in this manner. In the case of the revolution, rumors were circulating about discord within the party, but very few Grenadians could have guessed the extent to which the party was at odds with itself and the degree to which these problems would escalate. The warning rhyme is cited as proof that the rumors must be wrong. October is the end of the hurricane season. But the reality is that the political storm of October 1983 had been brewing behind closed doors for several months as the relationship between Maurice Bishop, Bernard Coard, and the Central Committee disintegrated and Bishop found himself at odds with the party.[53] These poems never mention revolution or politics, nor do they refer to any of the leaders by name. For readers familiar with the revolution, names are not necessary. The month of October alone is enough to evoke the entire history. This is something that is emphasized in Collins's poetry, which is the most compressed form of the genres in which she writes. The catastrophe is taken as a collective history that is always present and evoked in ways that remind readers how the revolution was a shared experience for the nation, no matter one's political affiliation. Responsibility is never assigned to any particular figure or "side," as her aim is not to blame but rather to tell a story that in many ways developed in secret and is in desperate need of airing:

> You know
> hurricane develop in
> secret? Not a whisper in
>
> breeze till wind with its rumour
> shake roof in October.

The question of how the hurricane develops is important because it addresses one of the reasons why the end of the revolution was so traumatic—namely, before October 1983 the government did not give the general public many signs that things were crumbling. From the time Bishop took over as prime minister, the NJM and the People's Revolutionary Government insisted that the major threats to Grenadian security and sovereignty were Eric Gairy and (a somewhat disembodied) U.S. imperialism. The revolution's leaders forged the joint leadership proposal in secret, and this meant that when Bishop changed his mind and no longer wanted to share leadership of the party, the citizenry was not prepared for the scenes of filial strife and fratricide that unfolded in rapid succession. The public was not primed for the revolutionary leaders to become their own worst enemies. Collins has expressed her surprise at hearing Minister of Foreign Affairs Unison Whiteman explain to her that the internal party conflict was turning into "civil war" in the final days of the chaos.[54] In hindsight, mapping logic onto chaos by way of a folk rhyme allows her to attempt to make sense of the turn of events. The disjuncture between "natural disaster" and human-produced political violence, however, constantly undermines this attempt at sense-making, so that the poem does double work, highlighting nature's internal logic while forcing readers to face the stark illogic that defined the actions of the government and party members in those final days.

In "Shame Bush," Collins makes a case for why certain patterns in Grenadian history, of which the revolution is a part, must end.[55] The poem is about the silence surrounding the history of the revolution among Grenadians more than twenty years later. Throughout the poem she makes repeated reference to "the silence people keeping." The cause for this silence is the sense of collective shame of the Grenadian people at the way the revolution ended.[56] She depicts this shame by evoking the image of the shame bush (scientific name, *Mimosa pudica*), a plant whose leaves close in on themselves when touched. Collins describes the plant's reaction to touch as a defense mechanism: "Watch shame bush/see how it close to defend itself." So too, the poem suggests, Grenadians become quiet when the topic of the revolution comes up. Shame bush can be found just about everywhere in Grenada. As in "October, All Over," Collins draws on metaphorical imagery that is part of Grenada's natural ecology. "Study shame bush, let me see you do that reading," she writes, and "you will understand the silence people keeping." Through this poem, Collins espouses a vision of reconciliation whereby Grenadians give voice to their memories of the revolution rather than shut out their own history the way the shame bush shuts out the world when touched. The metaphors provided by natural phenomena such as flora and hurricanes give Collins a local language with which to broach the painful subject. She, too, is careful to claim the inheritance from her ancestors and Grenada's natural environment to create a poetry that is at once rooted and forward-looking.

Collins closes the "Se Mwe, Nutmeg" section of *Lady in a Boat* with a poem titled "I d Open the Gate."[57] The poet-speaker addresses one of the Grenada 17, former members of the NJM convicted of orchestrating the assassinations of October 19. The speaker explains that if she could, she would release them from prison. She explains her reasoning as the result of "feeling": "I trust in your spirit, that/unsettling word." There are some Grenadians, those related to the victims, who would find this action egregious, the speaker admits. The prisoners, if they still believed in the ideology of the revolution, would find the act lacking in "clarity." But the poet-speaker insists on her intuition because this "sentimentality" and reliance on feeling and spirit represent precisely what was missing from the revolution in those final months and what is most needed in the present moment to effect repentance and forgiveness. The speaker is willing to release the imagined reader, this "one" still incarcerated, because of her sense of their innocence in relation to the crimes for which they have been convicted: "And I know there must be/others not guilty," she writes. Most poignant, however, is the speaker's suggestion that perhaps guilt and innocence are no longer productive categories for grappling with the revolution's aftermath. In this regard, she suggests that the release of the Grenada 17 prisoners is a possibility that all Grenadians need to consider to facilitate the healing, reconciliation, and truth-telling that the nation needs:

> And even
> for less innocent ones who
> have had time to think, I would
>
> ask, whose is vengeance? And, knowing
> the question would hurt many,
> whose is guilt? And how to
>
> speak of double loss?

Collins makes the point that the entire nation has suffered tremendously, including those responsible for Bishop's death, because of October 1983 and subsequent events. To continue in the absence of open dialogue only further mires Grenadians in a cycle of grief. The "double loss" she describes is both the loss of life from October 1983 and the loss of the history of the revolution in the endless cycle of grief. The revolution was four and a half years of work, joy, national pride, and growth. It should not be defined solely by the events of October 1983. In their desire to forget the trauma of that month, Grenadians have distanced themselves from the entire revolution, both its positive and negative legacies and impacts. While the loss of the revolution can never be replaced, Collins suggests the Grenadian people reclaim the histories of this period, lest these unclaimed stories become another loss themselves. In making the gesture of opening the gate for one, the poet-speaker expresses a desire to see her friend go free; and this gesture opens the gates of history, thus bringing the revolution back into the open. The poem offers a model of forgiveness and reconciliation that relies on the production and exploration of Grenadian history among Grenadians, relying on affect, literature, and ancestral knowledge.

Collins's writing keeps alternative historical records of Grenada and its revolution alive. Her work explores the revolution through the lens of local epistemologies that make room for discussions of how women shaped the revolution and how Grenadians understand it. The next chapter explores black radical masculinity and the gendered anxieties that arise in response to the representational challenges of the Grenada Revolution.

## 2  After the Invasion
Masculine Authority and
the Anxiety of Revolution

ON NOVEMBER 7, 1982, Prime Minister Bishop addressed an audience of invited dignitaries, University of the West Indies (UWI) staff, and members of government gathered on Tyrrell Street, in Grenada's capital, St. George's. He told them a creation story that exemplified the tension between the nationalist culture that buoyed the revolution's popularity and the internationalist character that influenced the New Jewel Movement (NJM). The story was about the birth of a black radical tradition in Grenada, and it revolved around the figure of T. A. Marryshow, a Grenadian politician and statesman and one of the architects of the West Indies Federation, the regional organization, comprising British Caribbean territories, that had been established in 1958 and dissolved in 1962.[1] Known as the "father of the West Indies Federation," Marryshow was born in Grenada in 1887. He was a journalist, political activist, and statesman for Grenada and the entire anglophone Caribbean. In 1915 he cofounded a newspaper called the *West Indian,* which he edited until 1924. In the early stages of decolonization he lobbied for Grenadians to achieve more local representation on colonial legislative councils. Marryshow was a skillful orator and used his skill as an activist for suffragist and labor movements in Grenada, as well as to promote the West Indies Federation.

The occasion of Bishop's address was the opening of a new theater at Marryshow House, the site of the UWI Centre in Grenada. The day marked the ninety-fifth anniversary of Marryshow's birth, and the NJM had decided that in his honor, November 7 would be known as T. A. Marryshow Day and a National Day of Culture for Grenada. At the beginning of his address that evening Bishop explained his relationship to Marryshow in terms of a Caribbean radical tradition: "Why is the memory and example of T. A. Marryshow so vital for us now in Grenada, and now throughout the Caribbean region? It is because Marryshow was the creator of a tradition, a set of principles and attitudes that since March 13th, 1979, we have struggled to implement, consolidate and extend."[2] He describes the memory of Marryshow as an indisputable discourse, one that is "vital" to a national and regional imaginary. According to Bishop, the NJM performs this inherent memory of Marryshow, implementing, consolidating, and extending the tradition through the pursuit of revolution. Bishop goes on to link Marryshow to another revolutionary figure in Grenada's history—Julien Fedon, leader of a 1795–1796 revolt of slaves and free people of color against the British colonial authority. Marryshow "grew from the earth" of the "rebel slave" Fedon, Bishop insists, and was himself the "inheritor of a revolutionary tradition that extends to . . . Fedon and the Haitian Revolution."[3] A linear reading of the history would prioritize Fedon and the leaders of the Haitian Revolution as the progenitors of the tradition, with Marryshow and Bishop as their descendants. But while Marryshow's radical activity follows Fedon's and that of the Haitian Revolution, Bishop refuses the linear reading and chooses to focus on Marryshow as the center of Grenada's radical tradition. Here a fragmented Caribbean imaginary, echoing the archipelagic shape of the islands, comes to bear on narratives of cultural and political resistance so that radical traditions, while created retrospectively, are subject to nonlinear revisions. Tradition becomes a concept mediated by contingency and disjointed dispersals of time and space.

Toward the end of his speech, Bishop creates a historical hinge between Marryshow and Lenin, a sleight of hand meant to connect the Grenada Revolution to the Russian Revolution. To do so, he points to Marryshow's article "Cycles of Civilization." "Cycles of Civilization" was written in 1917, Bishop explains to his audience, the same year that Lenin was "directing the Russian masses to storm the palaces of the Tzar."[4] It is after learning of the Russian Revolution that Marryshow was inspired to write "Cycles," Bishop surmises. This bit of speculation was indeed a stretch, as Marryshow's own writing makes it clear that "Cycles" was a response to racist statements by the South African general Jan Smuts.[5] Bishop needs Marryshow at the center of a tradition of revolution, however, in order to link Grenada to Lenin and to justify the role of socialism in the NJM's plans for the revolution. The majority of Grenadians admired Marryshow and supported the Grenada Revolution without links to Russian revolutionary history. While the connection between Marryshow and Lenin is dubious, it seems Bishop and the NJM needed this connection to assure *themselves* of the legitimacy of their process.

In this chapter I examine the writing of George Lamming, V. S. Naipaul, Derek Walcott, and Andrew Salkey, analyzing how their visions of revolutionary leadership are shaped by intersecting ideologies of gender, sexuality, race, and class. In the case of Lamming and Walcott, this includes the leaders' attachment to Marxism as a site for the performance of black radical masculinity. In Salkey's work the presence of a strident anticolonial activism, imagined without the black Marxist masculinity, represents an attempt to steer the legacy of the Grenada Revolution in a direction that might better account for the interplay of gender, violence, and authority in struggles for Caribbean sovereignty. I analyze Lamming's 1982 "The Education of Feeling," Naipaul's 1984 "An Island Betrayed," Walcott's "Good Old Heart of Darkness," published in the same year, and Salkey's "After the Counter-Revolution, After the Invasion," published in 1998, to highlight how this literature functions as a political tool that (re)produces, represents, and contests revolutionary authority. Lamming, Naipaul, Walcott, and Salkey were part of a generation of writers whose visions of freedom focused on taking the reins from the British and proving they were equally capable of governing within a model of governance that mimicked the British parliamentary system. This was the first generation to benefit from the suffrage movement. In Grenada, folks of this generation would have been early supporters of Eric Gairy, who in the 1950s broke the back of the brown elite and championed the rights of rural workers. By the late 1970s, as the Grenada Revolution took off, however, these writers, and this generation more broadly, were grappling with Caribbean attempts to build new nations while adhering to the Westminster model. This mode of parliamentary democracy had failed to produce sovereignty in the form of independence in economic and international affairs, infrastructure development, fair access to education, improved employment, and living wages. Marxism-Leninism provided a roadmap to sovereignty for the NJM generation in a way that it did not for Lamming, Naipaul, Salkey, and Walcott. Black Marxism in the Caribbean moved away from the brand of black leadership represented by figures such as Gairy with strongholds among the rural folk. This form of Marxism was present among the town-based brown-skinned intelligentsia and the aspiring, upwardly mobile black middle class. The younger generation of radicals was also interested in improving the plight of the nation's rural population, but they did so via Marx, Lenin, Fanon, Nyerere, and even Garvey. During his speech on Marryshow, Lenin, and Grenada, Bishop's intention was to educate Grenadians about the version of revolutionary history that was guiding the NJM's leadership and to generate further support for the revolution. The awkward connection to Lenin in the midst of a speech that was otherwise concerned with regional history created the kind of narrative disruption that Lamming and Walcott would seize on in their critiques of the revolution.

Lamming, Walcott, and Salkey represent a range of views, but what their work shares is an interest in the potential for a distinctly Caribbean political future. The NJM's attachment to Marxism compromised the integrity of the Grenada Revolution by creating unnecessary distance between its leaders and the Grenadian people. Lamming had no grievance with the ideological content of Marxism, which he thought was sound. Rather, his critique centered on how the NJM communicated with the Grenadian public about Marxism and its role in the revolution. Lamming and Walcott were both concerned about how language was used by the revolutionaries. For all three writers, their critique of the NJM's treatment of language and writers was a way of arguing for the importance of Caribbean forms of expression. I read in their critiques, as well, attempts to take stock of their own literary authority, as the rhetorical spaces created by the revolution seemed to have displaced people like Walcott, whose troubled relationship with black cultural and political nationalism predated the Grenada Revolution, and to a lesser extent Lamming. While the discourse was not openly competitive, competing visions of nationalism and black masculinity are at play between these two generations. Lamming, Walcott, and Salkey came of age as writers who mastered English forms and found ways to make these forms their own, to reconcile the complex literary legacies of colonialism in the nascent world of Caribbean letters. For Bishop and his comrades to leap to Lenin exposes the tension between the nationalist narrative of a Caribbean, black radical tradition and the ideological leanings of the revolutionary party, which were decidedly internationalist. Indeed, the Grenada Revolution itself serves as an indication of a nationalist narrative in some ways at odds with itself and in other ways attempting to fashion a creolized political discourse in order to reimagine postcolonial independence in the face of U.S. imperialism. The inclusion of Lenin in the NJM's Grenadian black radical tradition calls into question the place of national or even regional imaginaries as discrete discourses. Bishop's insistence on this contingent relation between Marryshow and Lenin, between the Grenada Revolution and the Russian Revolution, points to the desire to make Grenada mean something beyond the region, to connect the NJM's vision to another tradition. At the same time, it highlights the troubling disconnect between the NJM's theory and the Grenadian public's praxis. This vision of world revolution reproduces certain colonialist ideas of national leadership as the domain of exceptional men.

## Peculiar Forms of Fervor, or Marxism and Caribbean Being

Born in Barbados in 1927, Lamming is one of the writers considered to be at the forefront of mid-twentieth-century anglophone Caribbean writing, along with Kamau Brathwaite, Naipaul, Salkey, and Walcott, just as islands such as Barbados, Jamaica, and Trinidad were gaining political independence. By 1966, when Barbados became a sovereign state, Lamming had already published an essay collection and four novels, including the classic 1953 *In the Castle of My Skin*. He was a cosmopolitan figure, moving from Barbados to Trinidad, thence to England, back across the waters to Jamaica, and finally to the United States. In the late 1970s, as the Grenada Revolution started, Lamming, then in his early fifties, was already an elder statesman of Caribbean letters. He was a vocal and visible champion of the revolution, but he was also vocal about some of the flaws he saw in the government's approach to articulating an ideology of revolution.

In November 1982, just a few weeks after Bishop's Marryshow address, Lamming spoke at the "Education Is Production Too!" conference in Carriacou, part of Grenada's tri-island state.[6] Sponsored by the People's Revolutionary Government (PRG), the audience comprised a coalition of Grenadian artists, educators, and intellectuals, as well as international intellectuals and activists such as the Kenyan writer Ngugi wa' Thiong'o, the British antiracism activist and educator Chris Searle, and the Jamaican American civil rights activist Harry Belafonte. The themes Lamming addressed would have been recognizable to anyone familiar with his literature. He spoke of class tensions between generations (parents and their children), the shifting political ethos of the times, and the challenges of identifying distinctly Caribbean solutions to the problems of colonialism and postcolonialism in the region. He summarized all these concerns under the rubric "The Education of Feeling," a need he saw to cultivate "the creative imagination" of Caribbean people.[7] This was Lamming asking what it would mean to theorize imagination, locally, with a specifically Caribbean population in mind. His answer: it meant learning how to value formal and informal education and to take seriously one's own thoughts and feelings, as well as the thoughts and feelings of one's neighbors and community members. In Lamming's view, a large part of the education he espoused had to do with language and ideology.

He used his address to question the disjuncture he saw between, on the one hand, the rhetoric and ideology of the Grenada Revolution, as promoted by the PRG and the NJM, and on the other the lived experience of Caribbean people, who were trying to move toward forms of political liberation that were more meaningful than "flag independence."[8] He addressed the audience with a wry sense of humor that helped to establish his comments as a friendly assessment of where Grenadians might need to exercise caution. Throughout his address he couched his critique in a series of anecdotes about his own life, including descriptions of his friendships, his relationship with his mother, and his fiction writing.

Lamming begins his speech recalling his time as a young teacher in Trinidad in the late 1940s, hanging out with a friend named Cliff. Perusing Cliff's bookshelf, Lamming noticed many books in Russian, including texts written by and about Joseph Stalin and Vladimir Lenin. Cliff and Lamming never read these books, he explains, because neither of them could read Russian. Still, having them on the shelves was of great symbolic importance to Cliff. The objects of cathexis, books related to the Russian Revolution were enough to secure their sense of themselves as young radicals. "Fervour can take peculiar form sometimes," Lamming notes. "As long as it was in Russian, you were doing justice." Lamming chastises his younger self for being naïve enough to think that owning books was somehow contributing to radical action. In mentioning Stalin, he implicitly invites listeners to engage in a retrospective evaluation of the Russian Revolution. By linking the image of a violent dictator to Marxism-Leninism as practiced in the Caribbean, Lamming was issuing a thinly veiled warning to his audience about dictatorship, violence, and the dangers of uncritical political fervor. This was a bold statement for him to make with the PRG as his host; however, it appears to have been offered in the spirit of self-criticism that the Grenada revolutionaries valued, in keeping with Marxism-Leninism. While he and Cliff felt they understood something about the spirit of the Russian Revolution, Lamming still represented Russian revolutionary writing as illegible to Caribbean people. With this anecdote, Lamming was asking whether a foreign ideology can be sufficiently adapted for Caribbean realities. Embedded in this critique is the notion that youthful revolutionaries may be preoccupied with the *image* of radicalism that an adherence to Marxism-Leninism provides; even with a project aimed at producing justice, they use Marxist-Leninist theory to amplify their message and secure a greater sense of legitimacy.

It was also important for Lamming to make a statement about language in Caribbean revolution. Central to his argument is the burdensome way he thought Marxism (in its form and content) had been used to structure radical politics in the postcolonial Caribbean. He muses, "I have spent a lot of my life in association with Marxists of a variety of colours. But I have never in my life met a Marxist baby. Never. Never. Nor have I ever met a Christian baby. When a man tells me he is a Marxist, that is of great interest, but there is a matter that fascinates me more. I want to know how he got there. I want to know what was the particular journey that took him from wherever he was to that point of perception and conviction and redemption which he calls Marxist." In sharing this idea, Lamming assesses that the NJM's increasing emphasis on Marxism was off-base, or at least that a clearer accounting for Marxism's prominence in the party's ideology was necessary. Whereas Marxists were quick to point out forms of false consciousness, Lamming's address questions whether Marxism itself might be considered a kind of false consciousness for a region deeply rooted in other epistemologies of radicalism and resistance.

In discussing his skepticism of doctrinaire ideologies, whether the political ideology of Marxism or the religious ideology of Christianity, Lamming reminds his audience that these are identities that we learn and perform, not identities to which we are born. His insistence that he has never met a Marxist baby cues listeners to consider how one is socialized into ideological identities. In the context of the postcolonial Caribbean, what does it mean to embrace Marxism as, in Lamming's words, "a point of perception, conviction, and redemption," particularly if that means choosing Marxism over and above another form that could be derived from the region's history of revolution and anticapitalist (via antislavery) traditions of resistance that predate Marx and Marxist theory? The NJM leaders might have argued that Marxist theory is a product of the historical period when New World slavery was being abolished and different social and economic relations were being negotiated. And Lamming might have counterargued: Yes, but the enslaved knew how to resist enslavement, understanding the relations of production on their own terms. Lamming's critique somewhat elides the importance of socialism to the Non-Aligned Movement and the south-south solidarities that shaped the later push for greater postcolonial sovereignty; but again, this only amplifies the generational difference between him and the NJM leadership.

The "particular journey" that Lamming refers to is a journey through language and affect. Traditional Marxist theory comes with a language and set of circumstances rooted in the European experience, and he questions whether Marxist political identity and the language associated with it are necessary to achieve freedom in the Caribbean. He exhibits a skepticism about Marxism and suggests that the best way to proceed in the region is through a language that is locally rooted and understood by its people. Throughout his address, Lamming offers other anecdotes that outline what this locally established Caribbean politics might look and sound like while also explaining its close relationship to language and storytelling. It is a line of argument that assumes a clear distinction between Marxism and Caribbean political identity, but it works for Lamming because he understands certain aspects of Marxism to be universally applicable. That is, Marxism's detachment from Caribbean reality is in its language, not necessarily its practice. Since language is a site for the contestation of power, when Caribbean people use a language without making it their own, they give up some of their power. His use of the anecdote, an informal mode of storytelling, is itself a reclamation of the power of the colloquial. These anecdotes re-center Caribbean life in local, revolutionary discourse. Lamming argues against the importation of what he sees as a European theory and language into a context where Caribbean people already have the theory, experience, language, and stories they need to confront the problems of neocolonialism. If part of the issue Lamming addresses is about the generational transference of theory and praxis, then the NJM revolutionaries just need to adopt the right "education of feeling" to recognize and value the wealth of the resources at their fingertips.

Another humorous story Lamming shares focuses on a meeting he had with Cliff years later in London. Cliff invites him over for Sunday dinner; on arriving, he is surprised to learn that Cliff has become a vegetarian. This is a great disappointment for Lamming, who claims he was expecting stewed pork with his Sunday meal. What irked him in this moment was that Cliff did not announce his new dietary restrictions in advance, and yet he expected Lamming to go along. Lamming insists that had he known, he would have brought his own provisions to the meal. He dislikes Cliff's assumption that others should be subjected to his new beliefs without warning or explanation. He suggests that Cliff's newfound interest in vegetarianism is linked to his time abroad in England, that London has changed Cliff. There is also a machismo underscoring these stories, an understanding that Cliff's and Lamming's political explorations were also explorations of Caribbean masculinity and male camaraderie. He uses these comedic anecdotes about his younger self and his friend Cliff to question the youthful enthusiasm around scientific Marxism that was characteristic of the revolution's leaders. Several of the NJM leadership were educated abroad, and their early exposure to Marxism took place in foreign contexts. In these parable-like stories, Cliff is a stand-in for the Grenada revolutionaries who were setting a new agenda that the Grenadian people were not quite prepared for or fully briefed on.

Lamming challenges his audience to think about how it might feel for the Grenadian people to be offered the revolution in a set of terms that was initially quite legible to them, only to later face a revolution whose rhetoric seemed to shift away from local concerns and toward an ideology that, at least in its language, was disconnected from large swaths of the population. Lamming's stories about Cliff illustrate betrayal on a small, comic scale, but they are reminders to the revolutionaries of the importance of making clear to their constituents the goals of the revolution and the processes through which those goals would be achieved. The Grenadian people have a right to expect transparency and communication around questions of national importance. In sharing these anecdotes, Lamming represents himself as an older and wiser version of the revolutionaries, someone who has experienced the earnestness and early passion of radicalism and is now willing to unsettle the assumption that revolutions are one size fits all. But as a foil to Cliff, he has also been in the position of the Grenadian public. Particularly in terms of language and rhetoric, he is demonstrating that the very content of the struggle must be specific to the Caribbean and to local modes of thinking, feeling, and speaking. The experience of being asked to adhere to an ideology and speech that do not reflect one's own experiences or values is disheartening, he reminds listeners, and undermines the Grenada Revolution's goal of national unity and sovereignty.

The most powerful anecdote Lamming tells is how, as a ten-year old boy, he came to understand class relations in Barbados. Unlike the other anecdotes, this example does not rely on humor. Instead his tone darkens as he describes being surrounded by his friends one day, walking home from school. He saw his mother walking in his direction, and she saw him too, but he chose not to acknowledge her. He was embarrassed to greet her because it would have been a tacit acknowledgment of the difference in class background between him and his better-off friends. The episode is one that produces a sense of shame in Lamming because even as a youth, he understood that was it wrong to dismiss his mother this way: He recognizes the perversity of a system that would require this of him. His mother had sent him to a particular school so that he could be upwardly mobile and lift the family's circumstances. They were both complicit in the decision not to acknowledge each other in public. It was troubling, Lamming thought, that he would be expected to deny his mother in order to promote the social and economic prosperity of their family, and that they would share in this understanding without ever vocalizing it. Indeed, he represents it as a grave taboo that shifts their relationship irrevocably. The encounter is a lesson in class consciousness that is painfully comprehensible for child and adult alike. The gender implications of the scene are also stark: a mother labors to provide an elevated social status for her son, which simultaneously creates distance between them. This version of class consciousness is a familiar Caribbean experience. As hard as the Caribbean left was working to counter the advancement of neocolonialism in the region, Lamming observes that it was losing the battle when it came to addressing the issue of communicating and translating its ideas for average people, who were already "victims of a scarcity of knowledge." This anecdote places the audience in a position to rethink its own relationship to Marx and class consciousness because it insists that there are ideas for which Caribbean people do not need Marx as a detour or theoretical guide. Grenadians can draw lessons such as these from their own lived experiences.

Lamming calls on his audience to recognize the multiple sites at which education, both formal and informal, takes place. The anecdote about his mother interrupts the male-centered discourse that he began with in reminiscing about the contents of Cliff's bookshelf. It also signals a need to rethink how women's labor is rendered invisible in the production and promotion of masculine agency and leadership. Speaking directly to the leaders of the revolution when he references the Caribbean left, Lamming asks them to combine their theoretical knowledge with attention to local epistemologies, including thinking about women and mothers as sources of knowledge and participants in radical struggle. He is concerned that Caribbean people risk liberating "ourselves into some other kind of being" when foreign ideologies, including those from Cuba and Russia, are taken up without sufficient attention to local realities. The revolution's leaders need to become better teachers to ensure that Grenadians do not lose essential parts of themselves in the pursuit of liberation. While Cuba is undeniably Caribbean, colonial divisions persisted, and some Grenadians were wary of Cuban influence on the PRG. For Lamming, the education of feeling is about the experience of liberation as a process that is rooted in local communities with local people and the different experiences and skill sets they bring to the table.

Lamming takes advantage of the conference's theme of education to stress language and literature as sites for liberation, without privileging the classroom as the main site of knowledge transference. Acknowledging a unique role for writers during turbulent political times, he analyzes the difference between writing that exists to serve an explicitly political cause and his own writing, which was always political but equally imaginative. This latter kind of writing, not wedded exclusively to a politics but instead prioritizing the development of Caribbean poetics, is necessary, Lamming argues, to produce and reflect on the feeling of sovereignty.[9] Caribbean writers, and fiction writers in particular, are essential to both producing and representing this education as a form of knowledge that springs from local, Caribbean visions.

## Writing Postrevolutionary Grenada

In September 1983 the party proposed that Bishop and Bernard Coard share party leadership, hoping such an arrangement would stop the tailspin the government had entered. Foreign aid was beginning to dry up, and key party members were suffering from exhaustion. Bishop was still the most charismatic and popular figure of the revolution. His image and his words were at the center of its representational apparatus, but there was always a tension between Bishop and his public. While his early speeches demonstrated a sense of openness and transparency, there was the unmissable fact that the revolution had been planned in near total secrecy. Further, the NJM had become a vanguard party without publicizing it, leaving many Grenadians in the dark as to how the party viewed itself. The change was carried out in relative secrecy and without the input of the Grenadian people. Neither the men nor the party's Central Committee could have predicted the consequences of the joint leadership plan and its failure, and the extent to which U.S. destabilization efforts contributed to the revolution's demise remains uncertain. It is clear, however, that the actions taken by the party and the military leading up to Bishop's assassination in October 1983 would have been different had the party felt a deeper sense of accountability to the Grenadian people not only in terms of ideology but also with respect to communication. Instead, Bishop's assassination signaled the end of the revolution and a crisis of identity for the Caribbean left. Throughout the region there was an overall sense that the Caribbean had lost one of its most important voices and that the will of the Grenadian people had been betrayed on multiple fronts.

Lamming's words were to prove sadly prophetic. "It is the tragedy of a whole region which has brought us here," Lamming pronounced in December 1983 at the Cathedral Church of the Holy Trinity in Port of Spain, Trinidad, during a memorial service for Bishop and others killed that October.[10] The service was convened by the Trinidad Oilfield Trade Workers' Union, a group that had stood in solidarity with the Grenada Revolution. Lamming's address is angry and mournful. Tasked with remembering the good that Bishop and the revolution had achieved, he blamed "a small gang of native military killers" for opening the door for America's invasion, characterizing those responsible for Bishop's assassination as a minority within the Grenadian military sphere. He lamented the impossible circumstances Grenadians faced in welcoming neocolonial forces. While he hoped that Grenadians would wake up to the reality of the U.S. violation of Caribbean sovereignty, he empathized with those who felt backed into a corner after Bishop's assassination.

In eulogizing Bishop, Lamming was also eulogizing the revolution and offering an inventory of what remained to be salvaged for the Caribbean left, shamed as it was by the events of October 1983. In an echo of C. L. R. James's roll call of Caribbean revolutionary thinkers at the end of *The Black Jacobins,* this inventory is offered almost entirely in the image of Caribbean men.[11] Lamming credits Trinidadian prime minister George Chambers with good leadership for showing Caribbean independence by refusing to join the group of nations that participated in the invasion. He speculates that another political giant, the late Eric Williams, would have done the same. Lamming also draws parallels between Bishop and another fallen Caribbean revolutionary, Guyana's Walter Rodney. His references to Rodney add to the regional dynamic of his address. Bishop and Rodney both broke ranks with the privileged order that afforded them "education and social opportunity" in order to serve those of lesser means, Lamming says, and they paid for their integrity with their lives. Lamming critiques Marxism implicitly here through his praise of Bishop as a man who "required no textbook, no sterile list of abstract principles to recognize where his duty lay." Here we see the beginnings of the oversimplified and in some aspects misleading narrative that would represent the October 1983 power struggle as a conflict between Bishop as a "moderate" socialist and Coard as the more hard-line Marxist. It is true, however, that of all the NJM's leaders, Bishop was singularly capable of communicating the revolution's goals in ways that the Grenadian public could easily grasp. It is this dedication to the Grenadian people that Lamming recognizes: "His head found a home in the hearts of his people at a mass level; and he tried to move forward from his concrete experience of their reality." This commitment to the people is what made Bishop and Rodney threatening to the new postcolonial order, Lamming argues, and they were martyred by a system that was still deeply tied to colonialism.

In late October 1983, the Trinidadian novelist V. S. Naipaul was also taking stock of what had transpired in Grenada, visiting the island to write a piece on the invasion for *Harper's Magazine*. Naipaul was decidedly antirevolutionary. His 1984 article, "An Island Betrayed," presents a three-part critique of the revolution and ends with a mocking dismissal of the four-and-a-half-year political process.[12] Naipaul argues that the Grenada Revolution failed because it was a revolution of rhetoric and not action. Unlike Lamming, Naipaul did not believe in any part of the revolution; thus he claims the government produced many slogans and various forms of literature but did little concrete good for Grenadian society. By defining the revolution as *merely* rhetorical, Naipaul claims that it was not real but rather a kind of political theater or make-believe. He points

**Figure 5.** "If You Know Teach, If You Don't Learn" billboard, Gouyave, St. John's, Grenada. (© Kathy Sloane, courtesy of the photographer)

to Grenada's smallness, both in census and in geography, as the critical reason for the inability of Grenadians to truly forge a revolution: "The revolution was a revolution of words. The words appeared as an illumination, a short-cut to dignity, to newly educated men who had nothing in the community to measure themselves against, and who finally, valued little in their own community. But the words were mimicry. They were too big; they didn't fit; they remained words. The revolution blew away, and what was left in Grenada was a murder story."[13]

Central to Naipaul's argument is the idea that the revolution was simply a coup in the course of which young Black Power radicals removed an older, incompetent prime minister. These young socialists then used military force and stylized rhetoric to keep unwitting Grenadians hostage under a spell of Cuban-influenced Marxist-Leninist politics. For Naipaul, the NJM and the PRG had adopted a series of narrative performances designed to mimic both Grenadian vernacular forms (such as carnival) and European political-ideological forms (such as Marxism-Leninism), and in doing so had created the specter of revolution where none actually existed. Where Lamming makes a genuine plea for greater attention to local epistemologies, Naipaul dismisses the entire process. He objects to the displacement of the recognizable norms of colonial and neocolonial governance in favor of Marxism-Leninism. Here we find echoes of Lamming's argument; however, Naipaul's critique is hollowed out by his disregard for Grenadians.

Naipaul's statement is contradictory and inaccurate on several counts. In calling the revolution a "short-cut to dignity," he concedes that independence had failed to restore a sense of dignity and world recognition to postcolonial Caribbean nations. His claim that the revolutionaries "had nothing in the community to measure themselves against" is inconsistent with his observation that they "valued little in their own community." The revolutionary leaders in Grenada demonstrated that they had much to measure themselves against, in light of the history of anticolonialism in the Caribbean and their attention to black radical traditions at home and abroad. Their recognition of this history is part of what motivated their actions. Acknowledging this history was inconvenient for Naipaul, who wanted to convince his Anglo-American readers that Grenadians were not capable of leading a truly radical movement. His choice of a minor literary genre, the murder mystery, to characterize the Grenada Revolution reduces the four-and-a-half-year process to one day in October 1983. It indicates his belief that what took place in Grenada was not worthy of the genres revolution usually evokes, epic and tragedy.

The conclusions Naipaul comes to about Grenada, however, are no surprise to readers who have followed his work.[14] His observations are in keeping with the opinions he has expressed about the Caribbean as a whole: it is a place too black, too poor, and too backward to produce anything worthy to be deemed "history" or "politics," both privileged categories for Naipaul because he believes they emanate primarily from Europe and to a lesser extent the United States and Canada. Implicit here is a subtle critique of the United States for overreacting to Grenada's political situation. One of Naipaul's blind spots in his reading of the revolution, however, was his focus on the leadership and his failure to consider the mass appeal and participation the revolution generated. The Grenadian public is mainly absent from his critique. While Naipaul's reading of the revolution's historical and political impact is grossly and purposely understated, his focus on the importance of writing and mimicry in revolutionary Grenada identifies a critical feature of the revolution—namely, the intersection of history, politics, and culture and the resulting centrality of language, rhetoric, and performance in the context of radical change on the island. A more nuanced discussion of the confluence of these features can be located in Derek Walcott's attempts to write the revolution.

**Tainted Regret**

Although the article was never published, the *New York Review of Books* (NYRB) commissioned Walcott's "Good Old Heart of Darkness" shortly after the U.S. invasion.[15] Walcott appears to have started the essay in late 1983 or early 1984. The latest versions exist in two incomplete drafts, one with handwritten edits from Walcott and the other bearing handwritten edits by Robert S. Silvers, editor of the NYRB. A letter from Silvers accompanies the draft that he edited. In this letter, dated November 11, 1984, Silvers asks Walcott to shorten the piece. It was almost 12,000 words in that draft. In the following discussion, except where noted I quote Walcott's words from the latter version, not Silvers's suggested edits. Walcott refused to visit Grenada during the revolution and had to rely mainly on published reports and to a lesser extent on word of mouth to decide where he stood on matters pertaining to the island. But he did a fair amount of research on the U.S. invasion of Grenada. His files include newspaper clippings, books illustrating the uniforms that were worn by the U.S. military, U.S. State Department reports, copies of Grenadian government documents seized during the invasion, and other ephemera. "Good Old Heart of Darkness" is a frustrated attempt to narrate the

Grenada Revolution. When he found he could not bring a sense of order to the place of Grenada in essay form, he aborted the project.

A reading of this archive makes apparent, however, that none of these materials were sufficient to help Walcott come to any conclusions about Grenada. The essay title references Joseph Conrad's 1899 novella *Heart of Darkness,* a classic work on the structural violence of colonialism. The "good old" in Walcott's tongue-in-cheek phrasing is a reminder that this violence will not go away. The essay captures his ambivalence about the role of the poet in revolution and at the moment of political trauma, an ambivalence that results in the bifurcation of a political tradition of nationalist revolution from a literary tradition of writing the nation. It is possible that Walcott never published his work on Grenada because the revolution upset both the literary and political traditions from which his work originates. The narrative of a triumphant, masculine leadership was preserved with the beginning of the Grenada Revolution in 1979, but in a very different form, breaking with notions of Victorian manhood that still undergirded the wave of nationalism of the 1960s anglophone Caribbean, when Walcott's reputation as a leading voice in the region was cemented.[16] Walcott experienced a crisis of authorial privilege when the end of the Grenada Revolution left no clear actors with whom he could side. Finding himself at a literary and political crossroad, he reads the revolution as an emblem for a Caribbean that may never truly free itself of empire. Again, anthropologist David Scott's image of "the aftermath without end" applies to the unending crisis of colonialism and anticolonial resistance Grenada presents for Walcott.[17] Scott argues that the Grenada Revolution, while once imbued with a sense of "messianic futurity" (the promise of something to be delivered), lives on in the Caribbean imaginary as a state of "ruined time," as it has never had the opportunity to deliver on its promise. In its wake, Caribbean people contend with the memories of this promise and the knowledge of its failure. Walcott's sense of this failure is at the center of the impasse at which he finds himself in "Good Old Heart of Darkness."

Like Lamming and Naipaul, Walcott was also critical of the revolution's Marxist influences, though his reasons were distinct. While other Caribbean writers, notably those who wrote and spoke favorably of the revolution, including Merle Hodge, Audre Lorde, and Earl Lovelace, along with Collins and Brand, were enthusiastic about the revolution and willing to look past the revolutionary government's censorship and detention of certain journalists and political opponents, Walcott remained staunchly opposed to censorship in any form.[18] His criticism was not unfounded.

The PRG shut down private newspapers such as the *Torchlight* and the *Grenadian Voice;* the latter had to close after publishing just one issue, in June 1981. Leslie Pierre, one of the journalists behind the *Grenadian Voice*, remained in detention in Richmond Hill Prison until the U.S. invasion. The PRG also spied on and harassed journalist Alister Hughes and members of the Grenadian Rastafari community. While Walcott was concerned about how writers were treated during the revolution, he was simultaneously disturbed by the U.S. military aggression, which he viewed as an unlawful occupation and a violation of Caribbean sovereignty. "Good Old Heart of Darkness" details his alienation, then, from the revolution and a community of politically engaged and vocal writers at the same time as it expresses a qualified solidarity with these writers. At a time when several Caribbean writers seemed, for the most part, to be closing ranks around the idea of supporting Bishop and the revolution, Walcott's critique of the NJM left him feeling like an outsider in the world of Caribbean letters. He writes: "I had begun to feel as if I were a kind of political albino, an outsider from the regime, with the taste of digested bile, perhaps treachery even, to the Revolution's ideals of racial and economic equality at the cost of poetry."[19]

While his use of albinism as a metaphor is problematic in its othering of those living with the condition, the metaphor captures Walcott's sense of the difference he felt between himself and the creative community surrounding the revolution. At the same time, he was deeply invested in the idea of writing the nation and upholding the freedom of the writer as emblematic of a nation's freedom. Though he agrees with the policies of racial and economic equality that the revolution stood for, Walcott is unable to tolerate the threat to any writer. To make his point, he invokes calypso, noting that in a region where calypso music is used as a vehicle to criticize politicians, the censorship of writers stifles artistic production. This, he argues, is a dangerous way of controlling public discourse.[20] He is pointing up the compromises some writers made to support what they viewed as the mainly admirable and urgent goals of the revolution. The military and Marxist-Leninist image of the Grenada Revolution was enough to make people afraid, he continues: "When I pictured a military Communist regime in Grenada, so close to my own island, my spine iced. The Caribbean was vociferous. You cursed the Government in the squares. Calypsos, immune from libel, slandered politicians without proof. If people were fraid to talk they would be scared to sing and scared to write. This was one of the sacrifices of the Revolution, perhaps its first. I was fraid too, from that distance. We learn to believe in our cowardice, we writers."21 Walcott implicates himself in his own critique here, suggesting that perhaps he could have spoken up earlier despite his own fear, since his distance from Grenada protected him. He would also have been aware of the writers in Grenada who were in favor of the revolution. They wrote and published freely, some of them even working for the government or

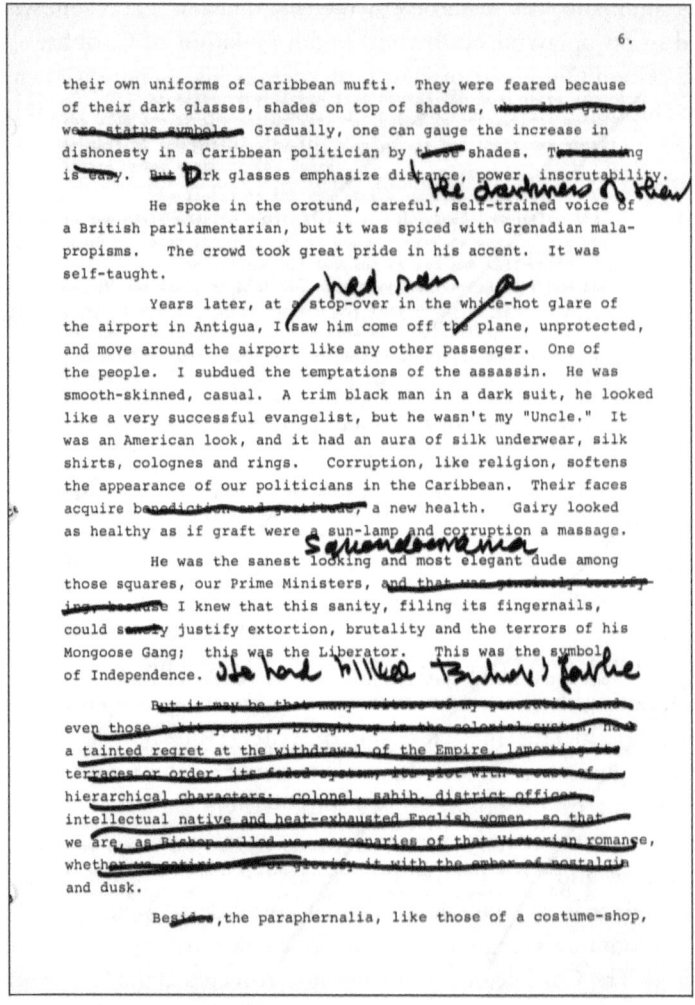

Figure 6. Manuscript page from "Good Old Heart of Darkness" with Derek Walcott's handwritten corrections. (Courtesy of the Estate of Derek Walcott and the Thomas Fisher Rare Book Library, University of Toronto)

beginning their careers as writers because of the revolution, Merle Collins and Jacob Ross being the most well-known examples. The Trinidadian novelist Merle Hodge is another important figure who lived and worked in Grenada during the revolution. The output of Lamming, Brand, and Collins, who each spent time in Grenada during the period and who wrote during and about the revolution, proves that not all writing was stifled by the government; rather, they all wrote in favor of the revolution. While some, such as Allister Hughes and Pierre, who were critical of the revolution, were silenced in crucial ways, others flourished, marking one of the key contradictions of the revolution.[22]

When Walcott insists that the revolution's pursuit of racial and economic equality comes at the cost of poetry, he is aware, of course, of the impossibility of separating poetry from politics. In the medieval origins of the term, *poetry* was the writing and representation of classical mythology. Walcott's concern for the preservation of poetry is also an attachment to certain myths that for him had come to define the Caribbean. The politics of the region, especially revolution, are essential to this mythology, as are various images from the region's colonial past. These competing and contradictory myths include nostalgia for the fiction of a politically stable colonial period (a myth that ignores the active ways the colonized resisted their oppressors), as compared with the myths of heroic rebels vanquishing the colonial power (an image that often elides the sacrifices made in quests for freedom). In the aftermath of the necessary anticolonial struggles and the disappointments of independence, the essay expresses Walcott's longing for a way to find order amid the challenges of postcolonial life. His struggle to reconcile the reality of Grenada with his vision of what the Caribbean could have been is tied directly to a literary imaginary of empire: "But it may be that many writers of my generation, and even those a bit younger, brought up in the colonial system, have a tainted regret at the withdrawal of the Empire, lamenting its terraces of order, its faded system, its plot with a cast of hierarchical characters: colonel, sahib, district officer, intellectual native and heat-exhausted English women, so that we are, as Bishop called us mercenaries of that Victorian romance, whether we satirize it or glorify it with the ember of nostalgia and dusk."[23] This passage describes hierarchies unique to the English domination of colonies while also alluding to an English literary tradition of colonial novels—in the vein of E. M. Forster's 1924 *A Passage to India* or Conrad's *Heart of Darkness*. Walcott's gloss implicitly cites the violence of this colonial period, hidden just beneath the superficial appearance of order. The novels he references are obsessed with this violence and the threat of it. His tongue-in-cheek yearning for this "order"—again, both political and literary—illustrates the feeling of being between a rock and a hard place when faced with the violence both of the colonial past and of the postcolonial present. He is naming the trauma of both realities and identifying the puzzle of imagining what Caribbean sovereignty could look and feel like, given these histories. There does not seem to be a good model.

As a writer whose life had played out under the system of colonialism until the late 1960s, Walcott was disturbed not by the unfamiliarity of a narrative of victory followed by tragedy so forcefully represented in the Grenada Revolution but rather by the too recognizable nature of that narrative, repeating as it did a painful pattern that Caribbean revolutionaries could not quit. He had already written about political jealousy and fratricide in the aftermath of the Haitian Revolution in his first play, *Henri Christophe*, published in 1949.[24] *Henri Christophe* was Walcott's attempt to complicate narratives of the Haitian Revolution that focused on enslaved Africans' heroic overcoming of colonial slavery and their efforts to replace the colonial order with black political power. Walcott had long been ambivalent about the efficacy of black power as a political ideology in a multiethnic Caribbean and critical of postcolonial governing structures that resembled colonial authority.[25] To his way of thinking, the revolutionaries in Grenada, in their preoccupation with shoring up authority and legitimacy in a hostile international context and their overarching fear of being attacked, had fallen prey to similar pitfalls as the ones that had plagued Jean-Jacques Dessalines and Henri Christophe in postrevolutionary Haiti. They could not escape the corrupting force of absolute power.

One of the key moments of the PRG's censorship that is absent from Walcott's discussion of the issue was the question of press freedom and the PRG's decision to close the *Torchlight* newspaper in October 1979. The *Torchlight* was privately owned by Grenada Publishers Limited. Its managing director and chief shareholder was Grenadian businessman, D. M. B. Cromwell. Cromwell was a former director of Grenada's Inland Revenue office and had close ties to Grenada's business sector. The *Trinidad Express* was another major shareholder with 25 percent interest in the *Torchlight*.[26] Because of Cromwell's background the paper was generally seen as representing the interests of the Grenadian bourgeoisie.[27] The headline of the last issue of the *Torchlight*, published on October 10, 1979, read "Rastas to Protest" and was accompanied by an illustration showing three dreadlocked men. The article detailed the dissatisfaction of a segment of Grenadian Rastafarians with the PRG. The Rastas were expecting changes but found that with the PRG in power, they were experiencing the same disdain they had been subjected to under the Gairy government. It seemed that capitalism and socialism had at least one thing in common in Grenada: neither mixed well with the cultural resistance of Rastafari. The *Torchlight* and the Grenada Rasta community were unlikely bedfellows; however, the newspaper's editors had already drawn the ire of the PRG by reprinting articles from international sources that were critical of the Cuban Revolution and that implicitly drew negative comparisons between Cuba and Grenada.[28]

The *Torchlight* editors took advantage of their shared moment of discord with Grenadian Rastas, who also found themselves marginalized by the PRG. Rastafarian leaders stated their solidarity with the paper: "The 12 Tribes of Israel congratulate *Torchlight* for its brave stand in this time. . . . If the PRG close down the *Torchlight,* is the same Gairyism they dealing with."[29] The article reported that Rastafarians would stage a protest to demand, among other things, greater political representation. One of their spokesmen was quoted as saying, "We are not supporters of Cuba and Russia, we see (these countries) as enemies of the Rasta since they do not acknowledge Rastafarian doctrine." Singling out Cuba and Russia as a source of contention between Grenadians and their government, this statement by a Rasta elder again highlights tensions in the public sphere around the idea that the revolutionary government was more interested in adopting foreign ideologies than in dealing with locally grounded frameworks of resistance. What was likely transpiring was not only the recognition that Marxism-Leninism as traditionally conceived was insufficiently able to account for the white supremacist aspects of colonialism that Rastafari condemned but also an acknowledgment that a distinct Caribbean middle-class respectability politics was seeping into the revolution, even as it professed class consciousness. Rastas were a threat both to this respectability and to any ideology for which race was not a principal category of analysis. For the Rastafarian community, Africa would have been the most potent symbol of revolution, not Cuba or Russia, as the elder explained. This article was the final straw in the PRG's conflict with the *Torchlight*. A counterprotest was staged against the *Torchlight* by Rasta members of the PRA, holding placards that read "Rasta Don't Work for No CIA," "Rasta Stand Firm with PRG," and "Rasta say Down with Torchlight, Up with People's Revolution." On October 13, 1979, the PRG ordered the *Torchlight* closed until further notice. The newspaper was never published again.

The critique launched by some Grenadian Rastas and the subsequent silencing of this critique by the PRG echoes the Communist Party of Cuba's treatment of certain radical Afro-Cuban groups that found that the CPC was eager to claim that the class consciousness of the Cuban Revolution had sufficiently addressed the problem of racism in Cuba. In the case of Grenada, the problem was not so much racism within Grenadian society but rather a clash between the race consciousness of Rastafari, which had developed in the region and circulated in the diaspora, and the class consciousness of the Marxism-Leninism adopted by the NJM. Walcott was not keen on the Marxist-Leninist leanings of the NJM, and the situation of Grenadian Rastas could have helped prove his point about the NJM's censorship of key aspects of Caribbean cultural production, but it was not in his purview to think through specific examples of how Grenadians engaged the revolution in critical ways, or even to examine contemporary sites of Caribbean resistance that could be placed in dialogue with the NJM's radical project.

Instead, the end of the Grenada Revolution triggered for Walcott a reevaluation of previous revolutions: he could now articulate all that he did not want in Caribbean revolution and postcolonial governance, but the aftermath of Grenada left him unable to articulate an alternative vision. On the one hand, his tainted regret is his lament for a previously legible structure of Caribbean nationalism now rendered obsolete. On the other hand, this regret is a response to the resurgence of that familiar narrative of violent failure. The United States asserted military power over Grenada, occupying the space left by the British—a space many Grenadians assumed had been filled when they won political independence—thereby cementing a neocolonial paradigm in the anglophone Caribbean. The fatal militarization of Grenadian politics was a summation of this regret: revolution was freedom-making, yes, but revolution was also a violent weapon that could be wielded against the people it was meant to serve. Walcott found this latter aspect most distressing.

Throughout the essay Walcott is highly critical of the U.S. government; however, he claims he supported the U.S. invasion of Grenada. This simultaneous critique and support is another of the ironies of colonialism in which he is ensnared. He had "grown up, as a colonial, on ironies, and ... [he] was not interested in violations of sovereignty, in comparing the invasion of the Falkland Islands with the landing in Grenada, in seeing the invasion in terms of Chile, Vietnam or Afghanistan."[30] With anger and sarcasm he invokes these places, reminding readers of the military incursions of either U.S., European, or Soviet colonial powers throughout the global south. The weight of learning both the ironies and the truths of colonialism and revolutionary resistance to colonialism burdens Walcott, as he concedes that U.S. intervention seemed the only solution for Grenada after Bishop's assassination. From his perspective, the critical flaw of the revolution was that it required "even more absolute and unquestioning" devotion than British colonialism.[31] He claims that in accepting the revolution in 1979, Grenadians had replaced one master with another. Walcott struggles to explain that what happened in Grenada was because of the revolution's contradictions in the way it both challenged neocolonialism and reproduced aspects of colonial power, in the way it championed creativity while muzzling certain writers, in the way it promoted freedom while dealing "heavy manners" to any of its perceived enemies.

But if this comparison equating the revolutionaries with British and American colonial powers seems a harsh evaluation of the NJM, we must remember that Walcott himself was displeased with either the sentiment or its expression. He crossed out many of the sentences in this essay draft. Perhaps he meant to revise these sections or to delete them altogether. His rejection of these lines highlights the status of this essay as an unpublished text, abandoned in a state of revision (see fig. 6). In its contingency we see a writer unsure of what conclusions to draw from this tragedy. For Walcott, in the aftermath of the Grenada Revolution, literature loses its nation-making power. Heroes in the traditional sense were assassinated or brought low, stumbling under the guilt of fratricide. He cannot make sense of the moment, and his writing cannot suture the nation back together again. When he recalls the order of colonialism with a qualified nostalgia, he is writing from a place of mourning for the cycle of colonial incursions the region has seen. Perhaps his nostalgia for Britain is somewhat justified in that even Prime Minister Thatcher was stunned at President Reagan's disregard for international law in the wake of the U.S. invasion of Grenada.[32] This text is best understood as an expression of the confusion, anger, shame, and grief that was 1984 in the Caribbean. Although it might be tempting to use these passages to dismiss Walcott's essay as an apologist's view of colonialism, a familiarity with his oeuvre does not permit any such dismissal. Instead we must grapple with how he represents a narrative of Caribbean revolution that is tied to traumatic repetition.

## The Long Hand of American Imperialism

In "Good Old Heart of Darkness," Walcott mourns not only for Grenada but also for the entire region. He was concerned about what the violent end of the revolution and the U.S. invasion would mean for the Caribbean. He was also dismayed at the participation of several Caribbean nations. It was clear to him that the governments of these islands were being used in the Cold War calculations of the American government. As an epigraph to the essay, he selected a quotation from *Grenada: A Preliminary Report*, a summary of the invasion released by the U.S. Department of Defense in December 1983. The passage describes the initial landing of external military forces in Grenada as an "Americas" effort: "In the early morning of October 25, 1983, elements of a combined U.S.-Caribbean security force landed on the beaches south of Pearls Airport and parachuted into the Point Salines Airport. This force included units from the United States, Barbados, Jamaica, and four member-states of the Organization of Eastern Caribbean States. U.S. forces provided airlift, sea, and mechanized support for the operation."[33] There is a tension in the paragraph between illustrating the "permissions" granted by Caribbean nations for the invasion and the idea that the United States was invited to invade. Even at the level of rhetoric, the United States cannot mask the fact that it was the only significant military force participating in the invasion. The pride of accomplishment is captured in the matter-of-fact final sentence, which shows the extent to which the whole operation was founded on U.S. military might and infrastructure, with U.S. air lift capabilities undergirding the entire effort. Even the minimal participation of Caribbean military operatives shows how the American neocolonial project of thwarting Caribbean sovereignty incorporates a complicity from within the region itself.

The dialogue between Walcott and his American editor, Silvers, in the margins of one of the essay drafts is illustrative of another kind of American intervention. From the earliest paragraphs, while Walcott is waging an unflinching critique of the United States, Silvers's feedback attempts to qualify this criticism, reading simultaneously like sound journalistic practice and grossly paternalistic commentary. In his first paragraph Walcott lays out his thesis about the dual character of the invasion: how it both helps and harms the Grenadian people. I quote Walcott at length:

> Was the liberation or invasion of Grenada, victory? The most difficult problem facing the American presence there is that it could outstay its welcome, and bleed gratitude white. Grenadians are getting irritable. They want to be trusted to go back to their own business, and the fear that even an elected government will be manipulated by Washington, places them in the shameful position of being puppets. The Empire has to temper its success and cool its

pride. Otherwise, victory becomes pyrrhic once the war is over and the administration of peace begins. New briefings, new "enemies lists." The Occupation begins to look worse than what it liberated people from. Peace becomes a ransom. "America glad they killed Bishop." More people must be thinking that.[34]

In his questioning of whether the military action was "liberation" or "invasion" and in his attention to Grenadian concerns about too much American involvement in Grenadian state affairs, Walcott is at his clearest. He looks for Grenadian agency in this equation and finds that American military intervention has denied the very freedom it claimed to bestow. Silvers places a square in bold, twice outlined, around "looks worse," and in the margins writes and underlines a question for Walcott: "Does it? Are people being killed etc?" Silvers is thinking only of the crisis, not able to see the revolution as a longer process that was not about "people being killed." Perhaps he is also unaware that an undisclosed number of Grenadians were killed during the invasion itself. He also queries Walcott's use of the term "occupation" and asks about the number of arrests that were made—again, seemingly unaware that Grenadians had been rounded up, interrogated, and in some cases detained for their connection to the revolution. Silvers's editorial input was likely informed by material on the revolution made available through American news outlets such as the *New York Times*. The American military kept foreign journalists out of Grenada until the most intense aspects of the fighting were over and the armed resistance of Grenadians had been neutralized. Silvers's position as an American editor challenging Walcott's authority to make certain claims about Caribbean revolution and its aftermath can be read as an example of how the U.S. intervention disrupted the ability of Caribbean people to narrate their own history. The American journalistic apparatus, often unintentionally, covered the tracks of the American military. Silvers might be fact-checking, but he does not seem able to understand Grenada in the context of other instances of U.S. intervention in different parts of the Caribbean and Latin America. This was not a new story.

In writing this essay, Walcott had to depend on secondhand information, American news reports, and research that consisted mainly of State Department documents. Even with the distance that Walcott places between himself and revolutionary Grenada, however, his analysis of the intervention acknowledges the gravely imbalanced geopolitics between the small Caribbean nation and the United States. While he concedes that the American presence was initially welcomed by many Grenadians, who feared chaos following Bishop's assassination, he is also careful to characterize this welcome as compromised by the violation of Grenadian sovereignty and international law. The metaphor of "bleeding gratitude white" evokes the image of killing something slowly by draining the life blood out of it. Indeed, Grenadians were drained of hope. They were infantilized and denied the right to self-governance. The sadness and anger Grenadians felt over Bishop's death and their fear around rumors that the Revolutionary Military Council (RMC) that took over on October 20 would bring an oppressive brand of communism to Grenada in 1983 provided the foundation for the welcome they offered American troops. The actual experience of Grenadians was, then, very different from the U.S. narrative, which justified the invasion by pointing to a people oppressed by the PRG. Walcott's essay tries to represent this important difference even as it critiques the revolutionary leadership.

Silvers's editorial influence shows the hand of American imperialism in print. This kind of editorializing represents the soft power of American neocolonialism shaping cultural production and discourse on the Grenada Revolution, sometimes shutting down that discourse altogether. Although the NYRB turned to Walcott for a story on Grenada, the magazine was equipped only to tell a certain version of the history. He is one of the few Caribbean writers at the time to have access to such a wide-reaching American media outlet, but he finds his voice on Grenada questioned and then contained. These are the limits of neoliberalism, where perspectives that complicate a liberal agenda are censured. Whereas the openness of the NYRB as a liberal magazine already precludes certain conversations about power, a view of the exchange between Walcott and Silvers emphasizes the importance of examining and critiquing liberal as well as conservative sources.

Walcott's efforts to work through this aftermath begin and end in the mid-1980s—a relatively short period when compared to the oeuvre of either Brand or Collins, which continued over decades. After his work on this essay he completed a stage play, *To Die for Grenada*. The play's action is set on the island of Monos, off the coast of Trinidad, on the day of the American invasion of Grenada. It follows the relationships and infidelity between upper-class Trinidadians and Americans working in Trinidad's U.S. embassy. Walcott takes on themes of race and class relations as the island's elite try to navigate the intersections of international relations, local radical politics, and sex. He dedicated the play to Robert Silvers, a gesture that signals his admiration for Silvers and an indication that he continued to have the editor in mind as he worked through his ideas on

Grenada. But this is not a play about Grenada. It has no Grenadian characters, and the inclusion of "Grenada" in the title and the sparse mentions of the revolution in the dialogue only highlight Walcott's struggle to imagine the revolution. His writing on Grenada overstates the importance of the capitalist/communist dichotomy by framing the revolution primarily as a Cold War conflict with the United States. His focus on journalists and the political leadership of the governments involved demonstrates the depth of Walcott's entanglement with nationalism as an expression of masculine authority. For Walcott, the assassination of Bishop and the U.S. invasion strip the concept of masculine nationalist authority of the logic and order it previously signified. The end of the Grenada Revolution left the island in a position of disgrace. The leaders of the revolution betrayed the principle of gentlemanliness that defined masculine authority, in Walcott's view. This crisis of masculinity, produced by and through revolutionary failure, evokes an ongoing trauma for Walcott because of an overidentification with masculine heroics and fraternity that lies at the foundation of his thinking on revolution. A leader's fall from grace in this model is necessarily framed as tragedy because no other genre can adequately capture the gravity of the moral lapse and its ensuing damage. He sees in Grenada a crisis that precludes any vision of a radical future.

## After the Aftermath: Salkey's Revision of Violence, Resistance, and Diasporic Solidarity

The May 1984 issue of the *Black Scholar* featured a section of poetry dedicated to remembering the Grenada Revolution, with contributors including Audre Lorde, D. L. Crockett, Pedro Perez-Sarduy, and Andrew Salkey. Salkey's contribution, a short poem titled "Maurice," is a series of tercets mourning the "dead-loss" of Bishop's passing while reminding readers of the optimism of the revolution, remarking the "truthful gift" of Bishop's service.[35] Salkey had been part of black radical circles, mainly composed of other Caribbean writers, since his time in London in the 1950s and 1960s. His *Havana Journal*, published in 1971, and *Georgetown Journal*, which came out the following year, detailing visits to Cuba and Guyana, respectively, reflect his commitment to Caribbean revolution and socialism while also providing a window on the fissures Salkey often identified in black radical politics and its intersection with black arts. His fictional reflection on Grenada, "After the Counter-Revolution, After the Invasion," was published posthumously in the short story collection *In the*

*Border Country*. "After the Counter-Revolution" imagines a grassroots anti-imperialist movement in Grenada in 1987, four years after the end of the revolution and the U.S. invasion of the island. Through his title, Salkey creates distance between the events of October 19, 1983, and the rest of the Grenada Revolution. He labels the assassination of Bishop and others a "counter-revolution." He brackets the invasion in a similar way, giving it its own temporal marker of "after." These moves are important for Salkey, whose main goal with this story is to paint a new vision of radical uprising in Grenada. Establishing a temporal setting that is concerned with aftermaths, Salkey effectively sets in gear a narrative that contains the crisis that ended the revolution, restricting the imaginative space it takes up in his literary representation. With the messiness and trauma of the revolution's end boxed in, so to speak, Salkey's story attempts to move on to other horizons of radicalism but stops short of producing new results.

The story follows the lives of the Axles, a Grenadian family at the center of a secret cell of community activists who dub their group "Heroic Action." The surname "axle" represents the idea of movement, of a communal circle, with each individual representing a spoke in a wheel and working together for movement. This movement is forward, backward, and cyclical in Salkey's telling. The members of Heroic Action are mainly former supporters of the revolution who want to steer the island away from the neoliberal agenda that has taken hold in the wake of the invasion and back to a more progressive and even radical governance, where power is shared among Grenadians for their mutual benefit. The story imagines a much longer American occupation, with U.S. forces physically present in Grenada into 1987, making the occupation as long as the original revolution. When Heroic Action organizes to resist the continued U.S. occupation of their country, however, it sets in motion a fatal chain of events. The story is a critique of the pre- and postrevolutionary governments in Grenada, and of the U.S. foreign policy of intervention in the Caribbean. Similar to Collins's *Angel,* it includes a figure based on Eric Gairy as one of its main characters, and it places women at the center of political organizing. Unlike Collins, however, Salkey does not use the 1950s labor movement to reframe the revolution but rather references Gairy's later, more troubled time in office in the years immediately preceding the NJM-led revolution. In this postrevolutionary context Gairy is reinstalled on the island and trying to regain political power. Gairy's role here is sinister, as he has to manipulate the United States and betray his fellow citizens to regain the prime ministership.

Salkey takes a split approach in his writing, painting intimate portraits of both political leadership and regular folk. He holds the military and the Central Committee partially responsible for the end of the revolution. "After the Counter-Revolution" says very little about the Grenada 17, noting only that they "had been rounded up and imprisoned during the aftermaths of the invasion, tried and convicted a very long time afterwards," and sentenced to death.[36] The NJM and the PRG are not his subjects. Bishop is referred to only in passing; Coard is not mentioned at all. This story is not interested in rehashing the events of September and October 1983 or in assigning blame for the revolution's collapse—at least not among Grenadians. Salkey's aim is to heap scorn on the United States for the invasion and to narrate the resilience of Grenadians (the main action takes place on the Easter Resurrection weekend). This split approach, between a critique of the United States and praise of the Grenadian people, shapes the gender politics of the narrative as it allows Salkey to home in on the work of radical Grenadian women. What he revives in this piece, through his representation of Evelyn, the matriarch of the Axle family, is the sense of hope and possibility that Grenadians had developed during the course of the revolution. Evelyn explains this as the sense of optimism that necessarily grows in places where progress would seem impossible: "Nothing ups and just dies, because it gets push down, one time. Whatever seems to die can come back alive in another shape or form, in another set of people action, in another time. In that way of thinking, hope is the best bet that folks like us have, true. Things only die, when we don't want them to live. Is really up to all of us, yes?"[37] Evelyn's take on their situation exposes the cycle of repeated traumas. A single instance of resistance will not squash all oppression. Their ongoing resistance and radicalism are necessary to fight colonialism and reimagine a postcolonial future. If colonialism reinvents itself as neocolonialism, then Grenadians must renew their efforts to defend their freedom. Evelyn is the classic mother of Caribbean literature, always portrayed installed at her Singer sewing machine, but Salkey adds a twist. She is also a key part of the radical vision for postrevolutionary Grenada embodied in Heroic Action. Her view is that of a black radical tradition that can survive periodic setbacks. When it meets resistance, this tradition recreates itself in other spaces and other times with different people. The development of the party was an outward expression of a hunger for freedom. The death of the party, therefore, does not kill that desire but simply opens a space for a new vehicle for its expression. Evelyn speaks from the viewpoint of an elder with experience and a sense of history.

Officially, Heroic Action is led by Marcus Breyerson, an expat architect recently returned to the island from Canada; however, Salkey gives him only a few lines of dialogue in the story. Evelyn is the character who articulates the ideology and vision of Heroic Action. She argues for the importance of the organization within her family and ends up recruiting her husband, Aaron, and children, Alton and Ennia, to play key roles in the group's plan. The pro-imperialist forces Salkey critiques are all men, including the American ambassador, the CIA station chief, the Grenadian governor-general, the prime minister, and Gairy. The anti-imperialist forces, by contrast, are led by women: Evelyn, Emelda, a friend of Evelyn's who works as a domestic helper in the U.S. ambassador's residence, and the market woman referred to as the "vendeuse." When the group faces its first crisis after being exposed by Gairy, Emelda and Evelyn are the first to meet and discuss the trouble.

Salkey weaves contradiction into the story, moving between a sense of hope and the oppressive violence that rises to quash any progressive action. The violence at the end of the story is graphic and the situation for the activists of Heroic Action seems dire. Mother and daughter Evelyn and Ennia are the only surviving members of the Axle family, as Aaron and Alton are killed in a violent conflict with the police forces who opposed the rebels.[38] Even as these two grasp hands in a sign of solidarity and resistance at the story's close, it is not clear what future is possible. Salkey gives Evelyn the final line of the story: "Evie, child, don't give in," she whispers, seemingly to herself.[39] She insists on continued struggle even in the face of violence and death. The story is ambiguous about whether Evelyn will succumb to her injuries.

One possibility for continuity lies in the budding relationship between Ennia and Carlton, an African American U.S. Marine stationed on the island. Carlton represents the subversion of American imperialism from within, as he uses his position with the Marines to assist Heroic Action in its plan. His union with Ennia represents the importance of diasporic solidarity between black Americans and Caribbean people as part of the anti-imperialist resistance. Still, if Grenadians try to organize peacefully, they will be met with violent, fatal force. Imperialism is ruthless, cruel, and relentless, Salkey says on the one hand. On the other hand, he writes about the importance of protecting Caribbean sovereignty anyway, suggesting that Caribbean people might come to expect this cyclical violence as a fact of their freedom struggles. The story's vision is about the kind of people who will be brave enough to put their lives on the line to resist imperialism even when they know it may harm them. It is about women leading by example in their practice of this kind of bravery. There are similarities between Salkey's representation of Evelyn and the other elder women in "After the Counter-Revolution" and the representations of women in Collins's work, including Doodsie in *Angel* and Willive and Mamag in *The Colour of Forgetting*. These are women who are leaders in their families and communities. In their own ways they envision building stronger families and stronger communities, which can lead to stronger nations. Salkey makes this point most emphatically, with Evelyn actually leading the charge. The idea is subtler in Collins's work: she examines how the democratic process and respect for the voices of women begins with interactions in the home. Of the works by male authors discussed in this chapter, Salkey's comes closest to the Caribbean feminist vision explored by Collins.

The end of the story provokes a reflection on how and why a return to revolution, in the form that Salkey imagines it, is not likely in Grenada. The beginning of the story foretells the ending in the following sentence: "After the counter-revolution, after the invasion, the island's land and water were the only true survivors. Aaron Axle and Evelyn Axle and their son Alton, and daughter, Ennia, were not."[40] Failure to survive the revolution can be read in two ways: either the family was indelibly damaged by the invasion or it had ceased to exist. The family is a product of Salkey's imagination; no such grassroots resistance movement like that portrayed in the story sprang up in 1987. From the beginning of the story, then, Salkey is interested in the idea that the aftermath he imagines could not happen. This is not about history but rather about the possibilities that history repeatedly denies.

## Will Grenada Respond Again?

Grenada has not had another revolution in response to the invasion. Salkey's imagined future remains fictional. But he was not the only one who conceived a radical response from Grenadians. At the memorial service in Trinidad, Lamming also drew on the victorious narrative of overcoming. "Grenada will respond again," he said, "as she has done in the past, from the deepest resources of her pride and self-esteem."[41] The response he imagines is not one of military dominance or political revolution, however. Instead he turns to the themes of writing and cultural production, indicating that these will be the avenues through which Grenadians, and Caribbean people more broadly, acknowledge their heroes, identify their enemies, and work out their futures. These are the future revolutionaries that neocolonialism should fear, he suggests. "Those Caribbean leaders who now luxuriate in the applause of the American aggressor will sooner or later become the targets of a different and more devastating kind of scrutiny by the historians, the novelists, the poets and all other intellectual and cultural workers from among their own people." Together, these historians, creative writers, and artists will form a coalition embracing diverse methodologies and perspectives. We see the masculine aspect of this vision in Lamming's claim that this cultural production will create a cult of personality and hagiography around Bishop. These historians and writers are "men and women for whom the name, Maurice Bishop, will blossom into one of the most fertilising symbols of creative expression in the culture and politics of this region. It is their judgement, not Mr. Reagan's, which will be decisive."

Lamming was correct in identifying the emphasis on Bishop as a charismatic leader that has developed in political science and history writing on the Caribbean. To date, however, the creative literature of the revolution has not blossomed around Bishop's image. If the oeuvre of Collins and Brand is accepted as indicative of the major writing on the Grenada Revolution, it seems this literature has gone to pains to avoid, or at least downplay, Bishop's image. Instead, writers have addressed other wounds and losses, focusing on the loss of Bishop as part of a larger narrative of trauma and loss that includes women, families, the poor, and the working class. By engaging in extended reflections on the political leadership of the revolution, Lamming and Walcott foreclosed producing narratives of revolutionary nation-making in the Caribbean. Instead they rehearse well-worn narratives that struggle to let go of the idea of the charismatic leader. This means that the temporal situation of their works, following the death of such a leader, is overly determined by tragedy. They confront either the absence of "great men" (in the case of Walcott) or the ongoing desire for new great men (in Lamming's case), which indicates an inability to contemplate truly new futures. At the end of his memorial address, Lamming quotes from the Guyanese poet Martin Carter's "Death of a Comrade": "Now from the mourning vanguard moving on/dear Comrades I salute you and I say/Death will not find us thinking that we die."

In this moment of heartbreak, it is difficult to imagine how the Caribbean left would continue to live. In Salkey's vision, the work of persistence and reinvention is voiced through women, through the intergenerational connection between Evelyn and Ennia and Ennia's ability to create strategic links across the diaspora. There is something distinctly feminist about Salkey's vision. He imagines ways forward for the Caribbean left that entail coming to terms with the scars of the past while also acknowledging the strong possibility of more violence, suffering, and struggle to come. Where Lamming's and Salkey's visions coalesce is in the surety that one of the ways forward for Caribbean leftist politics is in the realm of the literary, a site where the region's writers are free to create movements that may yet come to fruition out in the world.

## 3 "Comrade, Sister, Lover"
### Dionne Brand and the Limits of Radical Movements

NEAR THE end of her fifth poetry collection, *Chronicles of the Hostile Sun,* published in 1984, Dionne Brand writes, "I'm sick of writing history/I'm sick of scribbling dates."[1] The poem expresses the poet-speaker's feelings of frustration after witnessing the end of the Grenada Revolution and the U.S. invasion of Grenada in October 1983. The "sickness" the poet-speaker feels in writing is caused by the loss of friends and colleagues to the violence of that month, followed by her attempts to process her own trauma as a witness to and survivor of the military invasion. Her sickness is also the dread she experiences in having to use her art to correct North Americans' misconceptions about the Caribbean—misconceptions that came about as a result of American imperialism. And yet, in the tradition of many Caribbean writers before her, this writing of history is part of the task that the Trinidadian Canadian Brand takes on as she documents her time as a participant in the Grenada Revolution. She is a chronicler of history and dates. Her work is art, archive, protest, and pedagogy.

In the 1998 *Historical Thought and Literary Representation in West Indian Literature,* the literary critic Nana Wilson-Tagoe describes how colonial and postcolonial experiences keep Caribbean writers tethered to questions of historicity, the representation of subjectivities shaped by uneven development, and the difficulty of escaping the colonial past even as one claims the postcolonial contemporary.[2] "Traumatized by history, the West Indian writer is yet continually haunted by its specter and perpetually engaged with redefining it," Wilson-Tagoe writes.[3] Indeed, Caribbean literature is home to a tradition of writers revisiting, correcting, and resisting versions of history derived from archives with colonial roots. This tradition has developed because of the Caribbean's position as a site of colonial and neocolonial conquest, and it remains an ongoing legacy today, even though most of the region can be considered postcolonial. Brand's writing situates the Grenada Revolution in a black radical tradition whose many iterations across history (including the Haitian Revolution and slave resistance across the Americas, as well as African liberation movements and the Black Power movement) contributed to the pursuit of freedom on the part of black people the world over. For Brand, revolution has always been part of the practice of black freedom. The literary is home to discourse on this practice.

To speak of the postcolonial in the Caribbean in particular is to reference simultaneously the vestiges of colonialism that remain and the strategies employed by Caribbean people to create a contemporary moment that lives alongside these vestiges without being consumed by them. Brand's writing on Grenada is an example of this strategy playing out in literary form. Her oeuvre spans multiple genres, including poetry, essay, and fiction. With each generic assay, she grapples with the Grenada Revolution while imagining different relationships between the history of Caribbean anticolonialism and the present. Brand's work explores the limits of revolution as radical praxis by examining the aftermaths of revolution. She is interested in who experiences the aftermaths, under what conditions, and where.

In *Chronicles*, Brand writes about returning to Canada as a result of the U.S. invasion of Grenada. The Canada she enters is simultaneously foreign and familiar. The irony of Canada's neocolonial reach into the Caribbean is not lost on Brand: she considers that Canada is itself a former colony of both Britain and France and remains actively involved in extractive practices across the Caribbean.[4] It is also the place she had originally migrated to as a teenager from Trinidad in search of a better life. After Grenada, she describes Canada as a site of exile. But exile is not only a physical place, it is also a condition. In Brand's work, those who remain in Grenada might also be read as exiled, in the sense that the American invasion tried to prevent them from establishing sovereignty over their nation and their history. Grenadians are citizens of a nation that is politically independent by law; however, because of the U.S. invasion, they have experienced violations of this independence, which have served to remind them of how deeply colonial practices remain embedded in postcolonial experiences.

Acknowledging this simultaneous experience of sovereignty and nonsovereignty, this chapter examines the liminal spaces Brand creates in her writing to account for a revolution with a complex legacy. To create these liminal spaces, she represents historical events, refracting them through the genres of poetry, fiction, and nonfiction essays. This process of refraction gives Brand room for invention and imagination, allowing her to remember specifically the lives of black women, particularly black queer women, whose radicalism may not fit within traditional definitions of Caribbean revolution.

*Chronicles* captures the innocence, energy, optimism, and anger that characterized both the revolution in Grenada and the early stages of Brand's career as a writer. By the end of this poetry collection, however, the violence that marked the collapse of the People's Revolutionary Government (PRG) and the American invasion of Grenada destroys the sense of possibility the revolution initially generated. This violence would continue to haunt Brand's writing. Her first novel, *In Another Place, Not Here,* published in 1996, is Brand's most sustained meditation on Grenada after *Chronicles.* In a mode of positive critique, the novel sets forth a vision of queer love as a site of revolution. Set on an unnamed island that resembles Grenada in its history and geography, *In Another Place* is narrated from the perspectives of two women—one a Caribbean Canadian activist who returns to the island to participate in the revolution as a labor organizer and the other a sugar cane field worker who was abandoned by her parents as a child and now lives with an abusive man as an adult. The women narrating *In Another Place* occupy a space on the margins of the nation's socialist revolution even as they are living and working in its midst. *In Another Place* positions black queer love, and specifically women loving other women, as a constitutive part of political revolution at the same times as it resists the masculinity and heteronormativity of revolution as it is conventionally understood. This is an important difference between the experiences of the aftermath of revolution presented in *Chronicles* and in *In Another Place.* By analyzing these two texts, along with the autobiographical essays of *Bread out of Stone: Recollections, Sex, Recognitions, Race, Dreaming, Politics,* published in 1994, I explore how Brand's relationship to revolution and literary representation changes over time.

Poetry offers Brand an immediacy and distillation of thought that sharpens the feeling of trauma in the immediate aftermath of the revolution, whereas in the essay format Brand locates Grenada within a series of diasporic itineraries that shift between radical movements and the assertion of neoliberal, racist oppression. These autobiographical interventions offer readers a sense of the way Brand positions herself in the world and how she thinks through connections between the solitary work of writing and collective efforts to resist neocolonialism. Several years later, when she turned to fictional prose, she introduced an alternative vision of "grace," as she calls it, to her representation of the revolution. When she published *In Another Place,* she was in a different moment of postcolonial history. This temporal distance, coupled with the discursiveness of fiction as a genre, provided a more expansive canvas for her to reimagine what happened in Grenada. Together, *Chronicles, Bread,* and *In Another Place* draw on similar historical sources and personal memories of the Grenada Revolution while exhibiting different voices and formal outcomes.

Brand's insistence on the narrative multiplicity of Grenada as represented in three distinct texts decenters the colonial, patriarchal idea of a master narrative. Her return to similar material at later moments also illustrates how artists reinterpret the meaning of revolution over time. These texts reflect her numerous attempts to contribute to a discourse on revolution that is not entirely served by the historical method. Central to her work is the dual understanding of revolution as radical break and as cyclical condition. She revises representations of the Grenada Revolution because even in its failure, this revolution is continuously generative in modes that are theoretical, affective, and activist. Her writing forms part of a postcolonial and Caribbean feminist archive of revolution that is constantly rethinking how and why revolutions of the past remain a part of our ongoing present.

Brand's literary accounts of the revolution are poetic archives and attempts to find a grammar for postcolonial revolution. She describes the hypocrisy of the global north and the double bind faced by small countries in the global south that are forced to compete on the uneven playing field created by globalization in the postcolonial era. For Caribbean writers, she provides an example of how to create a counterpoetics that insists on regional particularity as opposed to North Atlantic universality.[5] Within this counterpoetics she not only writes against imperialist histories of the Caribbean but also establishes a strategy for using the historicity of imaginative writing to counteract colonizing epistemologies. By using literature to document history, Brand troubles the distinction between literary invention and historical truth. Can literary work be thought of as a historical source for Caribbean nations whose ability to produce more conventional histories is often thwarted by the collusion of historical convention with imperialist oppression? This is an especially pertinent question for Grenada, where Brand would have witnessed the destruction of troves of PRG documents as the U.S. military bombed Grenadian government buildings.[6] Brand's poetry and fiction expose a complex relationship among imperialism, postcolonialism, and black radicalism. In her work,

Caribbean people suffer trauma not only as a result of imperialism but also in the experience of revolution as a response to imperialism. Revolution itself visits a certain amount of violence on the very populations it purports to serve, and that violence is often pushed out of consciousness in order to forward the revolutionary project. Her writing is a space of confrontation and reconciliation where readers face this dual violence. Functioning as both archive and critique, her work asks, How can revolutions be better at producing freedom?

By the early 1980s Brand had a serious problem with the Black Power movement in Canada. Immigrating to Toronto as a young adult in the 1970s, she was drawn to the collective movement for black empowerment and politicization that had been gathering support in Montreal and Toronto. This movement allowed her to connect with blacks from Canada, the Caribbean, Africa, and the United States. She eventually became disenchanted with the masculine, macho rhetoric and tone of this activism. It did not provide any significant platforms for women and queer people of color. In petrifying old ideas of male leadership, it also curtailed the evolution of black masculinity. Unable to see a space for herself in the Black Power movement in Canada, Brand turned to Grenada—newly immersed in revolution—as a frontier of radical possibility. In some ways, travel to Grenada was one of Brand's earliest acknowledgments of the limits of the black radical tradition. Grenada was small, and its scale gave her the opportunity to do more impactful work than was possible in Canada. She imagined being able to get on with the business of building the revolution without having to contend with North American racism.[7]

From the beginning of 1983 Brand lived in Grenada, writing reports on foreign-funded agricultural projects.[8] She remained there for ten months, until just after the assassination of Prime Minister Bishop and his allies and the U.S. invasion. She survived the U.S. military assault and returned to Canada embittered, having witnessed firsthand the tragedy and trauma of neocolonialism. Since the revolution's inception the U.S. government had been deeply uncomfortable with the Grenadian government's close ties to Cuba. The Grenada Revolution represented, in part, a victory for Cuban internationalism and the willingness of a tiny, newly independent nation to chart its own course in the world. In the context of the Cold War, the tail end of both the Black Power movement, and the wave of decolonization across the third world, the United States was anxious about what the revolution's success would signal to the rest of the region, particularly the recently independent anglophone nations.

## The Revolution and Its Discontents

An explicit relationship between history and literature is postulated in *Chronicles*. Several of the poems' titles include dates and the names of places Brand traveled to when she worked for the PRG. With titles such as "Night—Mt. Panby Beach—25 March 1983," "Diary—The grenada crisis," and "October 19th, 1983," she documents life within a revolution and the new sets of possibilities she saw emerging and then destroyed in those months. These place names and dates force the reader to look back on a specific place and time. Brand's use of the poet-speaker to witness makes simple but important statements: This happened. I was there. The poems offer a sense of how one continues to live with those facts. Divided into three sections—"Languages," "Sieges," and "Military Occupations"—the poems in *Chronicles* are both discrete pieces that stand on their own and fragments of a larger project that seeks to narrate the revolution from the perspective of a Caribbean national who has traveled between the region and North America.

The term "chronicle" carries multiple connotations that effectively describe this work. The *Oxford English Dictionary* defines a chronicle as "a detailed and continuous register of events in order of time; a historical record, especially one in which the facts are narrated without philosophic treatment, or any attempt at literary style"; and "[a] record, register, [or] narrative, account."[9] Brand's use of dates and place names fits the first part of this definition, but the presentation of her account, her chronicle, in poetic form engages the question of literary style and philosophical treatment directly. It is not always clear to readers what material in her work is fact or invention; however, all of it is poetry. This is the license that Brand affords herself, given the genre she has chosen. The ambiguity with respect to the historical record is a reminder that whether it purports to be or not, all information in circulation about Grenada and the revolution is narrated with a philosophical treatment and in a literary style to suit the author and intended audience. Brand's work challenges readers to consider that no historical account can be produced independent of ideology, philosophy, or literary style. As she writes a poetic account of the Grenada Revolution, her formal choices point to the possibility of plural voices and thus plural personal histories. The multiplicity of these accounts disarticulates the U.S. master narrative on Grenada. I use *disarticulation* in the sense put forward by cultural critic Sarita See, who theorizes the "disarticulation of empire" as the erasure, misrecognition, or denial of American imperialist and neocolonialist histories. See argues that "the compulsive, organized nature of imperial forgetting has rendered inarticulate and incoherent the history of colonialism" in the United States.[10] She employs "disarticulation of empire" as a multivalent term, however, and I adopt it here to describe the artistic and literary responses of the colonized and racially subjugated to *dis*-articulate empire, that is, to dismantle it and throw off U.S. cultural, political, and economic hegemony. Brand addresses neocolonial erasure by writing counterhegemonic accounts of revolution in Grenada. In this way, *Chronicles* critiques the power of U.S. imperialism to dictate facts about the global south, and the Caribbean in particular.

At the same time as her text emerges from the North American publishing industry (*Chronicles* was published by the Toronto-based Williams-Wallace Publishers), it offers a corrective to U.S.-narrated versions of the revolution. While Brand refuses North Atlantic discourses on the "facts" of Grenada, her poems carry the weight of an eyewitness account. She invites readers to engage the poems of *Chronicles* as versions of the revolution narrated from specific and singular subject positions. They stand as an important record of the revolution precisely because they do not claim to speak to a universal experience. They are her own ethnographic account of the events she and others experienced.

Poems from the section titled "Languages" address the need for a counterpoetics of revolution in Grenada. A counterpoetics could portray the revolution as a unique experience while simultaneously putting Grenada (and the wider anglophone Caribbean) in the context of late twentieth-century radicalism in Latin America and the Spanish- and French-speaking Caribbean. During this period, Caribbean and Latin American radicalism often took the form of socialist (or socialist-inspired) governments and political parties, which saw themselves as of a kind with the nations of the Non-Aligned Movement. Founded in 1961, the Non-Aligned Movement was an organization of countries that committed to not taking sides with either the United States or the USSR during the Cold War. Many of its members were newly independent nations, and the organization was a vocal opponent of imperialism. The diversity of the nations involved in the Non-Aligned Movement meant that while most were opposed to capitalism because of its inherent links to colonial oppression, there was no widespread commitment to socialism among members. Nonalignment was, therefore, an important position for postcolonial nations navigating Cold War politics on a global scale. Brand's poems position Grenada in the context of such diffuse resistance to imperialism where governments of the global south were in search of a third way, beyond the capitalist-communist dichotomy. These efforts were about acknowledging a history and imaginary outside the bounds of Eurocentrism; hence the term "third world."[11]

The opening poem in *Chronicles*, "Night—Mt. Panby Beach—25 March 1983," describes an exercise where members of the Grenadian militia, including the poet-speaker, are staked out overnight on a beach, practicing a maneuver in preparation for a possible military invasion.[12] The poem is a statement about how one embodies the ongoing struggle to preserve and enhance the freedoms won with independence. It is a poem about how to be postcolonial in a Caribbean region thrust into the Cold War. Throughout the poem Brand repeats the phrase "this night may make it to a poem," drawing attention to the process whereby she edits her memories of the revolution to produce poetry. There is a documentary aspect to the poem, a sense that it gives readers access to events that Brand witnessed. She lays bare the apparatus of historical invention by making readers hyperaware of her authorship and situating the poem as a metatext: this bit of history might be archived in literature. There is also an awareness that, in fact, the literary might be the only place where the moment is recorded. The participants are nameless for the most part; it is not a "real" battle, merely a rehearsal. But even these small maneuvers deserve attention, and certainly the use of Mt. Panby Beach takes on new meaning after the events of October 1983, when these spaces were violated by the U.S. invasion.

The poem introduces the Grenada Revolution as if it were already a Grenada-U.S. conflict despite it being months ahead of the invasion—a reminder of the intense pressure the Grenadian government felt in defying the United States by maintaining relations with Cuba. She describes the threat "of american war ships in barbados" ready to approach Grenada.[13] Throughout the revolution the PRG repeatedly warned the nation that a U.S. invasion of Grenada was likely. The government knew that it was under U.S. government surveillance. It was also aware of an American navy maneuver (code-named "Amber and the Amberines") conducted near Puerto Rico during which U.S. Marines practiced invading a small island nation.[14] On the stark difference between the Reagan administration and the Grenadian militia, Brand writes: "they are comfy at Camp David/we are wet and always startled/though for once we have guns."[15] The "we" Brand constructs using the first person plural in this poem suggests a collective Grenadian people, represented in the characters she refers to, such as the "boy" and "Rose." "Rose belongs to the militia," she writes, and so does the boy, who "must put on his boots and his greens/and wake me up at 4 a.m."[16] The poet-speaker sees herself as part of this community, signaling a broader Caribbean solidarity. In this poem, Grenadians experience the revolution as an opportunity to arm and protect themselves against the threat of American imperialism. As such, the writer is positioned with a weapon, begging the question of what it might mean for the writer turned revolutionary to pull the trigger. This is a question that surfaces throughout Brand's writing on Grenada: How should an artist with simultaneous desires to write and to act engage in violent struggle? Through her attention to historical detail in the midst of poetic invention, Brand establishes the poem as an alternative source of history and thus a window onto the particularity of the Grenadian experience. She also positions the poet as a revolutionary fighter in the field and on the page.

## The Problem of Press Freedom

The poem "On eavesdropping on a delegation of conventioners at Barbados Airport" offers a defense of the PRG's 1979 decision to close down the *Torchlight*, a local, privately owned newspaper.[17] The poet-speaker calls out critics of the PRG as hypocrites who accept control of North American and British print media by a select group of wealthy white men while attacking the Grenadian government for disrupting the freedom of the press. The poem specifically indicts media moguls Rupert Murdoch and Kenneth Thomson for their monopoly of North Atlantic media.[18] Brand writes:

> because your wrist watches are one hour behind
> the whole damn Caribbean must wait
> because you do not know that Murdoch and Thompson
> owning all the newspapers in the world
> is a violation of free speech,
> we cannot close down the Torchlight.[19]

Her argument is that the first world media are constrained by the interests of a select few whose grip on the public is hegemonic, masking the scope and reach of their power. That is, in terms of media production, the nations of the North Atlantic are not as democratic as they purport to be. The domination of the media by a few powerful individuals is an example of the violation of free speech, she contends, but it remains invisible because it occurs in the first world. The very concept of a first world evokes a society that is shielded from such violations because it upholds particular values, including democracy and free market economics. The differences between the Caribbean and the North Atlantic are irreconcilable, she suggests, as distinct as their time zones. They exist in different temporalities. This difference is what makes first world ideas of "development" in the third world (including IMF loans, structural adjustment, and open markets) so unpalatable and oppressive for many in the Caribbean. The poet-speaker points out that when North Atlantic governments violate the sovereignty of Caribbean and Latin American nations by interfering in their politics, the actions of these governments are either ignored or reported on uncritically by the American and European media. She repeats the refrain "where were you," taking to task the Associated Press, Reuters, and other "liberal" North Atlantic news organizations for not speaking out against political injustice in Latin America and the Caribbean:

> you law unions and conventions of wellwishers
> looking to be delighted at problems
> where were you when they assassinated Allende
> and when El Mercurio tried to steal the peoples' revolution
> and when the gleaner shot down that timid jamaican,
> Manley[20]

The poet-speaker is angry at American imperialism. As she evokes Salvador Allende's Socialist Party of Chile and Michael Manley's People's National Party (PNP), which tried to bring democratic socialism to Jamaica, the implications are threefold: first, that the governments of Chile, Jamaica, and Grenada, despite their different postcolonial histories, shared a common political project of guarding their nations from neocolonial oppression; second, that political opposition, aided by the American government, deployed *El Mercurio* and the *Gleaner* to destabilize leftist governments in Chile and Jamaica, respectively; and third, that a similar tactic was deployed in the case of Grenada by means of false reports printed in the *Torchlight* newspaper.[21] The poem uses personification to represent the *Gleaner* as the violent agent that "shot down" social democracy in Jamaica. Brand's characterization of Manley as "timid," however, suggests that the forces of imperialism are not solely to blame in the events that led to the departure of the PNP from government and that the social democracy project failed in Jamaica in part because of Manley's own missteps. While I disagree with Brand's evaluation of the *Torchlight*-PRG conflict, the poem highlights the frustration the PRG experienced at not being able to sufficiently control the narrative of the revolution when faced with the international and local forces at play.[22]

The PRG feared that American efforts to destabilize leftist governments in Chile and Jamaica could be repeated in Grenada, and these fears were valid. Brand's poem sheds light on the pressure experienced by Caribbean governments confronting a new set of issues that emerged with their postcolonial status. The power of the American public sphere to manipulate Caribbean politics bleeds into a Caribbean literary imaginary where writers such as Brand use the outlets available to them to respond to the American media.

The poem represents North American convention-goers as only coming to the Caribbean for the sun.[23] Unwilling to recognize the particularity of Caribbean people and politics, North Americans and Europeans instead expect to import into the Caribbean the politics and values of the North Atlantic historical experiences. According to Brand, this North Atlantic hegemony in the Caribbean creates a context in which "truth is free to be fiction" and "counting is not an exact science."[24] At stake here are radically different definitions of freedom and truth. For Brand, the "truth" of the global north is often fiction when translated into a Caribbean context. The maps to freedom and sovereignty proposed by the United States for the Caribbean, with the promise of greater democracy and development, lead to greater U.S. influence in the region without improving the lives of Caribbean citizens. Discourses on economics and "objective" reporting can become as subjective as literary language when these North Atlantic universals are thrust upon the region. In many ways Brand's poems struggle with the burden of historical (mis)representation in the same way that the PRG did, as it battled local and international news outlets.

### Writing in the Fractures of Revolution

In "Military Occupations," the final section of *Chronicles,* Brand details the end of the revolution. She continues with the concept of poetry as chronicle. However, the perspective shifts from the national focus to a more personal evaluation of the politics of self in the midst of national crisis. The poems in "Military Occupations" convey a sense of urgency in their titles, rhythm, and sequencing. They announce themselves as if they were daily dispatches on the revolution's collapse: "Diary—The grenada crisis," "October 19th, 1983," "October 25th, 1983," "October 26th, 1983," "October 27th, 1983," "October 27th 1983—evening." Again, the poet-speaker's words stand as a correction to the neocolonial record, with an emphasis on the dates marking the assassination of Maurice

Bishop, October 19, and the American invasion, October 25. "Military Occupations" conveys the sense that the postcolonial, this time in the aftermath of a destroyed revolution, is experienced as a period of trauma. The loss of the revolution's promise becomes something that its survivors, including Brand, must face every day. This is what David Scott calls "ruined time," the experience of "temporal insecurity and uncertainty" whereby those deemed postcolonial subjects can never quite get to that horizon just beyond postcolonial.[25] Instead these subjects are stuck in a neoliberal paradigm that tries to coerce them to disavow their revolutionary process by deeming it unjust or undemocratic. This state of ruined time inaugurates what Scott calls the "aftermath without end."[26] Puri notes that the close attention to sequencing of the final days of the revolution in the work of writers such as Brand "produces the surreal effect of a dilated time."[27] Here she reads an attempt to "stay close to realism," while also pointing out the inability of poems like Brand's to truly order those final days. She reads this treatment of time as one of the signs of trauma in Brand's poetry. In *Chronicles* the invasion of Grenada is a harrowing example of how colonialism survives and reentrenches itself, even as postcolonial time is upon us.

"Diary—The grenada crisis" describes the U.S. invasion from a vantage point near St. George's, Grenada's capital.[28] Hours after Bishop was assassinated, the newly formed Revolutionary Military Council (RMC) claimed to have taken over the island's governance.[29] The RMC imposed a twenty-four-hour, shoot-to-kill curfew on the nation. The country was in total shock and chaos. Grenadians feared for their lives and were made to feel that external forces were necessary to restore order. For most Grenadians, the restoration of order meant bringing to justice those responsible for Bishop's death; that was more urgent than the need to protest an unlawful military invasion. A large percentage of Grenadians accepted the American invasion because they saw U.S. and regional intervention as the only way to restore order to the nation, but some also resisted. Brand represents the invasion as a war, stressing the often overlooked fact that the invading American forces encountered armed resistance from Grenadians.[30]

The Reagan administration sold the invasion to the American public as an effort not only to rescue American medical students at St. George's School of Medicine but also to liberate the Grenadian people from the clutches of communism. A *New York Times* article from that week cites a U.S. Defense Department official who claimed that U.S. Marines were being sent to Grenada to protect the 1,200 American citizens on the island.³¹ Another *Times* article quotes Reagan referring to Grenada as a "'Soviet-Cuban colony being readied' to export terrorism."³² Despite the alleged goal of leading a "rescue mission," the U.S. government prevented American journalists and other foreign reporters from traveling to Grenada until several days into the invasion, when the initial military assault was complete.³³ In so doing the American military could to a large degree control the narrative of the invasion, focusing on images of Grenadians and American medical students welcoming the Marines. This narrative of rescue did not recognize the complexity of the situation facing Grenadians, the majority of whom had supported the revolution and were aghast both at the deaths of October 19 and at the military invasion. The images offered by Brand communicate the banality, fear, and shock that the violence of invasion brings to Grenada. The incursion of American military personnel by sea and air seems out of place in the picturesque beauty of the island. The Grenada that is familiar to the poet-speaker is destroyed by the invasion:

> the ship and the cement
> drop against the metal skies
> a yankee paratrooper strangles in his sheet.
>
> prayers for rain,
> instead again this wonderful sky;
> an evening of the war and those of us looking
> with our mouths open
> see beauty become appalling,
> sunset, breaths of grey clouds streaked red,
> we are watching a house burn³⁴

The hostile sun is evoked in the image of the "wonderful sky" that provides the backdrop for the invasion. Here the sun's hostility is defined in the way it produces a clear day for the invaders instead of the rain that the poet-speaker hopes would interrupt the progress of the American forces. The sky is not only "wonderful" but also somehow "metal," transformed by the machinery of war. But Grenadians are not the only victims of the hostile sun. American paratroopers are strangled in their parachutes, falling like Icarus, too close to the sun.

Throughout the poem the shock of invasion and the onset of a neo-colonial reality are represented as keeping Grenadians in a liminal state between sleep and wakefulness, not unlike the feeling of the militia on the practice maneuver in "Mt. Panby Beach." In the second-to-last stanza the poet-speaker refers to "the last evening" of the war and the feeling of suffocation experienced by the survivors: "no air comes up,/we have breathed the last of it." The revolution was like oxygen for Grenadians, and it was sucked up by the invasion, marking the suffocation of their freedom. The poet-speaker describes a process of keeping vigil throughout the war, but there seems to be a combination of astonishment and inertia that prevents the speaker and those described in the poem from acting. They are static, crunched into defensive positions as they hope to stay alive. That an internal government conflict would set the stage for an American invasion was not something many Grenadians had expected. The American military was facing a completely fractured nation and a population that quickly resigned itself to a fate of neocolonial dominance once their revolutionary government crumbled.

The sense of resignation in the face of tragedy is communicated in the poem "October 19th, 1983."[35] The poem's opening translates shock at the inability of words to sufficiently account for the situation. Brand makes a self-reflexive reference to form, just as she did in "Night—Mt. Panby Beach—25 March 1983." Even though words are not enough, they must be put in service of all the emotions that the end of the revolution triggers:

> this poem cannot find words
> this poem repeats itself
> Maurice is dead
> Jackie is dead
> Uni is dead
> Vincent is dead
> dream is dead

Brand does not equate the revolution with Bishop, Jacqueline Creft (minister of education), Unison Whiteman (minister of foreign affairs), or Vincent Noel (a union organizer and NJM member); however, she suggests that the betrayal of trust that led to their deaths initiated the end of the revolution. The construction "is dead" appears to remove fault or agency from the act of their assassinations and instead emphasizes the finality of the fact. Further down, however, the poet-speaker names four other members of the NJM party and holds them accountable for the violence:

> Bernard, Phyllis, Owusu, H.A.!
> what now!

> back to jails in these antilles!
> back to shackles! back to slavery!

In naming Bernard Coard (deputy prime minister), Phyllis Coard (deputy minister of foreign affairs), Liam "Owusu" James (member of the Central Committee), and Hudson Austin (army general), the poet-speaker, echoing Grenadian public opinion, holds the surviving members of the NJM leadership responsible for the deaths of Bishop and his colleagues. Brand uses the term "fratricide" to describe the assassinations, in which black revolutionaries turned against each other and the nation. It is one of the rare moments in *Chronicles* in which she complicates her critique of the United States by acknowledging the problems arising from within the NJM itself.[36] The moment is important to the poem and to the wider text because it acknowledges tragic and fatal violence *within* the revolution. Here she not only names those who many Caribbean people believed were responsible for Bishop's assassination but also assesses the fate that now awaits Grenadians and other Caribbean nations in the wake of this crisis—that is, a return to imprisonment, foreign encroachment, and servitude. The self-inflicted violence under which the PRG collapsed left the Caribbean vulnerable to further violation by imperialist interests. The poem repeats itself just as the cycle of empire repeats itself. The metaphorical shackles the region is returned to echo the shackles of slavery, but this time the fault is shared (if unequally) between the proponents of the revolution and the forces of empire. The poet-speaker refers to the poem self-reflexively as a funeral song for the revolution, "a dirge sung for ever / and in flesh."[37] The survivors and the collective memory of those who died embody the mournful quality of the literary dirge.

Brand examines the radical alterity of Grenada vis-à-vis the North Atlantic, which was decidedly antirevolutionary during the late twentieth-century Cold War. Her work shows a commitment to black radicalism as a strategy for the advancement and protection of local epistemologies and political practices even as the threat of imperialism looms. Imagining Grenada beyond the limits of the American imperialism, her poems provide humanizing vignettes of the anger, pain, and confusion wrought by neocolonialism. She documents the disappointment when revolution proves an insufficient response to imperialism. These are not poems about the pursuit of independence but rather portraits of how Grenadians sought to make independence meaningful in a postcolonial context. By opening the collection with a poem about the militia, Brand appears to be sorting out how the atmosphere for violence was embedded in the culture of the revolution. Reading backward in time allows us to situate its violent end in a broader repertoire of violence that can be linked to histories of colonial slavery and the plantation.[38] Still, the collection overall is infused with a sense of shock that the revolution could turn against itself in this way. It is a sudden disappointment for the poet-narrator, who was fully immersed in revolution as a big idea and a part of quotidian life. While the last poems of this section of *Chronicles* document the poet's recognition of an unfolding tragic aftermath, during the years between the publication of *Chronicles* and *Bread,* Brand's perspective on how revolution rehearses the violent patterns of colonialism shifted, and she turned to the representation of neocolonialism and antiblackness across the diaspora. Her essays from this period form an important literary archive of the queer possibilities embedded in radical movements.

## Queer Genealogies of Revolution

At the beginning of Brand's essay collection *Bread out of Stone,* published in 1994, she writes about herself sitting on a beach in Cuba but thinking of a home elsewhere, in Toronto.[39] The vexed relationship between the Trinidadian Canadian's subjectivity and her citizenship requires that she detach from Canadian space and return to the Caribbean to properly render life in Toronto. She writes: "It is January. The weather is humid. In Toronto I live in the semi-detached, old new-immigrant houses where Italians, Chinese, Blacks, Koreans, South Asians and Portuguese make a rough peace."[40]

Brand's narrative is that of the diasporic writer. These are the artists whose work consistently reflects an "elsewhere" that informs their sense of "here." The images and words of diasporic writers often spring from a duality that can produce bifurcation or spawn uneasy assemblages. Movement is essential to their work—to their writing process and to the ideas that they represent. Brand is the epitome of the diasporic writer. She is constantly engaged in discourses of geographic and political movements. These are the itineraries that spur her writing. She has physically torn herself away from Toronto in order to write about it. This parallel relationship between rendering (i.e., representing) and rending (i.e., tearing or moving away) is central to Brand's operation within an African diasporic literary imaginary as she writes herself as a citizen of both Canada and the Caribbean.

*Bread* is a collection of thirteen essays. As the subtitle suggests, each essay reflects the intersecting aspects of Brand's activism, including gender, sexuality, race, and the politics of recognition. The chapters "Bread out of Stone," "Cuba," and "Nothing of Egypt" include images of Brand's movements between Cuba, Grenada, and Toronto in the 1980s. Movement is also central to her representations of the Grenada Revolution, when she was one of hundreds of internationalist workers who left their home countries to contribute to the efforts of the PRG. She writes, "I began leaving the house of bondage when I arrived in Grenada. Just being in the revolution, walking those hard hills, was walking out of bondage."[41] The essays in *Bread* draw attention to Grenada's inability to completely fulfill this romanticized role of revolution as a path out of bondage. Brand's writing demonstrates the difficulty of forging a truly feminist politics when the rhetoric and culture of revolution are so dependent on masculinist precepts deeply ingrained in Caribbean politics. Still, her representation of revolution as a process of becoming emphasizes the importance of movement and possibility in the experience of black radicalism. This is part of the queer temporality that Brand's work fuses together to account for the meanings that the Grenada Revolution can continue to generate for Caribbean futures. In *Cruising Utopia*, theorist José Muñoz identifies the work of queerness in envisioning political futures as such: "Queerness is a structuring and educated mode of desiring that allows us to see and feel beyond the quagmire of the present. The here and now is a prison house."[42] Brand's movements back and forth in time and space represent a strategy for queering the narrative practices we use to remember black radical movements. Her writing does more than simply document her time in the Grenada Revolution. She shows a sustained commitment to understanding the historical contexts that made Grenada and her presence there possible, while also using the literary form to think through what remains to be done in future movements.

There is a continued sense in Brand's work and movements that Grenada is but one stop in an ongoing itinerary of black radicalism that must keep moving in order to evade oppression and inspire new uprisings. Part of evading oppression is situated in the rejection of things as they are and the circling back to past moments of resistance to draw on different forms of memory—bodily, ancestral, cultural—to sharpen one's perception of the challenges ahead. As Muñoz reminds us, "Turning to the aesthetic in the case of queerness is nothing like an escape from the social realm, insofar as queer aesthetics map future social relations."[43] Brand's literary output highlights how internationalist participants project their hopes of a better society onto the newness of radical political movements elsewhere, so that even if Grenada cannot in the end fulfill their idealized vision, it at least stands as a moment of freedom-making that spurs maps of future social relations and revolutionary movements. A queer reconceptualization of revolution as a series of movements as opposed to a marked arrival at a single place or ideology, her writing disrupts ideas of revolution as a chronological project of achievement. Echoing Stuart Hall's ideas of diasporic identity as one constantly in production, the essays in *Bread* link diasporic subjectivity to the kinds of political movements that feed revolutionary action.[44] Brand's writing envisions the fullness of revolution in transformative acts of travel, in the potential that one experiences on the cusp of arrival, and in the embodied participation in anticolonial struggle that is figured as *becoming* free as opposed to *being* free.[45] The queer temporality of her work makes room to acknowledge the moments of failure and partial victory, learning and discovery that make up her multiple itineraries of revolution.

One of the earliest ways revolution is rooted in Brand's consciousness is through conversations among her family members about the Cuban Revolution and its regional implications for the Cold War. She understands her decision to travel to Grenada in early 1983 as a matter of inheritance. The chapter titled "Cuba" begins with a story about her uncle, who in 1959 left Trinidad for Cuba on a fishing boat. She offers limited details about the trip, emphasizing the work of memory in shaping this story. She insists that her uncle wanted to visit revolutionary Cuba to "see what was going on."[46] From an ideological standpoint, the politics of his decision are not defined by any clear stance in favor of communism or capitalism. Brand paints him as a figure who is simply curious about political change and methods of securing sovereignty in his region. He does not arrive in Cuba to perform any specific task; in fact, his story remains indeterminate—it is not clear that he stays in Cuba very long. She reports that he may have been turned away after landing at a small village; however, this is of little consequence. More important to Brand is that her uncle was motivated by a deep physiological desire to travel toward freedom: "He had style and he felt his body living in any place he chose, he felt it quicken at the thought of Cuba, he felt it move across the sand toward the fishing boat. He felt his hands loosen the rope, he felt his body climb over the side and push off. He felt it dip and wave and sicken into the sea, he felt it ignore its wretchedness for imagining Cuba."[47] The journey to Cuba and the act of imagining Cuba represent a physical escape from the wretchedness of colonial subjugation in Trinidad. Still, this escape precipitates a bodily wretchedness, figured here as seasickness. As her uncle prepares to leave Trinidad, the shore represents a place where the colonized subject can evade regimes of domination. The image of her uncle moving across the sand is reminiscent of Édouard Glissant's description of the cyclical nature of the shore in his 1990 *Poetics of Relation*. Describing the transformation of the shore between the dry season and the rainy season, he writes, "The edge of the sea thus represents the alternation (but one that is illegible) between order and chaos. The established municipalities do their best to manage this constant movement between threatening excess and dreamy fragility."[48] The shore is a place of possibility and constant movement, of simultaneous order and disorder. Uncle's movement toward the waves threatens the order of colonial authority that would keep him in Trinidad rather than encourage exploration to Cuba.

There is a queer vision of possibility in Brand's depiction of her uncle's solitary journey across the Caribbean Sea and her characterization of the bodily fragility and excess of feeling he possesses in this movement. We see this excess exhibited formally in Brand's repetition of the phrase "he felt" throughout the passage, as she describes him boarding the boat on his quest for freedom. Her uncle represents the centrality of the wandering traveler to a Caribbean imaginary: "He had style and he felt his body living in any place he chose."[49] The reference to the bodily impulse suggests a Fanonian concept of corporeal responses to colonialism and the figuring of anticolonial violence in the body of the oppressed. In *Black Skin, White Masks,* Fanon emphasizes the corporeal aspects of appropriation and humiliation experienced by the black colonial subject, describing his own body, after a racist encounter, as "returned to me spread-eagled, disjointed, redone, draped in mourning in this winter day. The Negro is an animal, the Negro is bad, the Negro is wicked, the Negro is ugly."[50] Similarly, in *The Wretched of the Earth,* he writes of the "muscular dreams, dreams of action, dreams of aggressive vitality" of the colonial subject.[51] This wretchedness and muscular resistance in the body signal the physiological burden of anticolonial resistance. For Brand's uncle the burden is the painful but necessary departure from "home" in order to experience the liberation of arriving elsewhere. Here rebellion is tied not only to the idea of revolutionary Cuba but also to the uncle's self-possession, adventurousness, and abandon. His rebellion is self-styled, creating his own bodily absence from colonial oppression through his migration beyond British-held territories. These kinds of migration, seen in the historical movements of Caribbean people throughout various territories in the region, must also be thought of as a form of revolutionary agency.[52] The act of moving toward revolution becomes as important as the site of revolution itself.

It is Uncle's decision to leave for Cuba that produces his freedom, his sense that Cuba held a utopic possibility he might grasp. The attraction to Cuba, for both Brand and her uncle, foregrounds the importance of the Cuban Revolution to Caribbean people across linguistic boundaries. The Cuban Revolution signaled a significant freedom-making moment for Caribbean people, and Uncle had a thirst for freedom—for its performance and its maintenance. Given Trinidad's colonial structures at the time, he felt he had to leave the island to experience this freedom: "It was Uncle's freeness. Just like that up and took a fishing boat to Cuba."[53] His desire to be a part of Cuba represents an embodied solidarity that speaks directly to his sense of a collective Caribbean identity. In her representation of Uncle, Brand focuses on the idea of freedom as it relates to perpetual movement, suggesting a model of dynamism and constant production of Caribbean cultural and political identity. The indeterminacy of her uncle's story speaks to questions around memory and imagination that are particularly salient for the diasporic writer, who necessarily works from a place of absence. Would her uncle really have been able to take a fishing boat all the way from Trinidad to Cuba? That is not as important as how she uses her uncle's story to contextualize her own experience of regional solidarity within the Grenada Revolution.

Growing up in a Trinidadian family prepared Brand to understand the multiple attitudes to communism and capitalism that shape a Caribbean imaginary. She recalls growing up in a family that simultaneously boasted that "Fidel had buried the Yankees in the sea" during the Bay of Pigs invasion *and* that "Kennedy had faced down Khrushchev and communism" during the Cuban missile crisis.[54] She attributes these seemingly contradictory positions to the "curious Caribbean nationalism my family held and to the propaganda of the Cold War and the red menace which they were equally steeped in. Or let me not lie—they also loved America."[55] This "Caribbean nationalism" she describes stems from a sense of regional solidarity coupled with an inescapable infatuation with American culture. Together the two produce a political ambivalence that subverts the Cold War binary. In a Fidel/Kennedy showdown they stood with Fidel in the burying of the "Yankees," in a Kennedy/Khrushchev conflict their loyalties lay with Kennedy. Her family seems to side with the protagonist with the best narrative.[56] Their vacillation between support for the United States versus support for Russia is not surprising in light of the very complicated relationship between Trinidad and the United States, especially during this period, when the United States maintained a military presence on the island.[57] Trinidadians had a firsthand experience of American cultural hegemony through their interactions with the American navy. Unlike the British, who had a clear and long-standing history of direct colonization in the region, the United States had managed to shore up neocolonial influence indirectly.

Political independence from Britain often led Caribbean nations to look to the United States, their largest and most powerful neighbor, for aid. Brand claims that her family "knew nothing about communism except for dire warnings against it and the way in which it was hauled out to discredit union leaders and anyone who seemed to be earnest or dangerous."[58] Clearly, in the Caribbean the coding of Cold War rhetoric takes on regionally specific meanings as the United States pressured newly independent Caribbean nations to side with it. Brand's family's view of communism functions in excess of the sanctioned American definitions of communism, which tend to focus on the absence of democracy and freedom, gross human rights violations, and fierce government control over the private and public lives of its citizens. Brand says her family was fascinated with communism as an idea: "Anyone who was serious or steadfast they called a communist. They would say, 'He is a communist, you know, so don't try nothing,' or 'You see my face? I is a communist, don't play with me,' or 'You lucky I is not a communist, you get away.'" Her rendering of Cold War rhetoric in Trinidad is comical, mocking the ideological boundaries that the Cold War stood for in American politics and rhetoric. In Trinidad, a communist is any person who gives the impression of being vaguely threatening, or a "bad john," in local parlance. While this popular conception of communism is not in line with U.S. Cold War perspectives, it speaks to a distinctly Caribbean politics linked to images of radicalism, masculinity, and aggression. It also illustrates the kind of hedging necessary for small nations, whose alliances with global superpowers might shift, depending on the political context.

With the story of her uncle and his relationship to Cuba, Brand articulates a Caribbean imaginary with deep but diffuse historical ties to revolution. Her "Cuba" chapter offers a view of revolution as something embedded in Caribbean consciousness at collective and individual levels. When she introduces her own story of traveling to the Grenada Revolution in 1983, she does so by invoking her uncle: "Uncle had infected me." The metaphor of infection again suggests the corporeal transmission of revolutionary fervor. It is Uncle's story itself that is "catching," and her fascination with his narrative inspires her own revision of the process. She recalls being careful not to ask her uncle why he went to Cuba so as to maintain the sense of enchantment with which she imbues his story: "I didn't want his answer to complicate my imagination of him; he might have answered foolishly or vainly, said the wrong thing, or he may have changed his mind, thinking of it now as something his body once did involuntarily." It is essential that she maintain authorial control over her uncle's story and that it become, in a way, her story. By focusing on her family, Brand is able to draw historical and political connections between Grenada and Cuba that go beyond the tremendous support the PRG received from Cuba between 1979 and 1983.

The story of Brand's uncle and that of her own personal journey together illustrate the impulse to migrate that shapes Caribbean consciousness. Drawing connections between herself and her uncle, Brand queers the concept of revolutionary traditions or genealogies. The line of kinship she maps between herself and her uncle circumvents heteronormative ideas of inheritance moving from parent to child.[59] Instead, Brand expresses a vision of revolution as something embedded in diasporic consciousness. She defines revolutionary inheritance as the nonfilial creation of relationships between generations and genders. What is most important is not the mode of transmission but the act of recognition that they share, seeing each other in their varied engagements with Caribbean radicalism.

While Brand performs her own "freeness" in her move to Grenada, her uncle remains a key part of the story. She is surprised to meet him in Grenada in 1983 and learn that he has again ventured into the revolution to "see what was going on," as with Cuba more than twenty years earlier.[60] Brand imagines that her experience is similar to her uncle's, with one crucial difference: while her uncle traveled to *see,* Brand travels to *know* and to *work.* She writes, "I know that it was twenty-four years later, after I had taken a plane to Grenada during the revolution, like my uncle but not just to see what was going on but knowing fully what was going on, to work at what was going on."[61] What does she know? That writing is critical to her role in the revolution. Brand's essays never detail the agricultural reports she wrote for the PRG. Instead she focuses on how she saw the revolution as a queer Caribbean woman, as a writer, and as a relative outsider to Grenada. She is constantly reminding herself and her readers that her diasporic ties extend north to Toronto and south to Trinidad.

For Brand, the act of writing is part of her engagement with the revolution. This physiological imperative is not simply an involuntary physical reaction; it is intentional on the part of the oppressed. The revolution is most impactful in this space of becoming and movement, in the space that is not always legible but always experiential. She is forthright about the challenges of describing her ties to the global north and south, and she is especially aware of this challenge in the case of Grenada, where the revolution eventually fails. A key question she explores is how to remember the full complexity of Grenada in the wake of such disappointment and trauma. Her response to this question involves a turn to the bodily experience of revolution: "Revolutions are not as simple as the words given to them after they fail or triumph. Those words do not account for the sense in the body of clarity of the sharpness in the brain, and they cannot interpret the utter vindication for people like me needing revolutions to reconcile being in a place."[62] Addressing the aftermaths of revolutions, she argues that whether any single revolution ends in failure or triumph, understanding revolution as process, as opposed to outcome, is the most crucial work. The clarity in the body she describes comes from movement, either moving through or moving toward one's desire for revolution. Here movement functions in both senses, as a physical return to the Caribbean and as organized protest for radical political change. To truly participate in the movement, Brand must make a "rough peace" with her diasporic condition. This reconciliation comes through an acknowledgment that the desire for liberation occurs naturally in the body. As such, the ideological categories thrust onto these movements will never sufficiently account for the intricacy of thought and experience that inform the pull toward freedom. Her challenge is to put this in print. Brand queers Caribbean radicalism by thinking Cuba, Grenada, and Trinidad through intimate, bodily engagements, as well as through "an insistence on potentiality or concrete possibility for another world."[63] These seemingly small, intimate movements are born out of the urge to experience freedom and to do so in ways that promote visions of freedom, rooted in the body but uninterested in strictly filial modes of transmission or masculinist visions of domination and aggression. These queer visions of radicalism imagine revolution as it should be instead of accepting revolution as it is.

### Revolution as a Feminist Act

One of the central preoccupations of Brand's work is the representation of women, including herself, forging their own visions of black radicalism. She is inspired by the women she observes working in Grenada, even as her representation of women laborers complicates her understanding of her own contributions to the revolution as a writer. She is drawn to images of Grenadian women who are able to do things with their hands and therefore make what she deems more concrete contributions to political change and nation-building. Brand emphasizes the connection between the Grenadian landscape and the work of women. Grenadian women are seen fixing the local roads and farming. Here feminist agency is embodied in the able hands of the woman laborer. She writes: "The patience of the eyes taking in the road to Gouave, the women fixing stones to it, the slick tar, the unbearable sun. The desire for the sight of the drop to water at Sauteres, the milk of ocean at Petite Martinique, how a woman digging yams in the bush can emerge, hands big as night. Things fell away, the slough of patriarchal life, the duty of female weakness, the fear that moves it, the desire grafted to it."[64] This focus on women at different sites across Grenada is essential to Brand's political intervention. As opposed to the spectacle of speeches and rallies led by the men who spearheaded the revolution, in the women's actions she sees the slow and steady clearing of roads and pathways. These inroads, figured literally and metaphorically in the women paving the road to Gouyave, illustrate the freedom Brand felt moving through the country. The emergence of women (as if suddenly from the bush) provides the political sustenance to wear down patriarchy and reject the idea of women's bodies as objects of heteronormative desire.

Brand makes women visible on other terms. In her writing, women's labor is recognized as critical to building the revolution. Observing these women, she imagines a departure from the "duty of female weakness" that defines the gender binary.[65] She feels the weight of her otherness, of being a Trinidadian Canadian in Grenada, and of her queerness, being a woman who desires other women in a predominantly heteropatriarchal society. This passage, while focused on other women, also gives readers a sense of Brand's itinerary throughout Grenada. While she writes elsewhere in *Bread* about living on the outskirts of St. George's, Grenada's capital, this passage places Brand in Gouyave, a fishing town on the island's western coast; at Sauteurs on the north coast, where Caribs leapt to their death to escape the French in the 1600s; and on Petite Martinique, the smallest of the three islands that make up the nation-state. What these three sites have in common is their rural location. They would not have been the easiest places to reach at the time—the revolutionary government was only working on the roads then, as the passage mentions. Clearly, the places in Grenada Brand traveled to had an impact on her imagination. She would return to a representation of rural Grenada in her fiction.

If this seems a somewhat romanticized representation of the work of subaltern women it is because Brand's portraits of these women are meant

**Figure 7.** Women farming lettuce and cabbages at River Sallee, St. Patrick's, Grenada. (© Kathy Sloane, courtesy of the photographer)

to stand in contrast to her image of herself and her anxiety about the writer's work. Brand's fiction and autobiographical essays share a self-reflexivity about the role of the diasporic writer in revolution. Her uneasiness with the role of the diasporic writer stems from issues of location and class and the intersection of these two issues with representations of authorship. She wants to decenter her role as a writer "authoring" the revolution because in comparison to the manual labor of rural Grenadian women, her work seems elitist and less significant. In the title essay she offers a portrait of herself in which her sexuality and her writing vocation set her apart in Grenada:

> I remember one noon in hilly St. Georges. I'm walking up that fatal hill in the hot sun. This is before those days when everything caved in. My legs hurt, I'm wondering what I'm doing here in Grenada with the sun so hot and the hill so hard to climb.... I'm here because I've decided that writing is not enough. Black liberation needs more than that. How, I ask myself, can writing help in the revolution? You need your bare hands for this. I drink my beer over my open diary and face this dilemma. I wish I were a farmer. I could then at least grow food.[66]

This is likely a description of Market Hill, one of the steepest inclines in St. George's, a town of several steep hills. Market Hill is at the center of St. George's, connecting the east side of the town to Market Square and the Esplanade on the west side. Brand assumes that to be part of the revolution, one must do more than write. The image she paints of herself struggling up the hill reminds readers of her status as an outsider who has to adjust to Grenada's topography. It also serves as a metaphor for her efforts to reconcile her vocation as a writer with her politics as an activist: it is an uphill battle. The terrain is both physically and socially challenging. She sees the farmers and rural workers as the ones who drive the revolution; she envisions being part of the Grenadian rural working class and doing something with her hands. This appears to be an early formulation of Brand's whereby she initially wants to define revolution as a utilitarian concern linked to the work of the lower classes. It would appear that she wants to write *writing,* and its implied elitism, out of revolution. And yet there is something that compels her to proceed with her writing as work and to continue with her documentation and theorizing of the revolution. The temporal hinge in this passage ("before those days when everything caved in") indicates the clarity with which she embraces her role as a writer and witness after the revolution's collapse.

Ultimately, in her representation of the Grenada Revolution, being a queer woman writer is also pivotal. Examining the genres in which Brand's work on revolution circulates, we find modes of writing that stand in contrast to the bureaucratic genres of reports and descriptions that she would have produced for the PRG. The genres she self-selects are expressive and subjective. Her oeuvre indicates her independence from the government and an interest in the makings of revolution outside the context of state power. This method of delineating boundaries of state-sponsored revolution is necessary for an understanding of how women and other marginalized figures shaped radical movements from the periphery of those same movements. For instance, if the mainstream narrative of the revolution emanating from the government made no mention of queer sexuality, she would write these stories into her own narratives. Brand's descriptions of herself working in Grenada also reveal the ways in which her gender marked her as an outsider: "The electricity has broken down. I decide to have a beer at Rudolph's. The customers, men alone or women accompanied by men, turn to look at me. I ignore this as I've been doing walking through town. I'm used to masculinity. It's more colourful on some street corners; in this bar it's less ostentatious but more powerful. A turn of the head is sufficient."⁶⁷ Rudolph's was a restaurant and bar frequented by locals and tourists on the Carenage, part of Grenada's harbor. In this scene, which gives her space to produce a commentary on local gender relations, Brand is clearly irritated by the expectation that women should be accompanied by men in order to move through certain spaces. The presence of this familiar masculinity signals the common thread of patriarchal power that runs through the various societies Brand has lived in, both in the north and in the south. It is also evocative of Grenada's smallness.

Many of the bar's patrons would have been able to identify Brand as an international worker. What does it mean for her to feel herself a lone woman in Grenada? How does this powerful masculinity complicate her desire for Grenada to serve as a venue for the potential redress of the shortcomings of previous radical movements? Throughout her essays, Brand changes the popular image of who represents Caribbean revolution by emphasizing the experiences of women. She insists that her own experiences be legible as part of the revolution, and this is especially important in the aftermath of the events of 1983, when the assassinations of Bishop and his comrades made it feel as though revolution in the Caribbean might never be possible again. Brand's representations of Grenada keep ideas of revolution alive in a Caribbean literary imaginary because they are centered on a population that has learned to survive epic tragedies and failures. Her memories offer roadmaps for understanding traces of the revolution that have survived the personal and ideological battles that consumed the NJM in its final days. By expanding the representation of participation as well as the historical markers of revolution, she rewrites definitions of the process and signals ways to make sense of the tensions produced by revolutionary violence in quotidian contexts.

### The Recitation of Violence

Brand's representations of revolution shift from the quotidian to the spectacular when she recalls the U.S. invasion of the island in the chapter "Nothing of Egypt." This chapter, whose title comes from the words of African American abolitionist and feminist Sojourner Truth, reflects on the experience of the military invasion of Grenada and Brand's difficulty reentering Canadian society on her return. Her descriptions of the invasion feature a dreadful stasis, marking the difference between the hopeful movement and cautious critique that characterized earlier descriptions of the revolution and the violent conclusion of her time in Grenada. For her, being trapped in the midst of the invasion calls to mind past colonial occupations. She focuses on the invasion as a primal scene of violation marking the end of the revolution, noting in particular the stagecraft of the American military assault and how this stagecraft is meant to be part of the assault's subduing power. Here is a prose version of the scenes she had described years earlier in the poems in *Chronicles*:

> I recall looking out at American helicopter gunships strafing the offices of the Prime Minister one afternoon of the war. The building hung tenuously to a hill of green from the rainy season. This day the sky was a dazzling white, the sun making the clouds silver and the American gunships like bees stung the building and the hill. The air seemed molten and the helicopters spewed metal, thickening the porous air white, leaving the ground bottomless. The building caught on fire and burned after they were gone and all night long.[68]

The conflict plays out like an action sequence in a film, an American fantasy of stamping out communism.[69] In juxtaposing the green hills and dazzling sun with the helicopters spewing metal and gathering "like bees," she contrasts the natural landscape with the destructive weaponry. The prime minister's office burning all night alludes to dreams of revolution gone up in smoke. Brand watches her hopes sink with the sun that evening: "From the verandah, where I stood limp against the wall, the ricketiness of the Third World fell as my heart's own."[70] What remained of the Grenadian military was no match for the most powerful military in the world. The idea of the "ricketiness of the Third World" suggests the inevitability of this kind of conflict and the instability that plagues the global south, as any attempts at crafting independent definitions of freedom can seem doomed to failure if those iterations of freedom do not coincide with Euro-American political ideals.[71] This sense of inevitability becomes an embodied experience for Brand when, trapped in a house, she anticipates her death: "It was only five days, but they took a long time to pass. I could hear each minute's temporal hum and the hum of the blood in my head. The skin burns. And the jaw clamps tight. And the mouth tastes like paper but sour. I could do nothing but think and notice the independence of my body and the disloyalty of the region of my brain which keeps notes on the present."[72] The time of waiting marks a partial self-betrayal for Brand. She cannot take up arms, and again, she feels the constraints of a cerebral response. The writer in her is always conscious of the need to witness and to document. The paces her body runs through—the hum of blood in the head, burning skin, clamped jaw—are a corollary to the wretchedness her uncle experienced on his trip to Cuba.

The violence raging outside the house will not bring liberation, however, but only confirm the subjection of Grenada, and places like it, to the might of U.S. imperialist power. She endures the waiting as her mind turns to the possibility of an escape, ostensibly back to Canada. This is the moment of transition when the possibility Grenada represented is foreclosed, slipping out of grasp. Yet again, Brand finds herself out of place, and in need of another itinerary.

The U.S. invasion leaves her searching for language to represent the disappointment that the end of the revolution brings. Brand says little about that power struggle in this text, the memory of friends lost too painful. At the end of Alejo Carpentier's *The Kingdom of This World*, set during the Haitian Revolution, the protagonist, Ti Noel, reflects on the "uselessness of all revolt" in the aftermath of the revolution.[73] Instead of the freedom he imagined, he faces the possibility of hard labor building King Henri Christophe's military fortress La Citadelle. A similar sense of the uselessness of revolution hovers over Brand as she witnesses American military aircraft bombarding the island. Following the trauma of the invasion, Brand searches for the appropriate terms to account for her disappointment when the U.S. invasion does not end with Grenadians defeating the invading forces. Describing the precise moment where she felt history fail her, she writes:

> This is why I do not believe in magic anymore. This is why my ancestors fail me with all their chants and potions. Because I wanted that day to rain sheets of water which would cover the island. I wanted a day when the enemy would be so overwhelmed by the sound of my ancestors dragging their chains that they would be killed by the clamour. I wanted a day when they would be compelled by that same spell which enveloped me, and their weapons would seize up or they would run away with screams in their heads. And at least if that did not happen I wanted to die.[74]

She rejects "magic," claiming that the American invasion of Grenada destroyed her faith in this mode. She never defines what she means by magic, but we can infer the term to reference the overwhelming power of the foundational narratives of the Caribbean that are based on histories of victorious revolution and uprising. Magic might also be the ability to escape the patterns of history in which colonial forces win. In this formulation, magic is the Caribbean imaginary she creates in which she, a black queer woman, is a subject, despite all the discourse to the contrary in colonial history dedicated to othering and objectifying people like her. Brand describes the collapse of the Grenada Revolution not only as the end of magic but also as the failure of the ancestors of the diaspora. Her invocation of the ancestors "dragging chains" evokes slavery. The Grenada Revolution was supposed to be a site for the emancipation of restless African and Caribbean ancestral spirits seeking both freedom and revenge for centuries of oppression. Instead of fulfilling its purpose as a means for redressing a long history of oppression and injustice, however, the revolution falls into a heartbreaking pattern. Her wish was that the American soldiers had been subjected to the madness of colonialism and neocolonialism. It is a call for Grenada to be great, to claim part of that regional history of resistance, but it also acknowledges the great burden of history carried by Brand and others like her fighting on the side of the revolution. This was not only for Grenada: the struggle was for Walter Rodney's assassination in Guyana, for the failure of democratic socialism in Jamaica, for the 1970 revolution in Trinidad, for the assassination of Allende in Chile, for the suffering of anonymous masses all over the global south.

Her invocation of the ancestors who fail her confirms that the Grenada Revolution was an experience guided by the spirit of prior moments of revolt in the Caribbean and throughout the diaspora. Brand accuses the ancestors of abandonment; however, she also acknowledges that this moment of abandonment is what allows her to develop a theory of revolution that fuels her writing. During this moment of abandonment Grenada represents revolution in dual senses—as a break with the past and as a continuation—revolving—of histories of revolution in the Caribbean. It leaves Grenadians with a sense of the "uselessness of revolt," but it also challenges them to remember the hopes and possibilities that inspired them when the revolution first began. The silence of the ancestors produces disillusionment with the black radical tradition. In this silence Brand writes a critique and revision of the tradition. When the ancestors do not respond to the U.S. military invasion of Grenada, writing itself must function as a way of making sense of the destruction the end of the revolution wreaks on the lives of its participants. Writing must represent a certain structure of healing. Brand makes legible this social and political crisis by moving through various forms of writing. She uses writing to face the failures of the revolution, including the fissures that were present before the crises of September and October 1983. The shift in genres creates a polyvocal archive that reveals intimate social relations whereby the characters she imagines find ways of articulating why the political and cultural space of revolution does not provide an escape from the trauma of empire and imperialism. She returns to Canada determined to reject the magic of victorious narratives of revolution and to produce a different kind of salve for what ails her.

With the essays in *Bread*, Brand uses the autobiographical mode to shed light on her experience as a diasporic writer in the midst of Caribbean revolution. She does not shy away from the contradictions of Grenada but uses them to think through the legacies of revolution that shape the region as a site of diaspora and black radicalism. These histories necessarily involved work, love, tragedy, and trauma, and Brand offers a language to map these experiences. While her themes in *Bread* are similar to those of *Chronicles*, *Bread* marks a sharper critique along the lines of gender and sexuality, a critique that becomes even more pronounced in her fiction.

### Resisting Revolution

*In Another Place* moves toward, and in many ways past, the tragedy of the revolution by recognizing the ongoing marginalization of women and queer people in black radical movements. Brand's novel provides a meditation on the limits of the black radical tradition in a way that *Chronicles* and *Bread* only allude to. With this novel Brand continues to write Grenada into a literary imaginary, using the revolution as a site for articulating a black, feminist, queer politics. Her persistence in remembering Grenada can be read as an attempt to address its unfulfilled promises, situating Grenada alongside previous revolutionary moments when liberation for all was pledged but not achieved. If Brand's writing in *Chronicles* stresses urgency and the violation of sovereignty, and *Bread* locates Grenada in a diasporic, anticolonial dialogue with Toronto and Cuba, her work in *In Another Place* continues these themes while emphasizing the coexistence of the intimate and the political. *In Another Place* demonstrates how the personal and the political are necessary to register black women's experiences in the Caribbean.

A crucial part of Brand's revision of revolution in this novel is her attention to the politics of gender and sexuality in the postcolonial Caribbean and her quest for what the literary critic Donette Francis calls sexual citizenship. In the 2010 *Fictions of Feminine Citizenship: Sexuality and the Nation in Contemporary Caribbean Literature,* Francis describes sexual citizenship as a means of accounting for "the political significance of the intimate sphere as a cornerstone of imperialists' and nationalists' projects and thus the private sphere's importance to understandings of colonial and postcolonial subjectivity and citizenship."[75] Within this framework the concept of citizenship, in both nation and diaspora, is seen as indelibly shaped by sexuality, sexual intimacy, and the private sphere. With *In Another Place,* Brand outlines the intersectionality of race, class, gender, and sexuality as they inform the circumstances under which black queer women are excluded from full citizenship in Canada and the Caribbean. This exclusion is part of what underscores the relationship that develops between Verlia and Elizete, the novel's protagonists. By placing queer women's desires at the center of the revolution, the text exemplifies the connections between queer sexuality, racism, and colonial histories that Gayatri Gopinath describes in *Impossible Desires:* "Queer desire does not transcend or remain peripheral to [colonial] histories," she argues, "but instead it becomes central to their telling and remembering: there is no queer desire without these histories, nor can these histories be told or remembered without simultaneously revealing an erotics of power."[76] The histories of entanglement between Canada and the Caribbean, between the Grenada Revolution and the women who lived through and participated in that revolution, cannot be told without also thinking through sexuality, erotics, and the politics of privilege.

The novel tells the story of a same-sex relationship between the two women, describing how their love makes them outlaws in the midst of revolutionary politics. Brand draws outside the lines of a patriarchal black radical tradition, making the women the center of a novel that is a queer chronicle of revolution. The text shifts between the perspectives of the two lovers, Elizete, a peasant laborer who works in the sugar cane fields, and Verlia, an expatriate who, having lived and worked in Canada for several years as part of the Black Power movement, returns to the unnamed island in order to contribute to the revolutionary movement. Here the revolution intersects with narrative strands on immigration, African Canadian life, and the translocal circuits of activism that animate the African diaspora in the late twentieth century. Queer desire pulls all these narrative strands together. This desire demands a feminist decolonizing politics to expose the exclusion of poor and queer black women from the discursive practices of black radicalism and Caribbean revolution.

*In Another Place* does not represent revolution by way of the usual stock characters of heroic men. Thinking through the frames of gender and sexuality, Brand finds that the site of revolution needs revolutionizing itself. She explores the way the gender divide in day-to-day Caribbean life and politics functions as a microcosm of the center-periphery power dynamics that define the relationship between the microstates of the Caribbean and imperial forces to the north. Brand's writing situates gender and sexuality as sites for struggle in revolution. The relationship between Elizete and Verlia serves as an example of the networks of queer sociality that work in part because they are almost invisible to the wider society, and at the same time it is demonstrative of what the critic Rosamond King calls the trope of "near-invisibility" that often accompanies representations of "female same-sex desire in the Caribbean."[77] Brand's centering of sexual citizenship is radical in the sense that it represents a departure from the issues that are typically emphasized in nationalist, revolutionary struggles and shines a light on an aspect of Caribbean women's lives that has been ignored in most accounts of the revolution to date.

Elizete's is the most demanding and fearless voice in the novel. Through her we understand rural working-class life on the island. By rendering a large part of the narrative from Elizete's perspective, Brand explores the possibilities open to a rural woman who shows little interest in the politics of the revolution. Elizete is not a political leader, but she is a worker and a lover. She and the other cane workers are not much interested in revolutionary leadership in the conventional sense; instead, they view Verlia as a leader who matters. They can identify with her anonymity and her work ethic. As Elizete explains, "I suppose not only me see rescue when she [Verlia] reach."[78] They are intrigued by Verlia, a woman who comes to the field to cut cane with them and who arrives with an eagerness to learn from them. By framing Verlia as a leader, even on a microscale, Brand sidesteps the need to make the novel about the more central figures in the revolution's history, such as Maurice Bishop, to whom she assigns the pseudonym Clive. Elizete never mentions Clive—or the government, for that matter; and Verlia mentions him only briefly toward the novel's end. But the "rescue" Elizete sees in Verlia is far more about the romantic connection the women share than it is about Verlia's labor organizing. In her intimate relationship with Verlia, Elizete experiences a liberatory feeling. Verlia came with her ideological views and faith in the revolutionary government; however, her initial goal of forging revolution in the traditional sense is transformed when she meets Elizete.

While she initially wants to avoid intimacy with Elizete, fearful of what she knows she cannot give Elizete as a woman, Verlia finds herself reluctantly opening up to something that feels bigger than party politics. It is the women themselves, and their shared intimacy, that serve as the central site of revolutionary praxis in this text—a crucial shift from *Chronicles*. The novel works as a response to the issue Brand raised in *Bread out of Stone* about wanting to avoid centering her own pain in Grenada: "Each time I speak I must say mine was not the only terror and not the most important but a small thing in my small self compared to the hundred thousand crouching in the other houses," she writes.[79] Brand's work in the novel is to identify alternatives to the more traditional black radicalism that has shaped dominant historical narratives of the Grenada Revolution. She focuses on the connection between activism and sexual intimacy, and on love between two poor black women, as the nexus of radical action. In doing so, Brand asks readers to consider the radical practices that fall outside the realm of how the revolution is typically defined. Elizete is indifferent to the politics of the revolution but finds freedom through a loving relationship with Verlia. Through her, Brand stages questions about what other forms of revolution are produced during this time and place and where one might look to recognize the full range of black women's radicalism.[80]

The novel opens with Elizete's expressing desire for Verlia after first sighting her in the cane fields. Brand gives over the first pages to Elizete's description of the sheer beauty she sees in Verlia:

> Grace. Is grace, yes. And I take it quiet, quiet, like thiefing sugar. From the word she speak to me and the sweat running down she in that sun, one afternoon as I look up saying to myself, how many more days these poor feet of mine can take this field, these blades of cane like razor, this sun like coal pot. Long as you have to eat, girl. I look up. That woman like a drink of cool water. The four o'clock light thinning she dress, she back good and strong, the sweat raining off in that moment I look and she snap her head around, that wide mouth blowing a wave of tiredness away, pulling in one big breath of air, them big white teeth, she, falling to the work again, she falling into the four o'clock sunlight. I see she. Hot, cool and wet.[81]

Brand immerses her readers fully in Elizete's gaze and her perception of Verlia's physicality. At the novel's beginning, Elizete's political consciousness does not seem much affected by the revolution in progress (she imagines that she will work under the hostile sun as long as she needs to eat); she does experience herself as a self-possessed and erotic being in relation to Verlia almost immediately after meeting her. Seeing Verlia, Elizete does not forget that she is a field laborer, but Verlia's presence makes her remember that there are other openings for pleasure that she can seize.

Writing about Caribbean literature and women's eroticism, the literary critic Omise'eke Natasha Tinsley calls for an engagement with women who love women as both lovers and "activists in their erotic and sexual practices."[82] Drawing on the work of Audre Lorde, Tinsley maintains the importance of eroticism and sexuality in black women's efforts to reclaim possession of their bodies. Within the matrix of colonial slavery, black women were denied personhood and therefore womanhood. "They were not supposed to feel," Tinsley writes.[83] Their eroticism, love, and feeling (both of and for each other) is a way of rejecting the commodification of their bodies as "the exclusive property of white men,"[84] she continues, referencing the racial dynamics of the plantation. At the beginning of *In Another Place,* Brand paints a picture of the ongoing legacies of the plantation complex. Elizete was caught in an abusive relationship with a man named Isaiah, a black laborer. Adela, the woman who raised Elizete after her parents abandoned her as a small child, handed Elizete over to Isaiah as if she were mere property. Several times Elizete attempted to run away from Isaiah but she never got farther than the village junction. When Verlia arrives, however, Elizete is suddenly able to envision her liberation in terms that are sensual and feeling. In her desire for Verlia, Elizete recognizes herself as a subject.

In his reading of *In Another Place,* the literary critic Ronald Cummings considers Verlia and Elizete's relationship a space of "erotic maroonage." Cummings defines erotic maroonage as "private erotic acts of desire and remembering between women."[85] Both Cummings and Tinsley note Elizete's "thiefing sugar" as both referring to a practice of theft that enslaved people and maroons used to resist the plantation and a turn of phrase to describe "the sweetness" of desire and eroticism.[86] Reimagining Grenada in this sense, Brand subverts heteronormative discourses on revolution. Her novel places political and economic liberation (via the worker-friendly policies of the revolution) in dialogue with sexual and emotional liberation. Elizete's desire for Verlia is taboo, but it is no less urgent and lifesaving for her than the workers' cooperative policies Verlia is promoting on behalf of the revolutionary government. The sovereignty she displays over her mind, body, and spirit in her embrace of this desire is, for Brand, another feminist vision of Caribbean radicalism. Elizete is representative of a population that has no reason to believe that political liberation has anything to offer it because that movement has never truly served it, even as the nation transitioned from colonial power to independence. Hers is a particularly postcolonial gesture, then, as she opts out of dominant politics (e.g., socialist revolution in response to the Cold War) to see what other forms of freedom are possible for her.[87]

Drawing on the linguistic origin of "radical" as the adjectival "root," thus connoting fundamental processes that are deemed vital, we can consider how Brand's approach in this novel takes gender and sexuality as foundational aspects of revolutionary discourse. Understood this way, attention to sexual citizenship is essential to alternative framings of Caribbean revolution. This is not to say that sexual citizenship is a new component of Caribbean revolution but rather that it becomes newly emergent when we turn to postcolonial narratives produced on the margins of revolution. In her revised narration of the Grenada Revolution, Brand creates a space where a black, queer, revolutionary subject can embody and inspire revolution more effectively than the more commonly accepted Caribbean heterosexual male subject figure. Her work changes the way sovereignty is defined in the Caribbean because of how she situates queer Caribbean women at the center of debates on liberation. Her writing allows readers to encounter Grenada not as a utopia but rather as a place from which to work through ideas of sovereignty and citizenship as they play out in a postcolonial context.

Through her narration of the relationship between Elizete and Verlia, Brand offers a vision of queer revolution. In this recasting of Caribbean resistance, women embody the possibility of liberation in both a collective and an individual sense. Here, as in *Bread,* liberation is a process more than an end point. Brand creates characters that explore possibilities for being and belonging. In her writing, women are best able to descry the contours of this liberation because they understand that the path on which this particular expression of freedom must proceed runs through a thicket of intersecting oppressions. Elizete imagines women as conduits to liberation, using the metaphor of a bridge: "A woman can be a bridge, limber and living, breathless, because she don't know where the bridge might lead, she don't need no assurance except that it would lead out with certainty, no assurance except the arch and disappearance. At the end it might be the uptake of air, the chasm of what she don't know, the sweep and soar of sheself unhandled, making sheself a way to cross over. A woman can be a bridge from these bodies whipping cane. A way to cross over."[88] Elizete's stream of consciousness reads like a manifesto for feminist liberation.

Brand focuses on scenes of vitality that involve women taking possession of their own bodies and minds, offering a different context for thinking about what it means to be revolutionary. The revolution, as defined by the party, becomes the backdrop for the radical act of women creating their own spaces for themselves and others to "cross over." Again, the act of crossing over, while connected to the idea of a bodily engagement, is not linked to a predetermined destination. The movement of crossing over, errant as it might be, is itself the revolutionary praxis. This is a praxis that works alongside (and beyond) intellectual or "scientific" engagement.[89] The intellectual is too narrow a frame with which to capture the complexity of experience for women such as Elizete. Of her confrontation with Verlia's impulse to lean on revolution in a theoretical sense, Elizete explains: "I tell she I not no school book with she, I not no report card, I not no exam."[90] Elizete's contribution to this movement is her lived experience, her resistance to being made into an abstract theory to be studied, and her seeming indifference to the rhetoric of a revolution that did not seem to inspire her. The fulfillment of radical potential is in the recognition that all possibilities are present in this Caribbean feminist movement—intellectual, spiritual, sexual. Being present in one's body is critical to the emancipation this book imagines through Elizete. Verlia and Elizete are each other's bridge away from "whipping cane" and into a space of possibility.

## A Caribbean Feminist Radical Tradition

In the loving and radical bond between Elizete and Verlia, Verlia is the skeptical partner. Where Elizete finds their intimacy liberating, Verlia struggles to reconcile her investment in the revolution proper with her investment in Elizete. She worries that falling in love with Elizete will only distract her from the work of the revolution and is not as sure as Elizete that their love can survive within the heteronormative boundaries of the nation. "I am not a man," Verlia tells Elizete. "I cannot take care of you like that; a man can promise things that will never happen not because he is lying but because they are within his possibilities in the world."[91]

Verlia's rejection of seduction in the midst of the affair allows Brand to explore the limits of romantic conventions of love for rural and working-class queer Caribbean women. Elizete confronts constraints on their love; Verlia is more focused on constraints on their politics. At the same time, they must come to understand love as a form of politics. Elizete and Verlia work to build their relationship and express their desire outside the confines of heteronormative romantic love; however, as Verlia points out, they are always already outside that structure. Together they model an alternative vision for revolutionary praxis in their pursuit of their mutual desires on the margins of a black radical political movement. Elizete represents a subjectivity that defines itself outside black power; she might even be described as part of a population that the Black Power movement forgot. Verlia and Elizete learn to appreciate their shared love even from a place of nonbelonging. From the margins, women such as Verlia and Elizete understand that the revolutionary project cannot be completed without the liberation of subjects situated at the intersection of multiple oppressions, and they pursue this freedom even as it stays under the radar of the revolution. This realization breeds apprehension within them about the black radical tradition, whereby black women often participate in black revolutionary movements while at the same time bracing themselves for the fallout, or the moment when a line is drawn that says their identities must conform to certain strictures for them to be properly "revolutionary." Often this line is drawn at the place where the revolution stumbles on its own exclusionary and oppressive policies. Queer sexuality compounds this exclusion. Brand takes up the incredible responsibility of articulating this critique through her own experience of love, grief, and trauma.

Verlia is an important contrast to Elizete because Verlia desperately wants national revolution to be sufficient for her liberation. She is terrified of the freedom represented in her love of Elizete. On the day of the U.S. invasion, when both Elizete and Verlia form part of the Grenadian resistance forces, Elizete observes Verlia and sees how deeply Verlia wanted the revolution to succeed: "She bet all of she life on this revolution. She had no place else to go, no other countries, no other revolution, none of we neither."[92] Elizete empathizes with Verlia's pursuit of revolution as a way of belonging in the diaspora; however, she herself has no such romantic attachments to the project. Even as she acknowledges that, like Verlia, she had nowhere else to go, Elizete still sees her participation in the revolution as an expression of her love for Verlia as opposed to an ideological conviction. For Verlia, as with the poet-speaker in "October 19th, 1983," the U.S. invasion and the end of the revolution are akin to a return to colonial enslavement because they destroy the place where she was seeking belonging. It brings her back to a conception of diaspora as a space of negation, the "not here" of the novel. At the novel's end, Verlia runs toward a cliff. An unnamed voice behind her (Elizete's, perhaps?) encourages her: "Comrade, run! Comrade, sister, lover, run, not today, not today."[93] At the edge of the cliff Verlia leaps. Brand offers the description of bodies falling down the cliff, breaking bones, but then suddenly taking flight across the sea.

The scene is Brand's rewriting of two earlier moments in Grenadian history—the October 19, 1983, massacre at Fort Rupert and the 1652 suicide of Caribs escaping French colonizers.[94] When the chaotic exchange of gunfire opened between the military and the prime minister's supporters on Fort Rupert, several civilians jumped from the fort to their deaths in an attempt to flee the bullets. Similarly, in 1652 a group of forty Caribs, indigenous to the island, jumped to their deaths from a cliff on the northern tip of the island rather than submit to the rule of French colonizers.[95] Brand's representation of Verlia and others jumping is a way of remembering the Grenadian dead. It echoes the diasporic trope of flying Africans who find their way back to Africa out of slavery and oppression in the Americas.[96] The passage from the novel also feels like a compression of time: Brand contemplates different historical events at once, linking colonial and postcolonial time. She recasts these histories in Verlia's likeness, allowing Verlia to cross over to another place once she confronts the end of the revolution. The narrator calls Verlia by the three names that express her multiple identities—comrade, sister, and lover. These names place her as a revolutionary, a black woman, and a lesbian. Verlia's leap is a liberating embrace of these identities even as it leaves Elizete alone to contend with the aftermath. In this scene Brand places black, queer women at the center of a foundational image of resistance in Grenadian history.

Elizete's sense of loss is tied to Verlia's transition from the land of the living to a place of the ancestors. It is distinct from the loss of the end of the political process of revolution. As a result, Elizete is not negated or otherwise forestalled by tragedy at the end of the revolution, unlike the poet-speaker of *Chronicles*. She experiences trauma, yes, but she has also witnessed Verlia's "crossing over," and this means she is compelled to think beyond the "here" of the revolution's end. In its wake, Elizete travels to Canada, seeking traces of Verlia. Diasporic movement is a choice she makes to help her make sense of the aftermath of their affair and of the revolution. Elizete's life in Canada is not a reprieve from what she experienced on the island before Verlia's arrival but simply a different kind of suffering. She is plagued by homelessness, poverty, the threat of deportation, police harassment, and sexual violence. Because of the novel's nonlinear form, we see Elizete in these Canadian scenes in the middle of the novel, before we learn how the revolution ended for her. In this way Brand avoids idealizing the revolution, Elizete and Verlia's relationship, and the idea of migration providing "greener pastures." None of these contexts provides a place where Elizete can truly settle. The healing work of this novel is in the redirection and transformation of mourning, achieved through its nonlinear form. If Verlia has crossed over, then she need not be mourned in the conventional way as she lived her convictions up to her final moments. The high points of Verlia's love for Elizete are represented as the best and brightest moments of the revolutionary period.

Years after the Grenada Revolution ended, Brand's narration of the lives and work of these women allows her to keep expanding the horizon of possibility for those whom revolution could work to liberate. The image of an affair such as Elizete's and Verlia's is what the novel offers as a way of making sense of history and loss. Whereas *Chronicles* was focused on the agenda of the revolutionary government and *Bread* gave readers Brand's personal and familial connection with revolution, *In Another Place* reflects her turn away from revolutionary politics shaped by governments and her embrace of queer desire as a radical act. This shift in her writing, thirteen years after the revolution fell apart, constitutes a reevaluation of what was truly possible in Grenada. Scott has argued that the violent end of the revolution was inevitable, given the American neoliberal impulse to stifle political formations that fail to replicate liberal visions of freedom, transparency, and democracy.[97] With the novel Brand acknowledges American liberalism's will to power in the postcolonial Caribbean, and she turns to the intimate lives of women to map a way out of this quagmire and toward something beyond political sovereignty. This other place is a vision of Caribbean radicalism that engages blackness and revolution as queer categories or ways of being, that is, as identities that are rendered queer vis-à-vis neocolonial hegemony.

The idealization of the Grenada Revolution that is apparent throughout *Chronicles* is a product of the time and place out of which the poetry emerges; the constant modes of comparison between the north and the south reflective of Brand's diasporic condition. As her focus shifts from an analysis of the destabilization of revolutionary politics as a result of American intervention in the Caribbean to an intimate account of revolutionary projects forged beyond the reach of American imperialism, Brand asks readers to consider what modes of repair can be enacted when postcolonial revolution is not enough. The problem that Brand's work highlights is the difficulty of forging feminist politics when the culture of revolution is overdetermined by precepts from the male, heterocentric black radical tradition that wants to keep queer identities as "unspoken revolutionary texts."[98] Brand's work highlights both the radical potential of transgressive sexuality while representing the trauma that often accompanies this radicalism. She wants revolution to *mean* something for the rural worker and the diasporic black activist, for people across genders: for it to be truly radical for queer and straight subjects, for citizens and immigrants. Queering the black radical tradition, *In Another Place* rejects the Cold War binaries in order to envision the broader frameworks of decolonization and postcolonialism within which the Grenada Revolution can be read. These frameworks reflect certain patterns of postcolonial political formations that keep formerly colonized nations in cycles of revolution.[99] A primary achievement of *In Another Place* is its positioning of the cane field worker, Elizete, on equal footing with the intellectual, Verlia. This relationship illustrates Brand's vision for how black radicalism must continue to evolve. "All that touching," Elizete thinks, "Nothing simple about it. All that opening like breaking bones."[100] Brand's writing provides a surface on which to break the black radical tradition, like bones, to broaden its scope and make it speak into silences where black queer women struggle within and alongside the revolutionary collective.

# 4 Legacies of Mercy
## Neoliberalism and the Disavowal of Revolution

THE TRIAL of the Grenada 17 ended in December 1986 when the Grenada High Court sentenced fourteen people to death by hanging for the crime of murder.[1] In 1991, Joan Purcell, then known as the "minister of mercy," decided to commute their death sentences to life in prison. Purcell's decision to show clemency to the fourteen facing death saved Grenada from falling into another cycle of political violence. Purcell's choice laid the groundwork for the eventual freeing of the Grenada 17, the last of whom departed Richmond Hill Prison on September 4, 2009.[2] After leaving prison, all of the seventeen except Bernard and Phyllis Coard resettled in Grenada. The Coards now live in Jamaica. Bernard Coard, Phyllis Coard, and Ewart Layne have published memoirs, and it is expected that some of the others may one day decide to share their stories in print as well. Part of what rests in the preservation of the lives of the seventeen is the possibility of more narratives and oral histories of the period, and the opportunity for Grenadians and Caribbean people more broadly to share in a greater sense of clarity about this interval in history. It is ironic, therefore, that Purcell who was not a supporter of the revolution and who had no formal legal training, was entrusted with the full weight of this transformative decision.

This chapter examines revolution and embodiment in Purcell's autobiography, *Memoirs of a Woman in Politics: Spiritual Struggle,* published in 2009. I analyze her representation of disavowal of the revolution, an experience she describes in spiritual, bodily, and psychological terms. Although she was a supporter of the New Jewel Movement (NJM) before the revolution, Purcell rejected the party after it seized power through a coup. Purcell's method for working through the collective shame of the revolution's aftermath is to highlight the fear the revolution caused her and to represent the entire process as an aberration and a momentary turning away from Christianity, a heritage that she interprets as essential to Grenadian history. After distancing herself in this manner, Purcell's postrevolutionary stance involves attempting to identify with the Grenada 17, representing herself as a channel for redemption and reconciliation.

I do not read *Memoirs* as a Caribbean feminist text. I include an analysis of it here, however, because I believe it is exemplary of the complex ways in which Grenadians of various walks of life have attempted to come to terms with the consequences of the revolution. Purcell's intervention makes peace where the legal system threatened to open the door to another period of political catastrophe. In this chapter I am thus concerned with how to read Purcell's intervention from a Caribbean feminist perspective, evaluating the experiences that shaped her worldview and set her on a path to play a key role in the ongoing project of healing in the lives of the surviving revolutionaries and all Grenadians. While I am not surprised that a woman took critical action to avert further political violence in Grenada, Purcell's role in normalizing the neoliberal turn in Grenadian politics is a reminder not to simply essentialize or idealize the role of women in Grenadian politics. She has also contributed to the island's turning away from the socialist-inspired framework that came into view with the revolution. Still, Purcell's story is important to include in any account of how Caribbean women have woven complicated narratives of remembrance of the revolution as she, too, pushes readers to think beyond the simple binary of innocence and guilt. Her *Memoirs* does this and more, suggesting that there may be countless other stories of women's crucial contributions awaiting recognition.

Because of her political conservatism and evangelical Christianity, Purcell holds a very different perspective from that of the other authors discussed thus far on gender and how women survive during and after radical movements. She is the only one to have held elected political office in Grenada. Unlike Brand and Collins, she was against the revolution, and her writing avoids presenting the revolution (or much of Grenada's political history, for that matter) in terms of colonialism and race. Still, there are clear connections between the thematic and formal characteristics of her work and that of Brand and Collins. From the outset, her story is both explicitly personal and political. She writes about the revolution in multiple genres, including memoir and popular historical accounts, and her representations do not follow a strict, linear timeline. In *Spiritual Struggle* the revolution is presented nonchronologically in an otherwise linear text. Finally, Purcell's objections to the revolution, and her observations of Grenadian politics more generally, are not entirely unrelated to Brand's and Collins's implicit critiques of the gender politics of black radicalism. Part of what she objects to is the authoritarian strain of the leadership. While she does not identify it as such, this concern is clearly tied to the gender dynamics of Grenada's political landscape.

Born on Carriacou in 1942, Purcell attended high school at St. Joseph's Convent in St. George's. She married at twenty-six and within two years, after some anxiety about conceiving, gave birth to a son. In 1973, at the age of thirty-one, she left Grenada to study social work at the University of the West Indies (UWI) in Mona, Jamaica. The decision to leave her husband and child for Jamaica weighed heavily on Purcell and was one of the most trying instances of confronting traditional gender roles in her personal life.[3] Upon her return to Grenada in 1977, she worked as an assistant principal at Wesley College, a local high school, before assuming the position of island supervisor at the Canadian Save the Children Fund (CANSAVE), a social welfare NGO. She would later go on to found GRENSAVE and serve as executive director of this organization. In November 1983 she accepted a position on the Advisory Council of the interim government convened by Governor-General Paul Scoon.[4] It was charged with governing the nation until elections could be held and parliamentary democracy restored. On this council Purcell served as minister of social services, youth, sports, culture, community development, and women's affairs.[5] The Advisory Council saw the nation through to the December 1984 elections. The following year Purcell left Grenada to pursue a master's degree at the University of Toronto. She returned to Grenada in 1987 and resumed her role at GRENSAVE. She served as resident tutor in UWI's Department of Extra Mural Studies in Grenada from 1988 to 1989 and joined the National Democratic Congress (NDC), then led by Nicholas Brathwaite. Purcell ran for and won election as representative for the Town of St. George's in 1990.[6] She formed part of the NDC's coalition government for that term. In August 1991, as chair of the Advisory Committee on the Prerogative of Mercy, she made the final decision to commute the death sentences of the surviving members of the NJM and People's Revolutionary Army (PRA) who were incarcerated in Richmond Hill Prison in Grenada. Since then Purcell has held various positions in Grenadian political and civilian organizations, including the post of minister of women's affairs, member of parliament for Carriacou and Petite Martinique, acting political leader and leader of the NDC, and board trustee of Youth for Christ Grenada. The two books she published independently—*Memoirs of a Woman in Politics: Spiritual Struggle*, in 2009, and *From Wilderness to Promise: A Spiritual Perspective of*

*Grenada's History,* in 2014—are both geared toward an audience of Grenadians at home and in the diaspora.⁷

*Memoirs* offers a woman's perspective on the political climate of Grenada in the post-1983 years, identifying the revolution as a moment of political coming into consciousness. In part 1 of *Memoirs,* "Servant Leadership Challenge: Personal Preparation," Purcell recounts her life from her birth in 1942 through marriage, motherhood, and undergraduate studies in Jamaica in the 1970s. She refers briefly to returning home and to participating in the workforce in Grenada, introducing her work with CANSAVE. The final chapter of this section details the nine months she spent at the University of Toronto pursuing a master's degree. Part 1 ends with her second return to the island in 1986 and her continued work with GRENSAVE and the UWI Extra Mural Office in Grenada, ending in 1989. She makes no reference to the revolution in this part of the book, which covers the years 1942–1989. Part 2, "Servant Leadership Calling: State Power," comprises chapters 6 to 11 and picks up the action in 1979 with the beginning of the revolution. Two chapters in this part detail her reaction to and her involvement in the fate of the Grenada 17: chapter 6, "Restoring Democracy," and chapter 9, "Balancing Justice with Mercy." Purcell structures time in *Memoirs* in such a way as to both skirt the greater part of the revolution's four and a half years and focus on the events of March 13, 1979, and October 1983. While this triaging is not representative of what the revolutionary process was about, this truncated temporal framing allows her to narrate the revolution as *only* a violent aberration in Grenadian political history. This is a representation that justifies the neoliberal turn she supports.

### Legacies of Trauma

"Don't!" The first voice to alert Purcell to the March 13, 1979, coup by the NJM was that of her husband, stopping her in her tracks as she was about to leave home for the day. "Revolution! **They** overthrow GAIRY," he explains.⁸ While Purcell was a supporter of the NJM in that organization's capacity as part of the official opposition to Gairy's Grenada United Labour Party, the revolution marked the end of her support for the party and the beginning of what she experienced as a political nightmare. The revolution awoke deep-seated feelings of fear in her because it seemed such a departure from what she knew to be the norms of governance, introduced during colonialism. Her fear of what the revolution might bring is cloaked in genuine nostalgia for Grenada's former identity as "a colonial outpost of Britain." Even though she spends several paragraphs outlining the corruption of the later years of the Gairy regime, Purcell does not greet the ascendance of the NJM to power as a sign of progress. For her the very idea of revolution, and further to that the overthrow of an elected government by violent means, was an aberration and a catastrophe.

While taking seriously Purcell's descriptions of her resistance to the revolution from its earliest days, I also want to highlight parallels in the strategy of representation she uses in discussing both the beginning and the end of the revolution. Because there are so many similarities in the language Purcell uses to describe March 13, 1979, and October 1983, it is possible to surmise that the way the revolution ended shapes how she remembers its beginnings. In her recollection of the four and a half years of the PRG government (documented in one chapter of just under thirty pages), she focuses almost entirely on March 13, 1979, and October 1983, giving little attention to the time between those dates. In effect, her memoirs collapse the time of the revolution, reducing it to the two most jarring and, in the case of October 1983, most violent aspects of the process. This skewed focus ignores not only much of the effort of the NJM and PRG to build the revolution, it also passes over the creative and enthusiastic ways in which thousands of Grenadians participated in and took ownership of the process as a collective endeavor.

As was the case for many Grenadians, Purcell's earliest impression of the revolution came from the radio broadcasts through which she and her husband heard the initial announcements from the NJM about the coup. "An unfamiliar authoritarian voice belted over the radio," she writes, sensing immediately that the NJM's seizure of the government by a coup would mean the restriction of certain personal freedoms. Whereas she had previously experienced the Gairy government as "increasingly authoritarian and despotic," she now had similar feelings about the NJM. Though the NJM planned and executed the revolution in secrecy among a small vanguard, after the party's paramilitary arm captured the army barracks in True Blue and the radio station, the NJM's efforts that morning quickly became a national collective action as members of the public joined in the work of securing police stations across the different parishes in order to neutralize Gairy's forces and consolidate their control over the nation. Still, Purcell's depiction of the revolution as "authoritarian" from its earliest moments points to a tension that existed for the duration of the PRG's existence between the actions taken by the government on behalf of the people of Grenada and the actual will of the people. In most cases the people of Grenada cooperated with the vision of the NJM as implemented by the PRG, however, in key moments the will of the party and the desire of the people diverged. In addition, there was always a small but sizable minority, including Purcell, that was at best indifferent and at worst hostile to the revolution. For these people the NJM's method of achieving and maintaining power would have felt particularly authoritarian as it left them with little or no say in the matter.

The tone of the initial radio broadcast as described by Purcell is paralleled in several accounts of the October 19, 1983, evening statement of Hudson Austin alerting Grenadians to the shoot-to-kill curfew instated by the Revolutionary Military Council (RMC), another moment of political power shifting swiftly and in the absence of elections. Purcell was not in Grenada on the evening of October 19, when Austin made this radio broadcast, because she had to travel to Barbados to meet delegates for a conference scheduled to take place in Grenada that week. She left the island on the morning of October 19, before Bishop was assassinated, and she did not return until two weeks later, on an American airlift out of Barbados. Still, she would have heard accounts of the RMC's announcement, which many have said did strike them with terror.

I point this out not to discredit or doubt that the morning of March 13, 1979, was frightening for Purcell and others but rather to highlight the possibility that memories of this period could have been overdetermined by the pain and shame of the end of the revolution. That is, because Grenadians know how things ended, they might be more likely to assign feelings of fear, abhorrence, and skepticism to their memories of the earlier days of the revolution, whether they initially had these feelings or not. Purcell describes her husband's "rigid face" and "bulging eyes" as if the news of the revolution alone was enough to transform his visage, the rigidity conveying a hardening resistance and his bulging eyes relating his shock. For her part, Purcell recalls feeling "dumbfounded" and "petrified" at the initial news of the revolution. Fear set ins, and with it comes a sense of numbness. The dawning of a new political reality starts to chip away at her physical and psychological well-being, and she notes "a general weakness taking charge of my body as my mind became confused with so many more questions than possible answers."

By describing her experience of the revolution as mainly physiological and psychological deficit, Purcell frames the process as a threat to her well-being while avoiding any sustained discussion of the policies the PRG put in place in the years following the coup. Though Gairy had "despotic and authoritarian" tendencies, he still represented something familiar to Purcell. He was in many ways a continuation of the order of colonialism. With the onset of the revolution she lost the security of this political heritage: "Slowly, reality dawned, my beloved country, a colonial outpost of Britain for centuries, and in my lifetime an independent, democratic, Caribbean state, was now a revolutionary state." Unlike the irony with which Walcott expressed a longing for the colonial past in his essay "Good Old Heart of Darkness," Purcell's nostalgia here is genuine. In comparison with Grenada's colonial past, she finds revolution anathema. She presents the revolution as a dangerous departure from both Grenada's colonial and early postcolonial history. She also seems to connect the two, the island's colonial past and its recent postcolonial history, in such a way as to erase the struggle that transformed Grenada from an "outpost" of Britain to an "independent, democratic, Caribbean state." This further minimizes the challenges that would have been involved in getting Gairy—whose government, she concedes, was corrupt and "undemocratic"—out of office through the conventional means of elections. Caribbean independence, in her formulation, exists essentially in its proximity to its colonial past.

Purcell's view of what defined Grenada at this time offers some insight into her political consciousness and helps to explain why a revolution whose goals from the outset involved a more complete decolonization would feel like such a catastrophe for her. At the moment she becomes aware of herself as a person with political impulses and agency, she is more comfortable with a form of governance that closely mimics colonial structures. The NJM's leap, pushing the nation into the realm of revolution, fills Purcell with uncertainty because it signals an immediate departure from the colonial and neocolonial status quo. She feels her body giving way, unable to resist the force of the news, and she is overwhelmed both psychologically and intellectually. This is someone for whom revolution, in principle, could never be a legitimate form of governance, and it affects the ways she writes about this period in her memoirs.

Although Purcell's descriptions of Grenada's social, political, and economic situation before the revolution are relatively thin, focusing mainly on her own life, in her memoirs she uses the occasion of the revolution to backtrack and offer a brief summary of the later years of Gairy's time in office. She mentions that Gairy was a close acquaintance of her husband's but that she kept her distance from him and his government, turning down an invitation to meet with him privately to discuss the possible job opportunities for her in public service. She also provides an outline of the violent oppression the NJM and its most vocal supporters endured under

Gairy. The revolution was clearly a moment of political provocation for Purcell, compelling her to think about Grenadian politics as a changeable, dynamic platform and about the kind of consequences produced by Gairy's mismanagement and abuse of power. But the NJM's success in deposing Gairy was not nearly enough to convince her of the revolution's promise: "I experienced no comfort from the comment that the coup was 'almost' bloodless. In fact, I convulsed in mind and body that the Grenada I knew, as a daughter of the soil, could have come to this. The effect on me was profound. Psychological trauma hit me. Indeed, the effect of this impact has lasted in some measure until now." There is considerable irony in the idea that while she was aware of the violations of public welfare endorsed by Gairy and his armed supporters, Purcell reserves her charge of "political trauma" for the revolution that removed Gairy from office.

Purcell acknowledges that the beginning of the Grenada Revolution has had a long-term negative affect on her. The way she emphasizes the "psychological trauma" of the events suggests, however, that this recollection is influenced by what she knows, at the time of writing, about how the revolution ended. We can contrast Purcell's descriptions of psychological trauma from the revolution's early days to her feelings around the end of the revolution. Just as the PRG brought about radical change that she says left her (and others) feeling uneasy, so too the October 1983 crisis and the U.S. invasion mark a period of shock, uncertainty, and rapid transformation: "The people of Grenada were caught unprepared for the radical political and social upheaval they experienced in so short a compass of time. The people were caught in a cocoon of grief at the violent, one might say, senseless deaths of family and friends, neighbors and colleagues." One difference between these two quotations is that her point of view shifts from a subjective account of her individual experience to a collective account of a grief that spread across all Grenada. While it is certainly plausible that the surprise formation of the PRG was traumatic for her (she says it "struck terror" in her heart), it is also plausible that some measure of this trauma about the beginning of the revolution was produced retroactively following the events of October 1983. Especially in narrations such as Purcell's, which is mostly silent about the middle of the revolution, it can be difficult to separate the affective power of the beginning from that of the end. By conflating her anxiety over the coup of March 1979 with her anger and sadness over the assassinations and violence of October 1983 and reducing the revolution to these two moments, Purcell narrates the Grenada Revolution as trauma, ignoring other aspects of the majority of the time the PRG was in power.

## The Illegitimacy of Revolution

It is important to take seriously Purcell's claim that the means by which political change was effected—revolution—was a significant problem for her. She knew many of the NJM leaders personally, and counted Maurice Bishop as a friend. Her discussion of the NJM at times sounds as though she would have supported the party had it won power through the ballot box. She writes, "I felt a sharp sense of conflict because I knew quite well several of the leaders of the 'Grenada Revolution' having given unstinting support to the NJM yet I could not with integrity support the action taken to gain power and to redress wrongs. I realized then that it was important for me to be cautious both in sharing my views on the 'revolution' and in any future involvement of the process." In this passage and throughout this chapter, Purcell uses quotation marks around "Grenada Revolution," for reasons that are unclear. This choice of punctuation, along with her tone, might convey her feelings about the PRG's legitimacy. Certainly, the PRG feared being perceived as illegitimate, and these fears dictated much of the rhetoric and action that was deemed censorious. It seems that Purcell did not accept revolution as a legitimate means of effecting political change. In another passage she describes her growing suspicions of the revolution after observing what she deemed intolerant behavior. "I started having misgivings," Purcell writes, "when I began to discern certain signals of distress. I began to observe acts of intolerance of local and internal dissent, and paranoia over external threats from the leadership of the People's Revolutionary Government." She is disappointed that the promised elections never materialized, that perceived political opponents were detained without trial while others were branded "counter-revolutionaries," and that the press was criticized and newspaper offices were shut down. Her description fits some of the PRG's responses to criticism they faced in the local and regional press, including in Grenada's *Torchlight* newspaper.[9] She also describes the sense of there being no privacy for citizens with regard to one's political views, as she felt one always had to make clear an allegiance to the revolution. There was little room for any gray area. "Everywhere one turned," she writes, "in all public spaces—there were huge billboards and ideological labels." Purcell's critiques have been validated, in part, by former members of the NJM themselves, who in recent years have conceded that their anti-U.S. rhetoric and their treatment of perceived opponents were overzealous and marked some early errors in judgment.[10] Some of the very things the revolutionaries did to safeguard their process are what led to critiques such as Purcell's.

**Figure 8.** "Women Committed to Economic Construction" billboard, Grenada. (© Kathy Sloane, courtesy of the photographer)

Purcell reveals her dismay at attempting to discuss her discomfort with the revolution with a friend and having that friend shut her out, refusing even to entertain Purcell's complaints. This, too, provoked a strong physical response for her. "When she did that," Purcell writes, "I felt the blood literally leaving my head and rushing to my feet."[11] She also describes feelings of "isolation and aloneness" after confronting another friend who was also a supporter of the revolution and being dismissed by this person. The chapter in which these encounters are related includes several descriptions of how the revolution changed some of her relationships with friends as she felt increasingly silenced in her attempts to ask questions about and to critique the revolutionary process. In the same passage she describes the time of the revolution as "one of the most tense and conflicting periods of my life." Purcell's descriptions of the exact policies she wants to critique are thin, however. Her most clearly articulated critiques are that the PRG's staunch opposition to Gairy was polarizing and that its leadership was unconstitutional and therefore illegitimate. She dedicates a total of three paragraphs to describing the policies of the PRG. She collaborated with the Ministry of Education to develop a new curriculum for preschoolers, and she credits the PRG for its literacy program, Maternity Leave Law, and the launching of the National Insurance Scheme (NIS), which paid various government benefits, including pensions. She recognizes the increase in the number of scholarships available to Grenadians to study abroad and the decrease in unemployment (though she takes a narrow stance here, attributing the drop in unemployment to the "mushrooming" military). She also offers vague praise for the revolution's many "national programs and projects," again without delineating any of the substance of these programs but simply recognizing them as being "people-oriented" and mobilizing the nation.

What stands out in Purcell's account, then, is the imbalance in her representation of the revolutionary process. While she claims the revolution represented "disturbing new developments—much more disturbing than anything I had noted before in the life of the people of Grenada," she does not provide much evidence to support her claims. Because she wrote her memoirs as a former elected official, it is understandable that she would oppose the idea of a revolution displacing an elected government; however, that does not explain her failure to reckon with what the PRG achieved in cooperation with the Grenadian people. The process the PRG meant to inspire and produce freedom instead evokes pain for Purcell, and it appears that a large part of this pain is tied to her desire to disavow the entire revolution because of the way it started and ended. When the revolution unraveled and Bishop was placed under house arrest in October 1983, Purcell defended him and supported efforts to secure his release. Although she did not support the revolution, she cared about Bishop. He is a redeemed figure because his house arrest allows her to position him in opposition to the party's Central Committee and the RMC. She makes plans with a friend to join crowds protesting his release, and, contradictory though this might seem in light of her early views of his government, her willingness to join others in demanding his release is in keeping with the level of popularity Bishop had achieved as a political leader.

Purcell's memoirs serve as part of her effort to deal with the trauma of Bishop's death and the American invasion; however, her narrative is more invested in a catastrophic representation of the revolution that disavows the efforts of thousands of Grenadians to come together to improve their lives and the lives of their fellow citizens. By discounting the revolution as illegitimate, Purcell misses the opportunity to truly grapple with the initiatives put in motion by the PRG. Such an engagement would have rendered her critique more nuanced.

## The Legitimacy of Invasion

On first reading, Purcell's writing on the period of the revolution—and her insistence that politics is not the appropriate venue for achieving liberation—may seem inconsistent with the views she expresses later in her memoirs, when she enters politics herself. This reads as a contradiction because of the vast difference between Purcell's political aims and those of the revolution. The radical vision of socialist revolution that the NJM held out would have required a wholesale transformation of the social, cultural, and political fabric of the nation—not at all in keeping with Purcell's vision of politics. She would have liked to have seen changes to society, but the changes she imagined were far more gradual and for the most part incremental, with the status quo maintained in some areas. When she argues that spirituality and knowledge of God are the only venues through which true liberation can be achieved, she is conceding a large portion of Caribbean politics to the legacies of colonialism and the reality of indirect, neocolonial rule. Her critique of the revolution is that the NJM promised entirely too much, that the liberation the PRG wanted to build, and wanted Grenadians to imagine, was outside the scope of what was possible in politics, revolutionary or otherwise: "Hundreds and hundreds of the country's brightest and the best, increasingly devoured ideologically, but hopelessly skewed theologically—sincere but sincerely wrong. If only they would recognize that political 'liberation' is a shortfall," she writes. She presents political ideology as a false god, claiming that it leads to "new corruption" and champions instead the concept of the liberation of the soul. She claims that spirituality and knowledge of God are the only venues through which true liberation can be achieved. I disagree with Purcell's argument positioning spiritual liberation against other forms of liberation because it dismisses the need for anti-imperialist action in postcolonial Grenada and sidesteps the question of the right of Grenadian people to experience, and if necessary to fight for, political freedom. Her argument suggests that political and spiritual liberation are mutually exclusive, when they need not be.

In a spiritual sense, Purcell feels that the revolution is a turning away from God and a detour from Grenada's divine course. Though she understands the revolution as a response to the failure of democracy under Gairy, she abhors the idea that its popularity depended, in her eyes, on demonizing him. As far as she could tell, the only vision the revolution had to offer was an anti-Gairy vision: "The event of a political revolution was perhaps a logical end to the then societal realities, but in many minds, including mine, such was not a welcome development. At that stage in my thinking, whatever may have been left of possible options, faith had to be first examined before there would be unanimity on that position." She does not explain what it would mean to "examine faith," or how that would help clear a political path to freedom, but it is clear that she rejects the noncapitalist, socialist-inspired plan of action that the PRG began to execute. This was a model premised on a mixed economy, blending state, private, and cooperative sectors and led by the state. Even though what the PRG actually pursued, in terms of an economic model, was not strictly socialist, that did not prevent the party from being perceived that way.[12] The specter of Marxism was part of what unnerved Purcell.

In the time leading up to the October 19 assassinations, many rumors spread through the nation concerning Maurice Bishop and Bernard Coard. A dominant rumor was that a faction of the NJM, led by Coard, wanted to take the country in a strictly communist direction and that a separate faction, led by Bishop, was resisting this turn. While those who were eyewitnesses to some of the events leading up to the events of October 19 have disputed these rumors, citing an equal dedication to Marxism from both Bishop and Coard, most Grenadians were not clear about what motivated the party rift.[13] What registers at this juncture is the compounded sense of loss. Grenadians mourned the violence of October 19 and the violence the U.S. invasion brought to their shores. Many also mourned the loss of loved ones and the end of the revolution. As Purcell makes clear, it was a time of collective sadness that affected even those who did not support the revolution. Her attention to the general mood at the time complicates the narrative of American rescue in Grenada. For Grenadians who were not invested in the capitalism/socialism dichotomy, what was lost and what was restored during the period immediately following the U.S. invasion is not easy to answer.

Ultimately, Purcell sees her role as helping to set Grenada on a proper path again, as the title she selected for the chapter featuring her revolution story, "Restoring Democracy," indicates. In this way, the importance of the revolution is always in view, alongside its end. The PRG's attempt to use parish councils as a form of participatory democracy is elided, and the definition of democracy as electoral politics is upheld. The restoration she is referring to is mainly the process that begins at the end of 1983 and spans through December 1984, when Grenada's governor-general at the time, Sir Paul Scoon, appointed the Advisory Council to work in concert with the United States to reconstruct Grenada's political system.

Despite what is now known publicly about the U.S. invasion—that even after October 19 the medical school students did not feel threatened, that the United Nations deemed the intervention unlawful, and that the U.S. military had rehearsed a similar invasion just months earlier—Purcell still felt strongly that the United States rescued Grenada when it invaded on October 25, 1983.[14] The idea that the implosion of the NJM was such a catastrophe that only an international force could bring order is one that is shared by many Grenadians because of the fear and shame they felt at the killings on Fort Rupert and the RMC's announcements. Bloodletting on this scale had never been seen before in modern Grenadian politics. The freedom of the revolution was lost on October 19 with those fateful decisions by the party leadership. The United States cemented the reality of that loss by violating Grenada's sovereignty and violently introducing a new era of neoliberal dependency from which the nation has yet to extract itself.[15] The tone at the end of this paragraph suggests Purcell's resignation to nonsovereignty for Grenada: "The USA also came to our rescue. In response to the appeal of the political leadership of the neighbouring Eastern Caribbean islands and subsequently endorsed by the Governor General of the day, the United States President sent into Grenada a fighting contingent on Tuesday, October 25, 1983. Grenada experienced a war in the days that followed."[16] The passivity implicit in the last sentence allows her to avoid the contradiction inherent in this passage: The United States waged a war on Grenada, and at the same time Grenadians credited the United States with rescuing them.

Purcell returned to Grenada from Barbados on a U.S. military aircraft. She writes, "The truth is, I never quite knew how it was managed and the added truth is, I did not much care. I wanted most of all to return to Grenada." Purcell is not unaware, however, of the price Grenada pays for this "rescue." While she missed the experience of out-and-out warfare, she notes that the Grenada she returns to is now heavily militarized: "Guns greeted me. There were soldiers everywhere, it seemed. Nevertheless, I just had to be thankful to God." Purcell's perspective balances an implicit critique of the military route used by the United States with something that feels like pragmatism—she resolves simply to be grateful to God; but I would argue that this is actually part of her distinct worldview. It is a worldview that understands Grenada and Grenadians to be capable of a certain kind of limited agency while remaining in the thrall of either colonial or neocolonial powers. It is a form of productive resignation that makes up its mind to do the best that it can in challenging circumstances but not to rock the boat too much. Her insistence on describing the U.S. military presence is something that should not be glossed over, however, as it is a critique of the ways the invasion affected Grenadian society.

Governor-General Scoon insists that he developed the list of potential candidates for the interim government based on his own judgment and the recommendations of several NGOs (he does not specify which ones).[17] It is difficult to imagine, however, that the U.S. military and Department of State would have invested resources and personnel to invade Grenada without attempting to extend the U.S. influence to matters of governance. Scoon was already relying on American and Caribbean military forces to police the island after the invasion, when Grenada's police force was depleted of personnel.[18] On her surprise at being approached for a role on the council that would collectively govern Grenada until the country was stabilized and able to hold elections, Purcell writes, "For all who know me, a simple evangelical and true national, it was a moment of shock for me when Sir Paul indicated that he was inviting me to be a member of an **Advisory Council**." Purcell was a lot of things; simple was not one of them. When Scoon suggested she consult her husband before deciding, she called instead, lawyers, friends, and prayer partners she thought would be better equipped to help her make the right choice. Of its nine members, Purcell was the only woman. Scoon insists that he wanted at least two women on the team, but he found the women he interviewed mainly "timid or disinterested to take up that kind of responsibility." Purcell was one of two women offered a position; the other declined.[19]

While she admits that there were detractors who saw the Advisory Council as "mere tools of the U.S. government," she interpreted her role as serving as "an agent of reconciliation." As one of the key indicators of its success, she points to the 85 percent voter turnout for elections in December 1984. The high voter turnout was a sign of "the installation of democratic respectability to a land where such respectability had been violently destroyed." With this assertion Purcell condemns the fratricide at the end of the revolution as a moment of immorality and impropriety. When read alongside her earlier critique of its beginning, however, it is possible to interpret her observation as a comment on the revolution, being itself aberrant, with the U.S. invasion and the Advisory Council serving to correct the nation's course after such a violent and disreputable deviation. It is evident that part of Purcell's issue had been with the youthful militancy of the PRG and its flouting of many of the norms of Western democracy, elections being but one of these norms. The age and relative inexperience of the PRG members were other norms that would have been disrupted. They did not fit the elder statesman leadership mold of figures such as Marryshow, whom they admired and emulated in other ways, or even Governor-General Scoon, whom they tolerated as part of their plan to maintain diplomatic relations with Britain.

Respectability, as Purcell uses it, is also about what kinds of Grenadian politics could be acceptable to the United States. Beyond the voter turnout and the completion and opening of the Point Salines airport, Purcell's memoirs are relatively silent on the more than thirteen months Grenada spends in a state of political limbo, with no prime minister or government in place: "For some reason, perhaps because it remained for me a very stressful assignment, much of the period of the Interim Administration constitutes a blur in my memory," she writes. She leaves her readers with very little clarity on how the council members worked with each other, the people of Grenada, or the American forces that remained. This self-imposed silence leaves readers with questions about the transition, but it also protects Purcell from criticism about specific aspects of the Advisory Council's role in the immediate aftermath of the invasion. *Memoirs* omits much of the process by which the revolution was criminalized in the postinvasion context. Not only does Purcell not comment on the earliest legal proceedings of the Grenada 17, she also says nothing about the psychological operations work done by the U.S. military to help convince Grenadians that the revolution was a fearful time and the invasion was freeing them from tyranny. Perhaps she was not fully apprised as to the legal proceedings, but it is unlikely that she did not follow them enough at least to form an opinion on the treatment of the Grenada 17 and the workings of the legal system. This silence could be interpreted as a sign of her discomfort with the manner in which the criminalization and treatment of the remaining NJM leaders played out in the courts and public sphere. The other possible reason for her silence on this issue in this part of her Memoirs may be that in a subsequent chapter she is responsible for their fate. Purcell may have wanted to appear unbiased in describing the process she later took on to make the ultimate decision about how the revolution's leaders should be seen in postrevolutionary Grenada.

The snapshots she does offer of postrevolutionary Grenada suggest a splintered nation. She describes observing the body language and listening to the words of her fellow citizens, finding signs of duress and strain: "Their messages were more powerfully communicated in their faces and voices than in their words—their richly varied experiences of pain, fear, and anxiety of the past fourteen days. There were many persons who were wildly happy at the 'US intervention'; there were also those who were infuriated and angry at the 'US invasion.'" Alluding to how the U.S. military presence in Grenada became a point of political contention, she acknowledges that not everyone saw it as a rescue. Those who were pleased that the United States sent forces to Grenada called it an "intervention," while those who saw it as wrong for various reasons—the violation of sovereignty, the violence, the mischaracterization of the revolution to justify military aggression—referred to it as an "invasion."[20] To this day in Grenada, the choice between those two terms can signal one's position vis-à-vis this aspect of the nation's history. What is clear from Purcell's observations is that the arrival of the United States brought more complicated realities to Grenada than a simple restoration of democratic electoral politics and capitalist endeavor. While the postrevolutionary period signaled a return to the less controversial Westminster parliamentary system, it also heralded a moment of ascendancy for the influence of the United States in Grenadian politics.

Purcell's writing is representative of the ongoing anxiety Grenadians continue to experience about the role of radicalism in their politics (both past and present), continuously expressed in a disavowal of the revolution as too "ideologically" inclined, even if it did achieve some good during its four and a half years. One of the lasting legacies of this disavowal is the annual celebration of "Thanksgiving," in Grenada, on October 25 to mark Grenadians' gratitude for the U.S. invasion. In many ways what was restored in Grenada was a sense of insecurity. The nation was not permitted to protect its own borders from foreign intervention, and further, it could not, it seemed, be trusted to run its own affairs. In this particular Cold War moment, Grenada was part of a global shift, what David Scott describes as "the emergence of a world in which the socialist past can appear in the present only as a *criminal* one and in which liberal democracy parades as the single—and, if need be, militarily enforceable—direction of a worldwide political order."[21] This has indeed been a lasting legacy of the invasion, and Purcell's memoirs offer a firsthand account of how this state of insecurity is achieved in the moment of disaster.[22] Especially after the shoot-to-kill curfew instated by the RMC, the end of the revolution left some Grenadians feeling they could not trust one other: "Grenada was deeply polarized then, and unfortunately, to some extent, remains like that, in need of national healing. The scars and distrust, though largely underground or faded, are nevertheless, still there." Purcell concedes that the nation was at odds with itself at the time of the invasion, a situation that the United States exploited to its own ends.

**Legacies of Mercy**

The trial of the Grenada 17 had ended in December 1986, when the Grenada High Court sentenced fourteen of those incarcerated to death by hanging for the crime of murder.[23] In her chapter "Balancing Justice and Mercy," Purcell recounts her part in deciding the fate of those sentenced to hang. Her recollection of this period is focused on her self-defined role as purveyor of divine will. She is firm in her belief that God is guiding everything, including the fate of the prisoners. At first glance, Grenada's colonial and postcolonial history are almost negligible in her analysis of their treatment. She does not comment on how the geopolitics of the region, including the interventions of the United States and certain Caribbean governments, influenced how the case against the former revolutionaries was handled. Still, a line can be drawn from Purcell's actions, which she classifies as "mercy," to more recent prison abolitionist thought advocating for alternatives to incarceration and corporal punishment.[24] The release of these political prisoners and the reintegration of most of them into Grenadian society (except Phyllis and Bernard Coard, who have resettled in Jamaica), points to the wider possibilities for rehabilitation and redemption. These are principles that are embedded and legible in some of Purcell's Christian ideology *and* part of a history of Caribbean radical thought on community building in the wake of trauma and violation.

In the context of Grenadian law, which draws heavily on British law as a model for both statutes and precedent, the Prerogative of Mercy, of which Purcell was the judge, meant that she was to act as the arbiter of common law (or precedent) over statutory law. In other words, she was not limited to the statues of codified law in her decision-making. What is left out in this formulation of the legal and the religious, however, is the question of what makes life itself valuable, and why systems of justice consider ending someone's life an adequate form of justice.[25] By

July and August 1991 the Grenadian courts were expected to respond to an appeal that had been launched on behalf of those convicted. Despite her attitude toward the revolution, Purcell's decision-making process led her to recommend clemency. She was not alone in this feeling. Others, including journalist Leslie Pierre, who was imprisoned by the PRG for launching a privately owned newspaper, later argued for clemency for the fourteen as well. But the final decision rested with Purcell, and she felt that that level of bloodshed would have imposed another tragedy from which Grenada might not have recovered. Her decision is an example of the complex ways Grenadians from different walks of life contend with the revolution at different moments in its history. Purcell's decision opens up the possibility of absolving the legal system of responsibility for its questionable practices with regard to these defendants, conceding that the legal system was simply not equipped to handle this case fairly because the assassinations of Bishop and his colleagues were inextricably tied up with revolutionary socialism, which had to be criminalized as part of the return to neoliberal democracy. A former critic of the revolution, she helped create the potential for reconciliation by commuting the sentences of the prisoners. She faced members of the public who felt that the executions should have gone ahead but held the conviction that the humanity of those incarcerated was more important than vengeance. What Purcell balances in this section of her memoirs is her personal sense of what is just, alongside her religious views and her responsibility to Grenada as a public servant and elected official. While she insists that she is motivated primarily by God, it is apparent that she separates her sense of God from what she views as fundamental or extreme evangelical views.

To lend an additional air of authenticity to her narrative, Purcell informs readers that she is consulting her journal for this portion of the memoir, offering contemporaneous commentary on the events. Eight years after the collapse of the revolution there is a mix of pride and humility in her measure of the importance of the role she played: "No matter how much I tried to avoid the responsibility, according to law, there was no way out. From a secular viewpoint, fate had chosen me. From a Christian perspective, God had ordained my part in the making of this judgment. . . . My reality was that I had no legal training. I had no seminary training. I was in essence a simple woman of faith who had committed herself to serve her God in public life with honesty, integrity and transparency." She is confident that she is divinely chosen for the task, and therefore endeavors to keep God at the center of her process. Purcell determined that the nation could offer compassion or forgiveness to the defendants. As with her reaction when the revolution first began in 1979, Purcell has a bodily response to dealing with the aspect of its aftermath, but this time it involves putting herself in the position of the prisoners and allowing herself to imagine what they might feel. She identifies with them: "I agonized in mind body and soul. Each day I awoke to the weighty ordeal, and each day I dragged myself along as if it were I facing the gallows."[26] She is anxious about having to take responsibility for the lives of fourteen people and their families, but she also senses the wider impact this decision would have on the nation's psyche. These are not the words of a woman prepared to send the prisoners to death. Purcell is interested in how the revolution can be re-narrated as a story of redemption, not unlike a biblical parable or psalm. "In the reality of that 'dread' situation," she writes, "my spirit rebelled. My conscience cringed. My heart was pained. Even my body ached." Her bodily discomfort shows her awareness that her decision would be a defining part not only of the legacy of the revolution but also of the legacy of her party, the NDC. She had the power to affect how the revolution was remembered by changing the course of its legacy.

In Purcell's retelling, the revolutionaries are fallen figures who, through the grace of God, are redeemed and set on the right path. It is the story of their deliverance, and of her own personal deliverance after a time of testing. She writes, "What I went through during a period of approximately six weeks may be likened to that of the Psalmist who spoke of passing through the Valley of the Shadow of Death." Referring to Psalm 23, Purcell summarizes how, from her perspective, the history of the path by which the surviving revolutionaries escaped the death penalty provides an opportunity for Christian testimony. Within many Christian traditions the act of testifying involves telling a conversion story attesting to the presence and recognition of God. By extension, Purcell is also presiding over a collective moment of redemption and she frames her decision as part of a "national act of forgiveness."[27] Her immersion in religious thought and prayer are an attempt to work through the revolution's traumas. In her formulation, however, mercy is only possible after a disavowal of the revolution and what it stood for. While I do not wish to discount Purcell's opinion of the revolution, it seems plausible that meaningful reconciliation and healing cannot be achieved without attempts to account for the complexity of the revolution, its flaws and its achievements.

The narrative of redemption Purcell sought played out quickly that summer. On July 27, she met with the prime minister and attorney general and was surprised to learn that they wanted to schedule the executions for that day. She hastily asked the governor-general for more time to think. That afternoon she met with the family and loved ones of the fourteen prisoners. On July 29, after attending a moving church service the previous day, she decided that the death sentences should be commuted. She attended a cabinet meeting, at which she shared this news with her colleagues, and they accepted her judgment. At the same time, lawyers for the fourteen were filing a motion of appeal to stop the executions. On August 4 she attended another church service, during which she felt herself receiving a prophetic word, and on August 9 she made a formal request to the governor-general for the death sentences to be revoked and replaced with sentences of life imprisonment. The reactions were different across the region. Grenada's public relations representatives in North America were relieved, as they had feared the executions would have damaged the nation's tourism industry. Others, including regional heads of state, were disappointed that the executions would not go ahead as planned.

Purcell's memoirs and career reflect her choice to follow a relatively conservative and cautious political path, shunning radicalism and its attendant challenges to the limits of postcolonial sovereignty. Her work is an attempt to use Christian values in political discourse as a corrective (or perhaps *overcorrective*) to any future radical impulses that might arise in response to Grenada's challenges. In her memoirs, Christianity is the redemptive antidote to the political aberration that she feels the Grenada Revolution represented. In turning to Christianity for a solution, Purcell rejects the violence, trauma, and general disorder of revolution. Instead she leans into the embrace of neoliberalism—a different type of violence, perhaps, but one that can appear less ostentatious than the bravado of black radicalism.

# Conclusion

## In Search of Our Mothers' Revolutions

THE PRECEDING chapters were concerned with how visions of the Grenada Revolution figured differently in the creative literature of Caribbean women writers as compared with the work of Caribbean men writers. Even as Caribbean women writers have participated in revolution, they have tried to point out the limits of, or problems with, certain conventional and popular conceptions of revolution in the region. I have chosen texts that reflect on how the revolution intersects with the private lives of women to highlight the underrecognized, often invisible labor required of women to reckon with revolution and its consequences. I close by examining a documentary that brings a black feminist aesthetic together with the story of how an African American woman sought refuge in the Grenada Revolution in response to being deemed a problem by the American state.[1] *The House on Coco Road*, released in 2017, was directed by Damani Baker, son of Fannie Haughton, the black feminist activist and educator whose story is at the center of the film.[2] The film recounts how Haughton decided to move to Grenada with her two children, Baker and his sister Kai, during the revolution, and how they found meaning in their lives there. I highlight this film as an example of black feminist storytelling in dialogue with Caribbean and third world feminisms because of its focus on decolonizing revolution by turning attention to the organizing work of women, because of the way it moves between storytellers of different genders and generations, and because of the insight it provides into the legacies and losses of radical action. In telling Fannie's story and his own, Baker connects the U.S.-based Black Power movement to Caribbean revolution, tracing the patterns of destabilization that tend to plague movements that speak out against American imperialism and white supremacy.

*The House on Coco Road* tracks a feminist genealogy. Nonteleological and hewing to a diasporic, as opposed to national, vision of freedom, the film weaves together voices across time and borders. Similar to Collins's storytelling in *Angel* and *The Colour of Forgetting*, Baker goes back several generations, investigating histories of racial oppression that help him better understand the politics and personal sacrifice of revolution. Baker examines how antiblackness only grows wilier in response to the Black Power movement. He also reveals where antiblackness intersects with neocolonial capitalist expansion and how it circulates simultaneously in the Caribbean. Focusing on black women's activism and resistance to antiblackness between the United States and Grenada, the documentary offers a framework for thinking, organizing, and loving in the diaspora on terms dictated by black women.

## Finding Black Feminist Form

The film opens in 1999 with Baker and his mother, Fannie Haughton, in the gate area of an American airport, waiting to board a flight to Grenada. There they will reopen a history that has lain dormant between them since October 1983, when their family was airlifted off the island. It has been twenty-eight years since Baker and his family left Grenada on a U.S. military aircraft, blending in with the American students who were being evacuated from St. George's University. The film represents Baker's second attempt to make a documentary about Grenada. His first attempt came while he was a graduate student at the University of California, Los Angeles, film school. Initially he wanted to make a film about the history of the revolution and the U.S. invasion, but after a weekslong shoot on location in Grenada, the film did not come together in the editing room.[3] He abandoned this first effort, boxing up the footage and setting it aside for a decade. When Baker found some old home videos and audio recordings of his mother's first trip to Grenada, he developed a new vision for the film: he decided to tell his mother's story instead of the history of the invasion. *The House on Coco Road* is thus a second take on Grenada that transports viewers inside Baker's reevaluation of which voices have a story to tell about Grenada. In making explicit that the film is a second attempt, Baker highlights the black feminist perspective as a choice that emerges when more conventional methods of narration fail. He builds an aesthetic around reflection, constantly reminding viewers of the questions that motivated his journey. These questions—enunciated in the film by Baker—include "What happens when your past is a matter of life and death?" and "Why would you tell your children stories that hurt?" The film combines home movies, archival footage, newspapers, and interviews, with Baker often turning the lens on himself and his filmmaking process. Baker proceeds in a self-reflexive style, showing the ways his narrative develops as he listens to the histories shared by his mother and grandmother instead of trying to piece together the history of why the revolution collapsed.

Weaving together voices across time and borders, Baker goes back several generations, investigating histories of racial oppression that help him better understand the personal sacrifice of revolution. Baker traces his family's postemancipation sharecropping years growing potatoes in Louisiana to their journey to Los Angeles as part of the Great Migration. They were in search of a better life—less racial segregation and a greater sense of safety to raise their children. Grenada, it turns out, was part of this pattern of wandering that pushed his grandmother and mother to seek better ways of life. The film demonstrates the similarities between the racism of the American state as enacted in black communities in the U.S. South, in Los Angeles and Oakland, and in Grenada. Baker examines the role of women in expanding the reach of the Black Power movement. In the scenes where he details his mother's involvement in black radical activism, including her work as one of the organizers of the 1970–1972 campaign to free Angela Davis, Baker acknowledges the different ways injustice and violence have interrupted the freedom dreams of black people in the United States. The film shows that learning the histories of his mother, grandmother, and great-grandmother, which helped him understand the private and public ways in which they participated in and shaped the radical movements of their day, is key to Baker's understanding of his present and future.

*The House on Coco Road* is an unlikely choice of title for a film concerned with events in California and Grenada. It makes sense, however, as the situational locus of his story. Coco Road refers to the route named after his great grandmother Sedonia Coco's family in Geismar, Louisiana. The house on Coco Road is the family home to which Baker traces his genealogical roots and the roots of the black feminist legacies he inherited from his foremothers. The grounding genre of Baker's film is the home movie, which played a critical role in how his family documented their history. Home movies record a range of activities, from the mundane to the extraordinary, typically of interest only to the filmmaker and that person's kin. As a form, home movies tend to be amateur. Filmed with low-budget equipment and seldom edited, they maintain a raw quality even when their subjects are actively engaged in performance. The subtext to Baker's use of home movies is that his family was motivated to document its own personal records as a way of resisting the ever-present threats of racist oppression and erasure. Baker's use of home movies as an archival record, informally preserved in boxes in an attic, opens up the potential for a more nuanced representation of social and political contexts for reading Grenada in conversation with other African diasporic freedom struggles such as the Great Migration, and the civil rights and Black Power movements in the United States. Baker includes footage of Sedonia and her family's life as sharecroppers in the South; they recorded family road trips, including their move from Louisiana to California; and captured on video the family home in South Central Los Angeles, where the Haughtons were among the first African Americans to integrate their neighborhood. As clips from these home movies play, Baker's voice-over commentary explains his family's history.

Part of why Fannie goes to Grenada is that she saw similarities between her goals and the goals of the women in Grenada. Taking her family to Grenada was a way to teach them the lesson she learned from her own mother about being willing to move to make a better life for oneself and one's family. Haughton's discomfort with revisiting the part of her history that involves Grenada is apparent in her interviews. Baker does not shy away from depicting the uneasiness between himself and his mother when they return to Grenada for the first time since 1983. He wants to piece everything together neatly. She is a reluctant subject dealing with the myriad emotions and memories of returning to the site of a dream interrupted. In one of these early conversations Fannie is seated at a table with Baker and Yvonne, a friend who lived with them in Grenada. They are debating what Baker knows or thinks he knows about his family's experience of the revolution. Fannie is aware that retelling her history will have consequences for others as well as for herself. Her lessons for Baker are multifold, and she is cautious about how she represents the revolution and the people she knew at the time. Part of Fannie's reticence about revisiting this history stems from the fear that her son might be penalized for telling this story. She knows that imperialism's narratives are disciplining forces and that to counter those forces is to invite potentially dangerous consequences.

Fannie asks Baker for patience and sensitivity as she determines how best to share her story on her own terms. These terms will not be straightforward: "That's the reality," she says. "There's a lot we didn't tell you. And we won't. . . . You'll discover stuff." She makes clear to Baker that there is no one method for gathering the histories he is in search of. First-person accounts, like other historical sources, will not be complete. The scene is awkward as they confront the reality that some silences between them will remain despite Baker's efforts to uncover truths. Fannie guides Baker in recognizing the necessary level of care he must bring to the telling of her story and his. Speaking of herself and Yvonne, she paints a picture for him of the pain entailed in a return to the island: "Coming in on that plane last night was very emotional for us. You know, the last time I was in that airport, we were going on a military plane, and my thoughts immediately went to the young people who gave their lives or are spending the rest of their lives in prison behind that airport. And so that was very emotional. I took my young children out of my country to come here to help this country. I left in pain. This is the first time I've been back, so you've got to be very sensitive." Baker has to learn to think about absences—the truncated lives of those killed or imprisoned. Fannie remembers them still as young people—the dead who would never know what it was like to grow old, and also the living, whose youth ended with their imprisonment and separation from their communities. He has to think about presences—what it means to land at an airport that remains the most visible legacy of the revolution, and how that airport continues to facilitate movement to and from Grenada for foreigners and locals alike, travelers moving physically through a legacy of the revolution.[4] In her pleas for sensitivity, Fannie also teaches her son a lesson about time and patience. This is not a story to be rushed. Baker must appreciate the trauma his subjects endure by revisiting their pasts. Altogether these lessons about absence, presence, trauma, and healing set the stage for viewers as well, shaping our expectations about how and why the story unfolds as it does. Patience is required of the viewer, as the film moves back and forth in time, slowly winding between Grenada and California, until the story of the end of the revolution and U.S. invasion, which serve as the film's climax.

Once Baker could bring together the voices and experiences of black women in Grenada and the United States, he was able to see and hear the histories these voices held and how their shared context could help him tell a story about black feminism and resistance to American imperialism, by thinking differently about what one's key archives are. Throughout the film he uses voice-overs from Fannie and Victoria Haughton as these women relay their experiences and explain why their families made certain choices, including how racism changed the way they moved through the world and the strength they found in their family and circle of friends. Their interviews tell of the ingenuity of people of humble origins, innovating to mitigate the influence of state-sanctioned antiblackness.

Baker is also heard on the soundtrack. At certain moments he layers his voice with his mother's and grandmother's, reciting parts of their story word for word. In these instances, history is a recitation, a choral arrangement Baker orchestrates, harmonizing his life and voice with those of the black women who paved the way for him. These sections of the film are at once instruction and homage. As a narrative technique, the vocal layering gives their shared family history the feel of a polyphonic, multigenerational testimony. It keeps the women's voices and stories central, and shows how understanding their stories makes his story possible. This device is central to the film's success in training its eye on a black feminist politics and aesthetics. It emphasizes that the passing on of oral history is not a passive activity. Baker is actively engaged in shaping the history even as he receives it.

The insufficiency of narratives that depend on any one historical source is another of the film's motifs. As Baker goes through his mother's timeline he chides her for leaving out certain parts, specifically how she met his father, Prestin Baker. "That's not part of my story," Fannie maintains matter-of-factly as she refuses to deviate from her narrative or center her biography on the part of her life that involved being married. Prestin Baker is present in the film but is introduced primarily as Damani's father and not as Fannie's ex-husband. Those are terms she has dictated, and they represent the choices she has made about how her story will be narrated.

At various points in the film Fannie is represented as a mother, daughter, comrade, activist, and friend. These different figurations are important because they allow us to think about the ways in which women come to be visible in private and public spheres, and how those spheres intersect. Her work as a parent is also represented for the way it intersects with revolutionary struggle. Once she becomes a parent, she takes on the role of community caregiver, minding the children of local activists while they are doing their organizing work. Though it appears she chose to be a mother more than an activist after her children were born, the way she explains her transition to parenthood is never only about Damani and his sister. Fannie describes her parenting as an integrated part of her political ideology and a new layer to her identity. She does not accept the false binary of being either a mother or an activist, instead finding ways to adapt her mothering labor to include activism. The influx of drugs and an uptick in drug-related violence in East Oakland had led her to take her children and leave their home. She had decided that to preserve the life of her children, she would leave behind everything she knew for a kind of exile in revolution.

At one point Baker finally admits, "There are so many parts to the story I am just now learning." As part of a later generation, it is up to him to make sense of the fragments and layers that form this history. These are not stories his mother can easily pass on. The work of listening to and repeating the histories of the Haughton women is all part of understanding more deeply what the activism of women looks like and of recognizing myriad sites of revolutionary politics, including motherhood. Silence becomes a theme in the film as viewers witness how and why certain silences develop between Baker and Haughton despite his efforts to document their past.

Fannie's silence is both protective and instructive. It is a way of training her son to tread carefully even as he seeks to uncover certain truths; her reticence makes him aware of the complexity of recovering this history. "I thought returning to Grenada with my mother and Yvonne would bring some closure," Baker shares in voice-over. "It didn't. I didn't realize how open the wounds were." *The House on Coco Road* is fascinating in how it exposes the impossibility of closure in some instances. Sometimes recognition and witnessing are more effective ways of acknowledging generational wounds, rather than insisting on closure. Fannie observes Baker's reconstruction, acknowledging he may arrive at questions her generation did not think to ask and also standing ready to correct him if he gets any part of her story wrong. This is also a form of mothering labor. By understanding this history through the point of view of his mother, however, Baker is able to focus on continuities, not only in the ways the American government oppresses but also in the ways black women work, love, and build in response to oppression and injustice.

## It Goes to the Heart

Throughout the film Baker navigates a tension between, on the one hand, offering a conventional narration of the revolution with Maurice Bishop as the hero, and on the other, telling the story of his mother, Fannie, as a woman whose willingness to say yes to different forms of radical action shaped his own worldview. "Bishop was a hero to me. He was my first black president," Baker claims in his voice-over. Revisiting the revolution as an adult, Baker spent time interviewing the prime minister's mother, Alimenta Bishop (known affectionately as Ma Bishop), and his sister, Ann

Bishop. Ma Bishop shares personal photographs of her son at different stages in life—as a Cub Scout in uniform, relaxing on the beach with his son, at the graveside during his father's funeral. The archive of personal photographs humanizes Bishop, setting aside the icon image and situating him as part of a family. Ma Bishop discusses how she navigated radical politics and the effects of those politics on her loved ones. The interview allows viewers to consider the resolve required for a woman in Ma Bishop's position to survive the loss of her husband and son to political violence in the span of a decade. Her memory of his 1973 beating at the hands of the Mongoose Gang centered on her son downplaying his injuries, not wanting her to worry. For Ma Bishop, the way to address her son's house arrest in October 1983 was not to weigh the question of joint leadership within the party but rather to place a phone call to Bernard Coard's mother to discuss what appeared to be an impasse between their sons: "They said we have to ask this boy [Bernard Coard] for permission to go to see Maurice. So I called his mother. I tell the mother. She tell me, 'Say that again?! Say that again?!' And all this stupidness. So I say well I'm told that your son is the one to give us permission to go to see my son. Well I didn't exactly know how terrible it was." There is defiance

**Figure 9.** Damani Baker interviewing Alimenta Bishop during the production of *The House on Coco Road,* Grenada. (© Ku-ling Yurman, courtesy of the photographer and director Damani Baker)

and anger in Ma Bishop's reference to Coard as "this boy," and I also think it indicates her awareness of herself as an elder to the younger generation represented by both her own son and Coard. Her decision to call Mrs. Coard does not come from any political playbook: This was the action of a mother calling on a family friend to help her resolve a conflict. Mrs. Coard's reported exclamation, "Say that again?!," suggests that the situation was equally for puzzling to her. These are women conferring about why their authority as mothers does not exceed military and governmental authority even when the latter is headed toward a fatal conclusion. Freedom for these women was the right to raise their families in safety; to see their sons through adulthood and to be able to be heard as elders—to pull rank where necessary. There is considerable power to the story of this phone call, even if it was not enough to halt the fatal spiral their children were locked in: Ma Bishop's call to Mrs. Coard shows how even in the most trying circumstances women can speak to each other, that in a nation the size of Grenada, community bonds can be tested and fortified by the willingness to dialogue.

Ann Bishop, Maurice's sister, recalls having upsetting premonitions at the time, making it difficult for her to even face her brother, so frightened was she about his future. Her premonitions are reminiscent of Merle Collins' poem "Dream Mourning" discussed in Chapter 1, where the poet-speaker mentions premonitions that arrive in the form of dreams but are ignored because this class of knowledge is not considered relevant by those with political power. Baker gives space to her testimony, validating it as a reasonable response to a terrifying reality. About her brother's house arrest, she recalls: "I only went once to see him. Mom was braver than me. She went twice. But I was so upset, you know what I mean, Damani? I couldn't face him, especially as I had all these premonitions and so already. And I went that day, and I saw my brother sitting there, and I could—I . . . I just felt I wanted to scream." Ann gives voice to the fear that she had begun to feel as the news of conflict within the NJM began to circulate. Her testimony puts critical pressure on a term such as "women's intuition," which is often used to describe how women express collective fears, concerns, and ideas that they develop through observation and experience, but outside of formal structures of education or what is recognized as reasoning. It is socially acceptable to use the label "women's intuition" to dismiss women's knowledge as *merely feeling*. But there are circumstances, such as the revolution's deterioration, in which the ability to feel, to acknowledge and name those feelings—making them transparent—is precisely the kind of intervention that is necessary to work through conflict. Her inability to muster the courage to see her brother a second time is the refusal to face the coming reality, that the revolution would consume him and change her own life dramatically, producing a lifelong wound. In this refusal was also the acknowledgment that there was little she could do to stop the worst-case scenario from taking place. Recalling the moment she learned of her son's death, Ma Bishop says, "I couldn't cry at all . . . it goes to the heart." In the absence of tears is the space of reckoning for a woman whose sacrifices barely scratch the surface of the archival record. While there are limited opportunities to think about the effects of the revolution on women such as Ann and Ma Bishop, it is important to consider the clues they offer as to the intimate burden of revolution. Alimenta and Ann Bishop represent the less examined side of black radical politics. Through the combined testimony of the Bishop women, Baker's film confronts viewers with the reality that the black radical tradition has different kinds of painful effects on women standing just outside the spotlight.

The work of this book has been to think about how the revolution is remembered, and especially how this work of remembering is done by women. In the context of the Grenada Revolution women's voices stand in the gap of archival omission and the heterosexist drive that upholds the idea of radical political change as the work of great men. Recognizing the difference gender makes in a revolution's legacy is critical to a view that seeks to account for the benefits and drawbacks of revolution so that future generations can work from a more intersectional analysis of the past as they make decisions about their political futures.

# Notes

## Introduction

1. Merle Hodge, "Caribbean Women and Politics," *Torchlight* 22, no. 45 (June 21, 1979), 4.
2. Ibid.
3. Ibid.
4. Anne McClintock, *Imperial Leather: Race, Gender and Sexuality in the Colonial Contest* (New York: Routledge, 1995).
5. Hodge, "Caribbean Women and Politics."
6. Juliet Flower MacCannell's *Regime of the Brother: After the Patriarchy* (New York: Routledge, 1991) examines the role of the brother as an authoritative figure in "post-Oedipal" literary and historical contexts. Rooted in psychoanalysis, her argument tracks the major characteristics of what she calls the "regime of the brother," a transformation of the superego into a new power structure in the absence of the father. MacCannell stresses that the symbolic brother steps in to replace the dead or absent father but does so in a way that allows him to avoid fatherly responsibility. A variation on Hegel's self/other dialectic, according to MacCannell this process sees the sister become the other required to consolidate the brother's identity as self. In this way the sister's subordination is guaranteed as her main role is to "replac[e] the mother as the primary other whom the new 'man' must reject in order to become a man" (5). Throughout this process the regime of the brother has the appearance of equality, self-sufficiency, and liberty as one imagines oneself finally free of the oppressive patriarch.
7. C. L. R. James, *The Black Jacobins: Toussaint L'Ouverture and the San Domingo Revolution,* 1963 (New York: Vintage, 1989), 391–92.
8. In *Foundational Fictions: The National Romances of Latin America* (Berkeley: University of California Press, 1991), Doris Sommer makes a different but related argument, linking the development of national literatures in Latin America to the romance genre, citing "proper," heterosexual relations as central to the ways Latin American writers imagined their new nations. "The books fueled

a desire for domestic happiness that runs over into dreams of national prosperity; and nation-building projects invested private passions with public purpose," she writes (7). While revolution is not critical to her formulation, she points out that idealized and proscribed concepts of masculinity run through the texts she examines and the nation these writers imagine.

9. See Belinda Edmondson, *Making Men: Gender, Literary Authority, and Women's Writing in the Caribbean* (Durham, NC: Duke University Press, 1999); Leah Rosenberg, *Nationalism and the Formation of Caribbean Literature* (New York: Palgrave Macmillan, 2007); and Patricia Saunders, *Alien-nation and Repatriation: Translating Identity in Anglophone Caribbean Literature* (Lanham, MD: Lexington Books, 2007).

10. Edmondson, *Making Men*, 39. Salkey fits somewhat uncomfortably here as his writing of gender performance in "After the Counter-Revolution, After the Invasion" (*In the Border Country*, 1998) places both men and women in leadership roles. I discuss this point in detail in chapter 2.

11. Edmondson, *Making Men*, 108.

12. Carole Boyce Davies and Elaine Savory Fido, eds., *Out of the Kumbla: Caribbean Women and Literature* (Lawrenceville, NJ: African World Press, 1990), xiii.

13. Ibid., 12–13.

14. Ibid., 13.

15. Ibid., 1.

16. Gayatri Spivak, "Three Women's Texts and a Critique of Imperialism," *Critical Inquiry* 12 (Autumn 1985): 243–61; Gayatri Spivak, *A Critique of Postcolonial Reason: Toward a History of the Vanishing Present* (Cambridge, MA: Harvard University Press, 1999); Chandra Talpade Mohanty, "Under Western Eyes: Feminist Scholarship and Colonial Discourse," *Boundary 2: A Journal of Postmodern Literature and Culture* 12 (Spring and Fall 1984): 333–58.

17. Kamau Brathwaite, *Roots* (Ann Arbor: University of Michigan Press, 1993).

18. Wayne Sandiford, "Economic Growth and Development during the Grenada Revolution," paper presented at a conference, "The Grenada Revolution 40 Years After: Commemoration, Celebration and Critique," True Blue, Grenada, May 27, 2019.

19. Nicole Laurine Phillip, *Women in Grenadian History, 1783–1983* (Mona, Jamaica: University of the West Indies Press, 2010), 103–4.

20. Ibid., 118–28.

21. Other creative writers have published shorter pieces on Grenada, but nothing to rival the volume of material produced by Brand and Collins. Other novels about the revolution include David Franklyn, *Mission Betrayed* (St. Peter, Barbados: Caribbean Chapters, 2012), and Maria Roberts-Squires, *October, All Over* (London: Heinemann, 2005).

22. The term "intersectionality" was coined by legal scholar Kimberlé Crenshaw in "Demarginalizing the Intersection of Race and Sex: A Black Feminist

Critique of Antidiscrimination Doctrine, Feminist Theory and Antiracist Politics," *University of Chicago Legal Forum* 140 (1989): 139–67. The term has since been taken up across disciplines and fields, while remaining a cornerstone of black feminist thought.

23. Patricia Hill Collins, "Mammies, Matriarchs, and Other Controlling Images," in *Black Feminist Thought: Knowledge, Consciousness, and the Politics of Empowerment* (New York: Routledge, 2009), 76–106. See also Hazel Carby, *Reconstructing Womanhood: The Emergence of the Afro-American Woman Novelist* (Oxford: Oxford University Press, 1987); Katherine McKittrick, *Demonic Grounds: Black Women and the Cartographies of Struggle* (Minneapolis: University of Minnesota Press, 2006); and Samantha Pinto, *Difficult Diasporas: The Transnational Feminist Aesthetic of the Black Atlantic* (New York: New York University Press, 2013).

24. Audre Lorde, "I Am Your Sister," *Women & Therapy* 6 (1988): 25–30.

25. Maurice Bishop, *Maurice Bishop Speaks: The Grenada Revolution and Its Overthrow 1979–83*, ed. Bruce Marcus and Michael Taber (New York: Pathfinder Press, 1983), 25.

26. George Brizan, *Grenada: Island of Conflict* (London: Macmillan Education, 1998), 378–79.

27. Even though mass participation in violent uprising was never a rallying call of the NJM, the literature produced by the party did include such slogans as "The Liberation of the Workers and Peasants Can Only Come through Violent REVOLUTION!!" (*Spark* 1, no. 2 [undated NJM newsletter c. late 1974]).

28. Rick Atkinson, "Estimates of Casualties in Grenada Are Raised," *Washington Post*, November 9, 1983.

29. The bodies of those executed on the fort have never been recovered. A group of Grenadian students, the Young Leaders of Presentation Brothers College, have used evidence gleaned from trial records, newspapers, and interviews to piece together a history of the manner of death for Bishop and the others on Fort Rupert, as well as what happened to their bodies after their deaths. They named their text *Under the Cover of Darkness* (Grenada: Ministry of Education, 2002). They concluded that the bodies were transported to Calivigny (near Grenada's eastern coast), where they were burned in a shallow grave on the night of October 19, 1983. The next day they were covered with soil (Young Leaders, *Under the Cover of Darkness*, 30). The remains were exhumed by U.S. soldiers and transported to St. George's University for analysis on November 9, 1983. After analysis the remains were transferred to a local funeral home for burial at a site that has never been located. The final report from the Armed Forces Institute of Pathology (AFIP) disputes the idea that the remains exhumed belonged to Bishop and his comrades; however, the Young Leaders' investigation proves that there are major discrepancies between the AFIP report and accounts of the pathology process by doctors who assisted in the examination of the remains (42–52).

30. Shalini Puri, *The Grenada Revolution in the Caribbean Present: Operation Urgent Memory* (New York: Palgrave Macmillan, 2014), 79–81.

31. Frantz Fanon, *The Wretched of the Earth*, trans. Richard Philcox (New York: Grove Press, 2004), 116.

32. For a discussion of structural violence in the Caribbean, and Jamaica in particular, see Deborah A. Thomas, *Exceptional Violence: Embodied Citizenship in Transnational Jamaica* (Durham, NC: Duke University Press, 2011).

33. Veena Das, *Life and Words: Violence and the Descent into the Ordinary* (Berkeley: University of California Press, 2006), 9.

34. Ibid., 8–9.

35. Both David Scott in *Omens of Adversity: Tragedy, Time, Memory, Justice* (Durham, NC: Duke University Press, 2014) and Shalini Puri in *The Grenada Revolution* have noted that a definitive history of the revolution has yet to be written. The closest account we have is Brian Meeks, "Grenada: Pitfalls of 'Popular' Revolution from Above," chap. 4 in his *Caribbean Revolutions and Revolutionary Theory: An Assessment of Cuba, Nicaragua and Grenada* (Mona, Jamaica: University of the West Indies Press, 2001). Nicole Laurine Phillip's "Women in the Grenada Revolution, 1979–1983," chap. 6 in her *Women in Grenadian History*, is invaluable for any study of gender and the revolution.

36. On the distinct character of shame in a postcolonial context, see Timothy Bewes, *The Event of Postcolonial Shame* (Princeton, NJ: Princeton University Press, 2010).

37. Marianne Hirsch, *The Generation of Postmemory: Writing and Visual Culture after the Holocaust* (New York: Columbia University Press, 2012).

38. Frantz Fanon, *Black Skin, White Masks*, trans. Richard Philcox (New York: Grove Press, 2008); Michael Rothberg, "Decolonizing Trauma Studies: A Response," *Studies in the Novel* 40, no. 1/2 (2008): 224–38; Irene Visser, "Trauma and Power in Postcolonial Literary Studies," in *Contemporary Approaches in Literary Trauma Theory*, ed. Michelle Balaev (New York: Palgrave MacMillan, 2014), 106–30.

39. Rothberg, "Decolonizing Trauma Studies: A Response," 224–34.

40. Visser, "Decolonizing Trauma Theory," 259–62.

41. Meeks, *Caribbean Revolutions and Revolutionary Theory*, 157.

42. Ibid., 179.

43. Scott, *Omens of Adversity*, 7, 88, 11.

44. Phillip, *Women in Grenadian History*, 133–36.

45. Puri, *The Grenada Revolution in the Caribbean Present*, 161.

46. Hirsch, *The Generation of Postmemory*, 5.

47. Joy and creativity are but two of the multiple, and at times opposing, aspects Puri identifies in the revolution. Puri, *The Grenada Revolution in the Caribbean Present*, 23.

48. Some of the key Caribbean literary texts depicting this relationship between revolution and trauma include Alejo Carpentier, *The Kingdom of This*

*World*, trans. Harriet de Onís (New York: Farrar, Straus and Giroux, 2006); Cristina García, *Dreaming in Cuban* (New York: Ballantine Books, 1992); Édouard Glissant, *Monsieur Toussaint: A Play* (1961), trans. Michael Dash (Washington, DC: Three Continents Press, 2005); and Derek Walcott, *The Haitian Trilogy* (New York: Farrar, Straus and Giroux, 2002).

49. See Devyn Spence Benson, *Antiracism in Cuba: The Unfinished Revolution* (Chapel Hill: University of North Carolina Press, 2016); and Alejandro de la Fuente, *A Nation for All: Race, Inequality, and Politics in Twentieth-Century Cuba* (Chapel Hill: University of North Carolina Press, 2001).

50. Sarah Z. Hoffman, "HIV/AIDS in Cuba: A Model for Care or an Ethical Dilemma?," *African Health Sciences* 4 (December 2004): 208–9; Rebecca Sananas, "Love, Loss and Beauty Pageants: Inside a Cuban HIV Sanitarium," National Public Radio, March 26, 2016.

51. Scott, *Omens of Adversity*, 21.

52. See Cedric Robinson, *Black Marxism: The Making of the Black Radical Tradition* (Chapel Hill: University of North Carolina Press, 1983). Robinson's work traces the black radical tradition through Africans' resistance to enslavement by European colonizers to the activism and scholarship of turn-of-the-century black intellectuals W. E. B. Du Bois, C. L. R. James, and Richard Wright. See also Robin D. G. Kelley, *Freedom Dreams: The Black Radical Imagination* (Boston: Beacon Press, 2002), who has more recently written about an expanded tradition reborn in black feminism and black surrealist art; Sandra Gunning, Tera Hunter, and Michele Mitchell, eds., *Dialogues of Dispersal: Gender, Sexuality, and African Diasporas* (Oxford: Wiley-Blackwell 2004); Katherine McKittrick, *Demonic Grounds: Black Women and the Cartographies of Struggle* (Minneapolis: University of Minnesota Press, 2006); Fred Moten, *In the Break: The Aesthetics of the Black Radical Tradition* (Minneapolis: University of Minnesota Press, 2003); and Christina Sharpe, *In the Wake: On Blackness and Being* (Durham, NC: Duke University Press, 2016).

53. "Meeting of Coordinating Council of Delegates: Agenda," *New Jewel*, May 19, 1974, 1.

54. An article in Grenada's *Torchlight* newspaper indicates that the public was aware of efforts by governments across the Caribbean to prevent certain black radicals from attending the congress. A journalist noted, "The Caribbean delegation is totally comprised of members of unconventional, revolutionary opposition factions, and there is a fear among delegates of a regional conspiracy by the various governments to prevent them from attending the Congress and airing the oppressive nature and general unsuitability of the Governments in power and in some cases, the very form of Government" ("NJM Bishop to Attend Pan-African Congress," *Torchlight*. May 26, 1974). See also Olayiwola Abegunrin, "Pan-African Congresses, 1893–1974," in *Pan-Africanism in Modern Times: Challenges, Concerns, Constraints*, ed. Olayiwola Abegunrin and Sabella Ogbobode Abidde (Lanham, MD: Lexington Books, 2016), 41.

55. "Still United in Our Cultural Heritage," *Free West Indian,* June 2, 1979, 6–7.

56. Bishop, "Heirs of Marryshow," *In Nobody's Backyard: Maurice Bishop's Speeches 1979–1983: A Memorial Volume,* ed. Chris Searle (London: Zed Books, 1984), 168. See also the satirical column "Cotay Si, Cotay La: What Is ah Likkle 'Coop' for Us?," *Torchlight* 22, no. 44 (June 17, 1979). The column's fictional writer, market woman Dame Sarah Chile, chides the U.S. ambassador to the Eastern Caribbean, Sally Ann Shelton, for claiming that the Grenada Revolution was orchestrated by the Cuban military. Chile reminds Shelton that Grenada's revolutionary history can be traced back to Henri Christophe and that Grenadians were capable of running their own revolution.

57. One of the most significant efforts to use culture to promote the revolution was the formation of a National Performing Company. The company of about forty Grenadian artists, ranging in age from seventeen to sixty-five years, was composed of smaller groups from around the country, including Tamarind Folk Company, Veni Vwai Dance Group, and the choir "A Group of Us." In November 1982, members of this company toured North America, making stops in Oakland, California, Washington, D.C., New York, Toronto, and Montreal. They were tasked with showcasing expressive culture from Grenada and creating some good will for the revolution.

58. Audre Lorde, *Sister Outsider: Essays and Speeches* (Berkeley, CA: Crossing Press, 1984, 2007), 184. For a reading of this essay and Lorde's complicated relation to Grenada and the United States, see the conclusion to Michelle A. Stephens, *Black Empire: The Masculine Global Imaginary of Caribbean Intellectuals in the United States,* 1914–1962 (Durham, NC: Duke University Press, 2005), 269–82.

59. Lorde, *Sister Outsider,* 189.

60. "Revolution, n.," in *OED Online* (Oxford University Press, June 2017).

61. Yarimar Bonilla, *Non-Sovereign Futures: French Caribbean Politics in the Wake of Disenchantment* (Chicago: University of Chicago Press, 2015). See also essays in Linden Lewis, ed., *Caribbean Sovereignty, Development and Democracy in an Age of Globalization* (New York: Routledge, 2015).

62. Phillip, *Women in Grenadian History,* 126.

63. Ibid., 133–34.

64. Ibid., 112–13.

65. *Torchlight* 22, no. 44 (June 17, 1979).

66. Ibid.

67. Another reading of this passage could be that the editor imagines that rural women only become feminists after interacting with more educated women. The government-run *Free West Indian* newspaper carried more detailed reporting on the National Women's Conference. The June 16, 1979, issue included a list of speakers: Ingrid Kirkwood from Jamaica, Susan Craig and Merle Hodge

from Trinidad, Diana Prescod from the Women's Democratic Organization of St. Vincent, and, from Grenada, Dessima Williams (Grenada's ambassador to the OAS), Beverly Steele (extramural tutor at UWI), and Jacqueline Creft (adviser on youth affairs, Ministry of Youth).

68. Wendy C. Grenade, "An Interview with Bernard Coard," in *The Grenada Revolution: Reflections and Lessons,* ed. Wendy C. Grenade (Jackson: University Press of Mississippi, 2015), 77.

69. These conflicting accounts are on display in eyewitness accounts of the confrontation featured in the documentary *Forward Ever: The Killing of a Revolution,* directed by Bruce Paddington and Luke Paddington (New York: Third World Newsreel, 2013).

70. Paul Scoon, *Survival for Service: My Experiences as Governor General of Grenada* (Oxford: Macmillan Education, 2003), 145. See also Patsy Lewis, "A Response to Edward Seaga's *The Grenada Intervention: The Inside Story,*" *Social and Economic Studies* 62, no. 3/4 (2013): 83–111.

71. Richard Bernstein, "U.S. Vetoes U.N. Resolution 'Deploring' Grenada Invasion," *New York Times,* October 29, 1983, 1, 4.

## 1. Generational Ties, Revolutionary Binds

1. Merle Collins, *Angel* (Leeds: Peepal Tree Press, 2011), 264. All references to *Angel* cite the 2011 revised version unless otherwise noted.

2. This and the next few quotations are from Collins, *Angel,* 264–65.

3. Puri notes that the genres of tragedy, romance, and epic have generally been avoided by authors recounting the Grenada Revolution because they overdetermine narrative outcomes and require a "grandeur of scale that is unnecessary to recognize the importance of Grenada." Shalini Puri, *The Grenada Revolution in the Caribbean Present: Operation Urgent Memory* (New York: Palgrave Macmillan, 2014), 274.

4. Jacqueline Bishop and Dolace Nicole McLean, "Working Out Grenada: An Interview with Merle Collins," *Calabash* 3 (2005): 59; Collins, *Angel,* 5. Born in Aruba in 1950 to Grenadian parents, Collins spent her childhood in Grenada before traveling to Jamaica in 1969 to attend the University of the West Indies (UWI), Mona. In 1980 she earned a master's degree in Latin American studies at Georgetown University in Washington, D.C., before returning to Grenada to work for the PRG in the Ministry of Foreign Affairs. She has written several texts reflecting on her experiences during the revolution, including a poetry collection, *Because the Dawn Breaks! Poems Dedicated to the Grenadian People* (London: Karia Press, 1985). After the U.S. invasion, Collins left Grenada to pursue a Ph.D. at the London School of Economics.

5. David Scott, *Omens of Adversity: Tragedy, Time, Memory, Justice* (Durham, NC: Duke University Press, 2014), 74–75.

6. Collins, *Angel,* 9–14.

7. Pedro Noguera, *The Imperatives of Power: Political Change and the Social Basis of Regime Support in Grenada 1951–1991* (New York: Peter Lang, 1997), 54.

8. Collins, *Angel*, 300–1.

9. Frantz Fanon, *The Wretched of the Earth*, trans. Richard Philcox (New York: Grove Press, 2004), 1.

10. Scott, *Omens of Adversity*, 86.

11. Collins, *Angel*, 20–30.

12. A commission set up by Dame Hilda Bynoe, governor of the Associated State of Grenada, investigated both the Bloody Sunday and Bloody Monday incidents. The investigation began in November 1973 after Bloody Sunday but was interrupted by Bloody Monday, and finally concluded in May 1974. See Duffus Commission, *Report of the Duffus Commission of Inquiry into the Breakdown of Law and Order and Police Brutality in Grenada* (St. George's, Grenada: Duffus Commission, 1975); "Remember Bloody Sunday," *Free West Indian* November 17, 1979, B1; "Bloody Sunday, November 18, 1973," in *The Grenada Revolution Online,* ed. Ann Elizabeth Wilder (2001), http://www.thegrenadarevolutiononline.com/bloodysunday.html.

13. Collins, *Angel*, 32–34.

14. Here Collins is not drawing a comparison between Gairy and the NJM in terms of their goals in political leadership. She never suggests that the NJM is corrupt, but rather that it becomes overly involved in the structures of power within the party, losing track of the people's needs and desires.

15. In the 1960s, postindependence Jamaica and Trinidad saw the power shift to local elites, a population that was predominantly high brown or mixed raced. The predominantly black (and in Trinidad black and brown) lower classes struggled to move up the socioeconomic ladder, and this led to periods of unrest by the late 1960s and early 1970s. See D. A. Dunkley, "Hegemony in Post-Independence Jamaica," *Caribbean Quarterly* 57 (June 2011): 1–23; Terry Lacey, *Violence and Politics in Jamaica, 1960–70: Internal Security in a Developing Country* (London: Frank Cass Press, 1977); and Carl Stone, *Stratification and Political Change in Trinidad and Jamaica* (Beverly Hills, CA: Sage Publications, 1972).

16. Collins, *Angel*, 202–17.

17. Manley, the prime minister of Jamaica from March 1972 to November 1980, came from an upper-class mixed-race Jamaican family, supported democratic socialism, and maintained close ties with Fidel Castro.

18. Jamaica Kincaid describes this phenomenon in *A Small Place* (New York: Farrar, Straus and Giroux, 1988). Dionne Brand hints at it as well in her own work. In her 1994 *Bread out of Stone,* Brand goes so far as to suggest that anyone who seemed vaguely intimidating could be labeled a communist.

19. Collins, *Angel*, 216.

20. Ibid., 201.

21. Ibid., 207.
22. Ibid., 295
23. Ibid., 305–6.
24. Ibid., 311.
25. Ibid., 311–12.
26. Ibid., 312.
27. The imagery here is very similar to that of "Dream Mourning," a poem from Collins's 2003 *Lady in a Boat;* however, the poem is more explicit in its exploration of the chasm between generations at the end of the revolution. I discuss this poem in detail later in the chapter.
28. Collins, *Angel,* 308.
29. Ibid., 8.
30. Ibid., 349.
31. Ibid., 349.
32. Merle Collins, *The Colour of Forgetting* (London: Virago Press, 1995), 17.
33. Paula M. L. Moya, "The Search for Decolonial Love: An Interview with Junot Díaz," *Boston Review,* June 26, 2012.
34. Collins, *Colour,* 18.
35. Just as blood mixes in *Colour,* so too does language, and Pax, the original name of the island, becomes Paz, with Paz City as its capital. Carib thinks the Latin name of the island, rather than connoting peace, is an ironic example of onomatopoeia—pax sounds like a "slap" she claims (Collins, *Colour,* 17). Both the passage of time and the sound of the word on the tongue of changing colonial populations change the name and identity of the island. The "peace" of Pax is always corrupted, never permitted to stand unperturbed.
36. Collins, *Colour,* 58.
37. Ibid., 58.
38. This and the following quotations are from Collins, *Colour,* 155–67, passim.
39. Edward Baugh, *Black Sand: New and Selected Poems* (Leeds: Peepal Tree Press, 2013), 109.
40. Collins, *Colour,* 3.
41. Ibid., 150.
42. The boat scene is described on pp. 205–13.
43. Collins, *Colour,* 4.
44. Derek Walcott, *Selected Poems,* ed. by Edward Baugh (New York: Farrar, Straus and Giroux, 2007), 137.
45. Merle Collins, "Dream Mourning," in *Lady in a Boat* (Leeds: Peepal Tree Press, 2003), 29–32.
46. Collins, "Morning Glory," in *Lady in a Boat,* 31–32.
47. Merle Collins, "Tout Moun ka Pléwé (Everybody Bawling)," *Small Axe: A Caribbean Journal of Criticism* 11, no. 1 (2007): 8.

48. Maurice Bishop, *In Nobody's Backyard: Maurice Bishop's Speeches 1979–1983: A Memorial Volume,* ed. Chris Searle. London: Zed Books, 1984.

49. Brathwaite, *Roots,* 265. More recently Shalini Puri has written about the "hurricane poetics" of some of the literature and art of the Grenada Revolution, including the writing of Merle Collins and the painting of Susan Mains. Puri uses the term hurricane poetics to discuss the cyclical patterns in Collins' poetry and to highlight the recurrence of natural and political disaster followed by rejuvenation and reconciliation. This history can be traced in what Puri calls the "hurricane historiography" found in literature by Brathwaite, Collins, and others. See Puri, *The Grenada Revolution in the Caribbean Present,* 206–23.

50. Collins, "October, All Over," in *Lady in a Boat,* 33–34.

51. On catastrophe in African American and Caribbean modern literature, see Sonya Posmentier, *Cultivation and Catastrophe: The Lyric Ecology of Modern Black Literature* (Baltimore, MD: Johns Hopkin University Press, 2017).

52. The idea of the cycle, the spiral, or repetition as a defining aspect of a Caribbean imaginary informs the work of several theorists. See, for example, Antonio Benítez-Rojo, *The Repeating Island: The Caribbean and the Postmodern Perspective,* trans. James E. Maraniss (Durham, NC: Duke University Press, 1996); Édouard Glissant, *Poetics of Relation,* trans. Betsy Wing (Ann Arbor: University of Michigan Press, 1997); Kamau Brathwaite, *M/R* (New York: Savacou North, 2002).

53. David Scott, "The Fragility of Memory: An Interview with Merle Collins," *Small Axe* 14 (March 2010): 127–28.

54. Ibid., 127–28.

55. Collins, "Shame Bush," in *Lady in a Boat,* 50–52.

56. Timothy Bewes, *The Event of Postcolonial Shame* (Princeton, NJ: Princeton University Press, 2010).

57. Collins, "I d Open the Gate," in *Lady in a Boat,* 56.

## 2. After the Invasion

1. While Marryshow was a key critic of the colonial system that kept Grenada and several neighboring isles tethered to Britain, he worked within the system to effect change. He sought and earned the respect of both British and West Indian officials and served on the Executive Council of Grenada from 1944 until his death in 1958.

2. Maurice Bishop, "PM Bishop Tells of the Great Marryshow Tradition," *Free West Indian,* November 13, 1982, 1.

3. Ibid., 1. While Fedon led the rebellion, he was a free person of color, not a slave. See Edward L. Cox, "Fedon's Rebellion 1795–96: Causes and Consequences," *Journal of Negro History* 67, no. 1 (Spring 1982): 7–19; and Curtis Jacobs, "The Jacobins of Mt. Qua Qua: Fedon's Rebellion in Grenada, 1762–1796" (Ph.D. diss., University of the West Indies, 2000).

4. Bishop, "PM Bishop Tells of the Great Marryshow Tradition," 1.

5. Theophilus Albert Marryshow, *Cycles of Civilization* (St. George's, Grenada: Printed at the office of *The West Indian*, 1917), microform. The copyright of a pamphlet version of *Cycles* indicates that the pamphlet was composed from a series of articles first published in the *West Indian* in September 1917.

6. George Lamming, "The Education of Feeling," in *The George Lamming Reader: The Aesthetics of Decolonisation,* ed. Anthony Bogues (Kingston, Jamaica: Ian Randle Publishers, 2011), 13–22.

7. Ibid., 20.

8. On "flag independence" and the concept of nonsovereignty in Caribbean society, see Yarimar Bonilla, *Non-Sovereign Futures: French Caribbean Politics in the Wake of Disenchantment* (Chicago: University of Chicago Press, 2015)

9. See also George Lamming, *The Sovereignty of the Imagination— Conversations III: Language and Politics of Ethnicity.* (Philipsburg, St. Martin: House of Nehesi, 2009); and David Scott, "The Sovereignty of the Imagination: An Interview with George Lamming," *Small Axe: A Caribbean Journal of Criticism* 6, no. 2 (September 2000): 72–200. More recently Deborah A. Thomas has written about affect and sovereignty in "Silence, Taboo, and Everyday Practices of Revolution: What Sovereignty Feels Like," paper presented at the New York University African-Diaspora Forum, October 22, 2014.

10. George Lamming, "Maurice Bishop Lives: Address by George Lamming at the Memorial Service for Maurice Bishop and Colleagues at Trinity Cathedral, in Trinidad, December 1983," in *In Nobody's Backyard: Maurice Bishop's Speeches, 1979–1983: A Memorial Volume,* ed. Chris Searle (London: Zed Books, 1984), 1–6.

11. C. L. R. James, *The Black Jacobins: Toussaint L'Ouverture and the San Domingo Revolution* (New York: Random House, 1963), 391–92.

12. V. S. Naipaul, "An Island Betrayed," *Harper's,* March 1, 1984, 61–72.

13. Ibid., 72.

14. For an equally dismissive representation of the 1970s Black Power revolution on an unnamed Caribbean island, see V. S. Naipaul, *Guerrillas* (New York: Vintage, 1990).

15. Derek Walcott, "Good Old Heart of Darkness," Derek Walcott Papers, MS Collection 136, box 1, folders 30–31, Thomas Fisher Rare Book Library, University of Toronto, Toronto, Canada.

16. Belinda Edmondson, *Making Men: Gender, Literary Authority, and Women's Writing in the Caribbean* (Durham, NC: Duke University Press, 1998), 39.

17. David Scott, *Omens of Adversity: Tragedy, Time, Memory, Justice* (Durham, NC: Duke University Press, 2014), 21.

18. The Guyanese writer and political activist Andaiye has discussed Walter Rodney's critique of the PRG's decision to close the *Torchlight* newspaper: Andaiye, "The Grenada Revolution, the Caribbean Left, and the Regional Women's Movement," paper presented at the Caribbean Studies 35th Annual Conference, Barbados, 2010.

19. Walcott, "Good Old Heart of Darkness," 12.
20. Ibid., 2.
21. Ibid., 22.
22. Author interview with Leslie Pierre, St. George's, Grenada, August 2, 2011. Surveillance reports on the Grenadian journalist Allister Hughes are among the Grenadian government documents seized by the U.S. military during the invasion. See Microfiche DSI-83-C-004403, Seized Grenada Document Collection 7/11/1919–12/31/1984, Group 242, National Archives, College Park, MD.
23. Walcott, "Good Old Heart of Darkness," 6.
24. Derek Walcott, *Henri Christophe* (1949), in *The Haitian Trilogy: Plays: Henri Christophe, Drums and Colours, and the Haytian Earth* (New York: Farrar, Straus and Giroux, 2002).
25. Derek Walcott, "The Muse of History" and "What the Twilight Says," both in *What the Twilight Says: Essays* (New York: Farrar, Straus and Giroux, 2014).
26. Ken Gordon, *Getting It Write: Winning Caribbean Press Freedom* (Kingston, Jamaica: Ian Randle Publishers, 1999), 80.
27. Author telephone conversation with Ray Roberts, Director of Grenada Information Service and former journalist for the *Torchlight* and the *Free West Indian*, January 25, 2012. See also Pedro Noguera, *The Imperatives of Power: Political Change and the Social Basis of Regime Support in Grenada from 1951–1991* (New York: Peter Lang, 1997).
28. For a discussion of representations of Cuba in Grenadian newspapers during the revolution, see Laurie R. Lambert, "The Revolution and Its Discontents: Grenadian Newspapers and Attempts to Shape Public Opinion during Political Transition," in "The Invasion of Grenada 30 Years On: A Retrospective," special issue, *Round Table: The Commonwealth Journal of International Affairs* 102 (2013): 143–53.
29. "Rastas to Protest," *Torchlight*, October 10, 1979, 1.
30. Walcott, "Good Old Heart of Darkness," 25.
31. Ibid., 8.
32. President Reagan called Prime Minister Thatcher the day after the invasion to apologize for proceeding with military action without her input. "Grenada: Reagan phone call to MT (throwing his hat in the door)" [audio] [declassified 2014], October 26, 1983, Margaret Thatcher Foundation Archives.
33. Walcott, "Good Old Heart of Darkness," 1.
34. Ibid., 1
35. Andrew Salkey, "Maurice," *Black Scholar* 15, no. 1 (May/June 1984): 15.
36. Andrew Salkey, *In the Border Country and Other Stories* (London: Bogle-L'Ouverture Press, 1998), 137. For another vision of postrevolution memory and aftermath, see Earl Lovelace, *Is Just a Movie* (London: Faber and Faber, 2011).
37. Salkey, *In the Border Country and Other Stories*, 139.
38. Ibid., 197–98.

39. Ibid., 202.
40. Ibid., 137.
41. Lamming, "Maurice Bishop Lives." This and the following quotations appear on pp. 1–6, passim.

## 3. "Comrade, Sister, Lover"

1. Dionne Brand, *Chronicles of the Hostile Sun* (Toronto: Williams-Wallace Publishers, 1984), 65.
2. Jini Kim Watson and Gary Wilder, *The Postcolonial Contemporary: Political Imaginaries for the Global Present* (New York: Fordham University Press, 2018).
3. Nana Wilson-Tagoe, *Historical Thought and Literary Representation in West Indian Literature* (Gainesville: University Press of Florida, 1998), 2.
4. For examples of the extractive practices of the Canadian private and public sectors in the Caribbean, see Irving Andre, "The Genesis and Persistence of the Commonwealth Caribbean Seasonal Agricultural Workers Program in Canada," *Osgoode Hall Law Journal* 2 (1990): 243–301; Agnes Calliste, "Women of 'Exceptional Merit': Immigration of Caribbean Nurses to Canada," *Canadian Journal of Women and Law* 6, no. 1 (1993): 85–102; Peter James Hudson, "Imperial Designs: The Royal Bank of Canada in the Caribbean," *Race & Class* 52, no. 1 (2010): 33–48; and Mimi Sheller, *Aluminum Dreams: The Making of Light Modernity* (Cambridge, MA: MIT Press, 2014).
5. I borrow the term "North Atlantic universals" from Michel Rolph Trouillot, *Global Transformations: Anthropology and the Modern World* (New York: Palgrave Macmillan, 2003), 29–46.
6. The U.S. military seized those Grenadian government documents that survived the bombings.
7. Dionne Brand, *Bread out of Stone: Recollections, Sex, Recognitions, Race, Dreaming, Politics* (Toronto: Coach House Press, 1994), 59.
8. Ibid., 12–13.
9. *Oxford English Dictionary Online*, www.oed.com.
10. Sarita Echavez See, *The Decolonized Eye: Filipino American Art and Performance* (Minneapolis: University of Minnesota Press, 2009), xvi.
11. Robert J. C. Young, *White Mythologies: Writing History and the West* (New York: Routledge, 1991).
12. Brand, *Chronicles*, 7.
13. Ibid., 7.
14. Brian Meeks, *Caribbean Revolutions and Revolutionary Theory: An Assessment of Cuba, Nicaragua and Grenada* (Mona, Jamaica: University of the West Indies Press, 2001), 168.
15. Brand, *Chronicles*, 7.
16. Ibid., 7.
17. Ibid., 20.

18. Rupert Murdoch is an Australian American media titan and the CEO of News Corporation. His holdings include the *Wall Street Journal,* Twentieth Century Fox, HarperCollins, the *Times,* the *Sunday Times,* and the *New York Post.* The late Kenneth Thomson was a Canadian businessman whose company, Thomson Corporation, sold the *Times* to Murdoch in 1981. Thomson also owned several smaller newspapers in Canada, as well as the *Globe and Mail,* Canada's largest national newspaper.

19. Brand, *Chronicles,* 20.

20. Ibid., 20.

21. Salvador Allende was elected president of Chile in 1970. An avowed socialist, he enacted several social reforms in Chile that were met with resistance from the Chilean elite. Allende's government was overthrown by the U.S.-supported General Augusto Pinochet in 1973. *El Mercurio,* a right-wing Chilean newspaper, received funds from International Telephone and Telegraph (ITT), an American corporation working directly with the CIA to destabilize Allende's government. ITT's cooperation with the CIA to oust Allende is detailed in "The Church Report: Covert Action in Chile 1963–1973," published by the U.S. Department of State in December 1975. Michael Manley, a democratic socialist, was first elected prime minister of Jamaica in 1972, leading the People's National Party (PNP). His plans for social reform met much resistance from the United States. See Anthony Bogues, "Michael Manley, Equality, and the Jamaican Labour Movement," *Caribbean Quarterly* 48, no. 1 (2002): 77–93; Darrell E. Levi, *Michael Manley: The Making of a Leader* (Athens: University of Georgia Press, 1990); and Beverley Manley, *The Manley Memoirs* (Kingston, Jamaica: Ian Randle Publishers, 2008). See also the documentary *Life and Debt,* directed by Stephanie Black (New York: New Yorker Films, 2001), for an interview with Manley. The *Gleaner* is a Jamaican newspaper noted for representing Manley as a communist and deriding him for his relationship with Fidel Castro. See Brian Meeks, *Narratives of Resistance: Jamaica, Trinidad, and the Caribbean* (Mona, Jamaica: University of the West Indies Press, 2000), 125. Manley eventually took legal action against the *Gleaner* for claiming he "sold Jamaica to Cuba." See "Manley to Sue Gleaner," *Torchlight,* September 26, 1979, 5.

22. The *Torchlight* was unfairly censored by the PRG. While the *Torchlight* was run by members of Grenada's business class, I have not found any evidence to suggest that the newspaper was funded in any part by the U.S. government or any American agencies. See Laurie Lambert, "Worlds Real and Invented: The Grenada Revolution and the Caribbean Literary Imaginary" (Ph.D. diss., New York University, 2013), 71–119, and idem, "The Revolution and Its Discontents: Grenadian Newspapers and Attempts to Shape Public Opinion during Political Transition," in "The Invasion of Grenada 30 Years On: A Retrospective," special issue, *Round Table: The Commonwealth Journal of International Affairs* 102, no. 2 (2013): 143–53.

23. The danger of having an economy that is overly dependent on tourism is a topic covered by many Caribbean writers. See Jamaica Kincaid, *A Small Place* (New York: Farrar, Straus and Giroux, 1988); Stephen Moss, "The Oxford Poetry Job Would Have Been Too Much Work," interview with Derek Walcott, *Guardian*, May 3, 2012; and Angelique Nixon, *Resisting Paradise: Tourism, Diaspora, and Sexuality in Caribbean Culture* (Jackson: University Press of Mississippi, 2015).

24. Brand, *Chronicles*, 20.

25. David Scott, *Omens of Adversity: Tragedy, Time, Memory, Justice* (Durham, NC: Duke University Press, 2014), 12.

26. Ibid., 21.

27. Shalini Puri, *The Grenada Revolution in the Caribbean Present: Operation Urgent Memory* (New York: Palgrave Macmillan, 2014), 165.

28. Brand, *Chronicles*, 37–39.

29. Reports of a rift between Bishop and Coard appeared on October 15, 1983, on the front page of the *Trinidad Guardian*. Although Coard resigned from his position as deputy prime minister to quell rumors that he was behind a plot to assassinate Bishop, it was obvious to the public that a power play was in effect within the party once Bishop was placed under house arrest on October 14, 1983. On October 19, the *Guardian* printed another article reporting that Unison Whiteman (minister of foreign affairs), Lynden Ramdhanny (minister of tourism), Norris Bain (minister of housing), George Louison (minister of education), and Jacqueline Creft (minster of education) had all resigned from office on October 18, 1983. The article also quoted Whiteman claiming that Coard was now running the country. On October 21 the *Guardian* reported that Austin was heading the RMC, and that he had announced over Grenada's national radio station that "security forces" had killed Bishop, Whiteman, Creft, Bain, and union leaders Vincent Noel and Fitzroy Bain. During this time Coard and his wife, Phyllis, remained in hiding.

30. Cuban construction workers who were staying at the airport construction site in Point Salines also put up armed resistance, but this fact has been over-reported in publicized U.S. accounts of the invasion. A CIA "Grenada Situation Report" from October 22, 1983, concedes that "the Cubans may have been suspicious of Coard and do not have a clear picture of the new regime's intentions" (Central Intelligence Agency, "Grenada Situation Report as of 1700 22 October 1983," Freedom of Information Act Electronic Reading Room, document no. 0000401538, October 22 1983). In sizing up the resistance American military personnel could expect to meet in Grenada, the document reports that the RMC was "mobilizing the remainder of the Army and the 2,000- to 4,000-member militia." In the parts of this document that have not been redacted, no mention is made of Cuban (or any other) military forces. Another CIA document cites Cuban media reports that there were approximately 784 Cubans in Grenada at the time of the U.S. invasion, including 636 construction workers and 43 military

advisers. Central Intelligence Agency, "Official Cuban Breakdown of Cuban Personnel in Grenada (According to Cuban Media on 28 October 1983)," Freedom of Information Act Electronic Reading Room, document no. 0000679137, October 30, 1983.

31. B. Drummond Ayres Jr., "U.S. Marines Diverted to Grenada in Event Americans Face Danger," *New York Times,* October 22, 1983, 1.

32. Philip Taubman, "The Reason for Invading," *New York Times,* November 1, 1983, 1.

33. William E. Farrell, "U.S. Allows 15 Reporters to Go to Grenada for Day," *New York Times,* October 28, 1983, 13.

34. The quotations in this section are from Brand, "Diary—The grenada crisis," in *Chronicles,* 37–39, passim.

35. The quotations in this section are from Brand, "October 19th, 1983," in *Chronicles,* 40–41, passim.

36. A similar moment occurs in the poem "Eurocentric," where she writes "(even male revolutionaries refuse to radicalise their balls)" (*Chronicles,* 21). This line, however, points to gender problems in radical political movements more generally, as opposed to identifying gender issues within the Grenada Revolution specifically. For an analysis of women's roles during the revolution, including attention to some of the problems they faced from within the NJM, see Nicole Laurine Phillip, *Women in Grenadian History, 1783–1983* (Mona, Jamaica: University of the West Indies Press, 2010).

37. Brand, *Chronicles,* 41.

38. Deborah Thomas, *Exceptional Violence: Embodied Citizenship in Transnational Jamaica* (Durham, NC: Duke University Press, 2011), 4.

39. Brand was born in Trinidad in 1953 and migrated to Canada in 1970.

40. Brand, *Bread out of Stone,* 9. The litany of nationalities Brand lists corresponds in part with the myth of happy multiculturalism characterized in the image of the cultural mosaic. The term "Canadian Mosaic" served as the title for John Murray Gibbon's 1938 book on Canadian immigration. The term was later adopted and modified by sociologist John Porter in *Vertical Mosaic: An Analysis of Social Class and Power in Canada* (Toronto: University of Toronto Press, 1965). The term "cultural mosaic" has been an important symbol of the Canadian immigrant experience since the 1970s, when Prime Minister Pierre Trudeau introduced what would become the Canadian Charter of Rights and Freedoms as part of the Constitution Act of 1982. Under section 27 of this charter, "the preservation and enhancement of the multicultural heritage of Canadians" was recognized as an essential aspect of the equality of all Canadians under the law. Brand begins to disrupt this myth of happy multiculturalism by conceding that new immigrants to Canada were largely segregated, for instance in impoverished areas of Toronto. The full text of the Canadian Charter of Rights and Freedoms is available at http://laws-lois.justice.gc.ca/eng/Const/page-15.html.

41. Brand, *Bread out of Stone,* 141–42.

42. José Esteban Muñoz, *Cruising Utopia: The Then and There of Queer Futurity* (New York: New York University Press, 2009), 1.

43. Ibid., 1.

44. On diasporic identity as production, becoming, and being, see Stuart Hall, "Cultural Identity and Diaspora," in *Identity: Community, Culture, Difference,* ed. Jonathan Rutherford (London: Lawrence and Wishart, 1990), 222–37.

45. Ronald Cummings, "Between Here and 'Not Here': Queer Desires and Postcolonial Longings in the Writings of Dionne Brand and José Esteban Muñoz," *Journal of Postcolonial Writing* 55, no. 3 (2019): 308–22. On queerness and diaspora, see Nadia Ellis, *Territories of the Soul: Queered Belonging in the Black Diaspora* (Durham, NC: Duke University Press, 2015); and Rinaldo Walcott, *Queer Returns: Essays on Multiculturalism, Diaspora, and Black Studies* (London: Insomniac Press, 2016).

46. Brand, *Bread out of Stone,* 85.

47. Ibid., 98.

48. Édouard Glissant, *Poetics of Relation,* trans. Betsy Wing (Ann Arbor: University of Michigan Press, 1997), 121–22.

49. Brand, *Bread out of Stone,* 98.

50. Frantz Fanon, *Black Skin, White Masks,* trans. Richard Wilcox (New York: Grove Press, 2008), 93.

51. Frantz Fanon, *The Wretched of the Earth,* trans. Richard Philcox (New York: Grove Press, 2004), 15.

52. On emancipation as self-liberation, see Hilary Beckles, "Caribbean Anti-Slavery: The Self-Liberation Ethos of Enslaved Blacks," *Journal of Caribbean History* 22, no. 1 (1988): 1–19. On the movement of enslaved people to the francophone Caribbean, when they believed slavery was going to remain abolished, see Laurent Dubois, *A Colony of Citizens: Revolution and Slave Emancipation in the French Caribbean 1784–1804* (Chapel Hill: University of North Carolina Press, 2004).

53. Brand, *Bread out of Stone,* 98.

54. Ibid., 89.

55. Ibid., 89.

56. Her family's choices might also reflect regional and hemispheric affiliations; perhaps they side with Fidel because they see Cuba as part of their region, but later support Kennedy because they see themselves as part of the Americas.

57. Between 1940 and 1967 Trinidad was home to a U.S. military installation in the town of Chaguaramas on the island's northwest peninsula. A deal was brokered between the British colonial authorities and the U.S. government whereby the Americans acquired bases throughout the British empire in exchange for destroyers. Antigua was another island colony with a U.S. military presence. At the end of World War II, when the British were eager to sever ties with many of their overseas colonies, the relationship between the anglophone Caribbean and the United States grew increasingly complex. The development of the West

Indies Federation and the period of decolonization that immediately followed the collapse of the federation saw the rise of a Caribbean nationalism that was eager to shed ties with Britain but curiously ambivalent about U.S.-Caribbean relations. Chaguaramas was thrust into the center of these developments when it was selected as the capital of the West Indies Federation and the U.S. government, citing its treaty with Britain, refused to relinquish the land to Trinidadian authorities. C. L. R. James discusses the Chaguaramas controversy and highlights the importance of the United States in shaping a postindependence Caribbean in the 1963 appendix to *The Black Jacobins: Toussaint L'Ouverture and the San Domingo Revolution,* an essay titled "From Toussaint L'Ouverture to Fidel Castro" (New York: Random House, 1963). On Caribbean-U.S. relations during the shifting tides of decolonization, see Colin Palmer, *Eric Williams and the Making of the Modern Caribbean* (Chapel Hill: University of North Carolina Press, 2006); and George Lamming, *The Pleasures of Exile* (Ann Arbor: University of Michigan Press, 1992), especially the essay titled "Ishmael at Home." For an excellent comparative analysis of Lamming and James on Caribbean-U.S. relations, see the "Coda" to Harvey Neptune's *Caliban and the Yankees: Trinidad and the United States Occupation* (Chapel Hill: University of North Carolina Press, 2007) 191–98.

58. Quotations in this section are from Brand, *Bread out of Stone,* 89–99, passim.

59. The cultural theorist Judith Halberstam argues: "Queer subcultures produce alternative temporalities by allowing their participants to believe that their futures can be imagined according to logics that lie outside of those paradigmatic markers of life experience—namely, birth, marriage, reproduction, and death." *In a Queer Time & Place: Transgender Bodies, Subcultural Lives* (New York: New York University Press, 2005), 2. See also Elizabeth Freeman, *Time Binds, Queer Temporalities, Queer Histories* (Durham, NC: Duke University Press, 2010).

60. Brand, *Bread out of Stone,* 95.
61. Ibid., 94.
62. Ibid., 96.
63. Muñoz, *Cruising Utopia,* 1.
64. Brand, *Bread out of Stone,* 142.
65. Ibid., 142.
66. Ibid., 12.
67. Ibid., 12.
68. Ibid., 131–32.

69. The story of the invasion would later be adapted in part for the film *Heartbreak Ridge,* directed by Clint Eastwood (Los Angeles, Warner Brothers, 1986). Scenes from the film were shot on location in Grenada.

70. Brand, *Bread out of Stone,* 132.
71. Scott, *Omens of Adversity,* 149.
72. Brand, *Bread out of Stone,* 138–39.

73. Alejo Carpentier, *The Kingdom of This World*, trans. Harriet de Onís (New York: Farrar, Straus and Giroux, 2006), 172.

74. Brand, *Bread out of Stone*, 132.

75. Donette Francis, *Fictions of Feminine Citizenship: Sexuality and the Nation in Contemporary Caribbean Literature* (New York: Palgrave Macmillan, 2010), 1–2.

76. Gayatri Gopinath, *Impossible Desires: Queer Diasporas and South Asian Public Cultures* (Durham, NC: Duke University Press 2005), 2.

77. Rosamond King, *Island Bodies: Transgressive Sexualities in the Caribbean Imagination* (Gainesville: University Press of Florida 2014), 102.

78. Dionne Brand, *In Another Place, Not Here* (New York: Grove Press, 1996), 9.

79. Brand, *Bread out of Stone*, 139.

80. Early drafts of the novel were provisionally titled *Elizet*, speaking to the centrality of Elizete's worldview to Brand's conception of the novel. See "Finding Aid to Dionne Brand Fonds," LMS-0248, National Library of Canada, Ottawa, Ontario. The material remains under embargo.

81. Brand, *In Another Place, Not Here*, 3.

82. Omise'eke Natasha Tinsley, *Thiefing Sugar: Eroticism between Women in Caribbean Literature* (Durham, NC: Duke University Press, 2010), 20.

83. Ibid., 21.

84. Ibid., 21.

85. Ronald Cummings, "Queer Theory and Caribbean Writing," in *Routledge Companion to Anglophone Caribbean Literature*, ed. Michael Bucknor and Alison Donnell (New York: Routledge, 2011), 329.

86. Ibid., 329; Tinsley, *Thiefing Sugar*, 3.

87. The literary critic Raphael Dalleo reads *In Another Place, Not Here* as a distinctly postcolonial narrative in its effort to "both inhabit and critique the narrative of revolutionary decolonization." For Dalleo, definitions of the postcolonial in the Caribbean must necessarily engage with the limitations of prior anticolonial projects, see *Caribbean Literature and the Public Sphere: From the Plantation to the Postcolonial* (Charlottesville: University of Virginia Press, 2011), 237.

88. Brand, *In Another Place, Not Here*, 16.

89. The image of a woman acting as a bridge also references Cherrie Moraga and Glora Anzaldúa, eds., *This Bridge Called My Back: Writings by Radical Women of Color* (Albany: SUNY Press, 2015).

90. Brand, *In Another Place, Not Here*, 77.

91. Ibid., 72.

92. Ibid., 114–15.

93. Ibid., 245.

94. In *The Grenada Revolution and the Caribbean Present*, Puri argues that the relationship drawn between these two events by Brand and other writers and the Grenadian painter Canute Caliste provides a way of breaking through imposed silences and "honoring the Revolution," 162–64.

95. George Brizan, *Grenada: Island of Conflict* (London: Macmillan Education, 1998), 23.

96. For a discussion of flying Africans, see Michael A. Gomez, *Exchanging Our Country Marks: The Transformation of African Identities in the Colonial and Antebellum South* (Chapel Hill: University of North Carolina Press, 1998) 117–20; and Georgia Writers' Project, Work Projects Administration, Savannah Unit, *Drums and Shadows: Survival Studies among the Georgia Coastal Negroes* (Athens: University of Georgia Press, 1986). Other contemporary novelists who have taken up the trope include Earl Lovelace, *Salt* (London: Faber and Faber, 1996); and Toni Morrison, *Song of Solomon* (New York: Penguin Books, 1977).

97. Scott, *Omens of Adversity*, 127–64.

98. Alison Donnell, *Twentieth-Century Caribbean Literature: Critical Moments in Anglophone Literary History* (New York: Routledge, 2006), 216.

99. Watson and Wilder, *The Postcolonial Contemporary*, 6.

100. Brand, *In Another Place, Not Here*, 78.

### 4. Legacies of Mercy

1. See Wendy C. Grenade, "Exploring Transitions in Party Politics in Grenada, 1984–2013," in *The Grenada Revolution: Reflections and Lessons*, ed. Wendy C. Grenade (Jackson: University Press of Mississippi, 2015), 247. See also David Scott, *Omens of Adversity: Tragedy Time, Memory, Justice* (Durham, NC: Duke University Press, 2014), 19–20, 140–64.

2. Scott, *Omens of Adversity*, 20, 170–71.

3. Joan Purcell, *Memoirs of a Woman in Politics: Spiritual Struggle* (Bloomington, IN: AuthorHouse, 2009), 15–19.

4. Paul Scoon, *Survival for Service: My Experiences as Governor General of Grenada* (Oxford: Macmillan Education, 2003), 168–72.

5. Purcell, *Memoirs*, 79–80.

6. Ibid., 100–101.

7. Purcell's *From Wilderness to Promise: A Spiritual Perspective of Grenada's History* (Maitland, FL: Xulon Press, 2014) is a history of Grenadian politics, read through the lens of evangelical Christianity. While Purcell describes aspects of Grenada's colonial history, from Columbus's encounter with the island's indigenous residents to its colonization by the French and British, the greatest part of the text is spent discussing the nation's late colonial and early postcolonial period. Here her analysis centers on local political leaders, including Eric Gairy, Maurice Bishop, Herbert Blaize, Nicholas Brathwaite, and Keith Mitchell. She focuses on the party politics of the nation, all the while making the case for her own political party, the National Democratic Congress. She concludes that while the nation's history has been one of violence dating back to the colonial encounter with the original indigenous inhabitants, the current state of the economy is primarily the fault of self-serving, short-sighted politicians. She calls for a new, community-centered politics, driven by a biblical worldview.

8. This and the following quotations are from Purcell, *Memoirs*, 55–65, passim.

9. See Andaiye, "The Grenada Revolution, the Caribbean Left and the Regional Women's Movement," paper presented at the Caribbean Studies 35th Annual Conference, Barbados, May 26, 2010; Laurie R. Lambert, "The Revolution and Its Discontents: Grenadian Newspapers and Attempts to Shape Public Opinion during Political Transition," in "The Invasion of Grenada 30 Years On: A Retrospective," special issue, *Round Table: The Commonwealth Journal of International Affairs* 102, no. 2 (2013): 143–53.

10. See Bernard Coard, *The Grenada Revolution: What Really Happened?* (Kingston, Jamaica: McDermott Publishing, 2017); and Ewart Layne, *We Move Tonight: The Making of the Grenada Revolution* (CreateSpace Independent Publishing Platform, 2014).

11. This and the following quotations are from Purcell, *Memoirs*, 63–67, passim.

12. Wayne Sandiford, "Economic Growth and Development during the Grenada Revolution," paper presented at a conference, "The Grenada Revolution 40 Years After: Commemoration, Celebration and Critique," True Blue, Grenada, May 27, 2019. See also Shalini Puri, *The Grenada Revolution in the Caribbean Present: Operation Urgent Memory* (New York: Palgrave Macmillan, 2014), 41–48; and Brian Meeks, *Caribbean Revolutions and Revolutionary Theory: An Assessment of Cuba, Nicaragua and Grenada* (Mona, Jamaica: University of the West Indies Press, 200), 160.

13. David Scott, "The Fragility of Memory: An Interview with Merle Collins," *Small Axe: A Caribbean Journal of Criticism* 14, no. 1 (March 2010): 116.

14. Puri, *The Grenada Revolution in the Caribbean Present*, 101, 289n4, 106; Meeks, *Caribbean Revolutions and Revolutionary Theory*, 168.

15. The participation of the OECS in inviting the United States to intervene militarily must also be remembered. Pasty Lewis details the involvement of Caribbean leaders in paving the way for the U.S. invasion in "Revisiting the Grenada Invasion: The OECS's Role and Its Impact on Regional and International Politics," *Social and Economic Studies* 48, no. 3 (September 1999): 85–120.

16. The quotations in this and the next section are from Purcell, *Memoirs*, 67–82, passim.

17. Scoon, *Survival for Service*, 169.

18. Ibid., 161.

19. Ibid., 170.

20. I have used "invasion" throughout to reflect my sense that this military action was an illegal violation of Grenada's sovereignty.

21. Scott, *Omens of Adversity*, 164.

22. For a description of the West's practice of using moments of instability, warfare, and disaster to push capitalist expansion and exploitation in weaker

nations, see Naomi Klein, *The Shock Doctrine: The Rise of Disaster Capitalism* (Picador: New York, 2008).

23. See Wendy C. Grenade, "Exploring Transitions in Party Politics in Grenada, 1984–2013," in *The Grenada Revolution: Reflections and Lessons*, ed. Wendy C. (Jackson: University Press of Mississippi, 2015), 247; see also Scott, *Omens of Adversity*, 19–20, 140–64.

24. See Angela Y. Davis, *Are Prisons Obsolete?* (New York: Seven Stories Press, 2003); and Ruth Wilson Gilmore. *Golden Gulag: Prisons, Surplus Crisis, and Opposition in Globalizing California* (Berkeley: University of California Press, 2007). See also the work of the prison abolitionist collective Critical Resistance at http://criticalresistance.org/about/.

25. As Ruth Wilson Gilmore puts it in an interview with the *New York Times*, "where life is precious, life *is* precious." Rachel Kushner, "Is Prison Necessary? Ruth Wilson Gilmore Might Change Your Mind," *New York Times*, April 17, 2019.

26. This and the following quotations are from Purcell, *Memoirs*, 121–32, passim.

27. In *Omens of Adversity*, Scott asks whether Grenadians, and Caribbean people more broadly, might owe an apology to the Grenada 17 for the way their cases were mishandled in the wake of the revolution, 170–71.

## Conclusion

1. The title of this chapter is a riff on Alice Walker's *In Search of Our Mothers' Gardens* (Orlando, FL: Harcourt Brace Jovanovich, 1984).

2. *The House on Coco Road*, directed by Damani Baker (Los Angeles: Array, 2017). Subsequent quotations from the film refer to this production. I thank Natasha Lightfoot for bringing Baker's work to my attention and Donette Francis for insisting that I write about it.

3. Remnants of this first attempt are still highly visible throughout the film, perhaps most obviously in the sections where Baker attempts to explain Eric Gairy's time in power and in the dichotomy the film sets up between Ronald Reagan and Maurice Bishop. In some of these moments the film flattens or omits details about the government leaders to keep the focus on the personal aspect of the narrative. For example, Baker's voiceover refers to Gairy's rule as a "dictatorship," overstating Gairy's authoritarian tendencies. He presents Bishop as a straightforward hero, with little attention to the collective role of the NJM. While neither of these extremes allows for the multilayered historical, cultural, and political work necessary to unpack the legacies of these men, the film is not about them. What it loses in the oversimplification of Bishop's and Gairy's leadership it gains in the time and care it takes to present the perspectives of the women it trains its eye on.

4. Shalini Puri, *The Grenada Revolution in the Caribbean Present: Operation Urgent Memory* (New York: Palgrave Macmillan, 2014), 141–45.

# Bibliography

## Archival Sources

### Canada

Derek Walcott Papers, MS Collection 136, 348, 504, 710, 772. Thomas Fisher Rare Book Library, University of Toronto, Toronto, Canada.

Dionne Brand Fonds, LMS-0248. National Library of Canada, Ottawa, Ontario.

### Grenada

T. A. Marryshow Library, University of the West Indies Centre: Grenada Invasion Papers; Grenada Newspaper Collection; Grenada Poetry File, 1, 2; Maurice Bishop folder. St. George's, Grenada.

Grenada Public Library: PRG Speeches folder; Grenada Social and Cultural History 1974–1998 folder. St. George's, Grenada.

### United States

Central Intelligence Agency Freedom of Information Act Electronic Reading Room, http://www.foia.cia.gov/.

National Archives Record Group 242, Seized Grenadian Document Collection 7/11/1919–12/31/1984; Record Group 330, Records of the Office of the Secretary of Defense; Record Group 373, Records of Defense, Grenada Document Index. National Archives, College Park, Maryland.

New York University Archives, Research Institute for the Study of Man Vertical Files RISM VF 1. "Evaluation of Marryshow Readers" (1984), Grenada—Reading, Studying, Teaching Folder, box 13, "Grenada: Facts and Figures" (1980), Grenada Central Statistical Office, Grenada—Statistics Folder, box 13. New York University, New York.

### United Kingdom

Margaret Thatcher Foundation Archives, https://www.margaretthatcher.org/archive.

## Interviews

Nunez, Clive, interview by author, Port of Spain, Trinidad, August 23, 2011.
Payne-Banfield, Gloria, interview by author, St. George's, Grenada, August 10, 2011.
Peters, Ann L., interview by author, Botanical Gardens, Grenada, August 4, 2011.
Pierre, Leslie, interview by author, Frequente Industrial Estate, Grenada, August 2, 2011.
Robinson, Shirley, interview by author, Sauteurs, Grenada, August 11, 2011.
Sloane, Kathy, interview by author, Oakland, California, March 25, 2012.

## Other Sources

Abegunrin, Olayiwola. "Pan-African Congresses, 1893–1974." In *Pan-Africanism in Modern Times: Challenges, Concerns, Constraints*, edited by Olayiwola Abegunrin and Sabella Ogbobode Abidde, 17–45. Lanham, MD: Lexington Books, 2016.
Alexander, M. Jacqui. *Pedagogies of Crossing: Meditations on Feminism, Sexual Politics, Memory, and the Sacred*. Durham, NC: Duke University Press, 2005.
Andaiye. "The Grenada Revolution, the Caribbean Left, and the Regional Women's Movement." Paper presented at the Caribbean Studies 35th Annual Conference, Barbados, 2010.
Andre, Irving. "The Genesis and Persistence of the Commonwealth Caribbean Seasonal Agricultural Workers Program in Canada." *Osgoode Hall Law Journal* 2, no. 2 (1990): 243–301.
Atkinson, Rick. "Estimates of Casualties in Grenada Are Raised." *Washington Post*, November 9, 1983.
Ayres, B. Drummond, Jr. "U.S. Marines Diverted to Grenada in Event Americans Face Danger." *New York Times*, October 22, 1983.
Baugh, Edward. *Black Sand: New and Selected Poems*. Leeds: Peepal Tree Press, 2013.
Beckles, Hilary. "Caribbean Anti-Slavery: The Self-Liberation Ethos of Enslaved Blacks." *Journal of Caribbean History* 22, no. 1 (1988): 1–19.
Benítez-Rojo, Antonio. *The Repeating Island: The Caribbean and the Postmodern Perspective*. Translated by James E. Maraniss. Durham, NC: Duke University Press, 1996.
Benson, Devyn Spence. *Antiracism in Cuba: The Unfinished Revolution*. Chapel Hill: University of North Carolina Press, 2016.
Bernstein, Richard. "U.S. Vetoes U.N. Resolution 'Deploring' Grenada Invasion." *New York Times*, October 29, 1983, 1, 4.
Bewes, Timothy. *The Event of Postcolonial Shame*. Princeton, NJ: Princeton University Press, 2012.
Bishop, Jacqueline, and Dolace Nicole McLean. "Working Out Grenada: An Interview with Merle Collins." *Calabash* 3, no. 2 (2005): 53–65.

Bishop, Maurice. *In Nobody's Backyard: Maurice Bishop's Speeches 1979–1983: A Memorial Volume.* Edited by Chris Searle. London: Zed Books, 1984.

———. *Maurice Bishop Speaks: The Grenada Revolution and Its Overthrow 1979–83.* Edited by Bruce Marcus and Michael Taber. New York: Pathfinder Press, 1983.

———. "PM Bishop Tells of the Great Marryshow Tradition." *Free West Indian,* November 13, 1982, 1.

Bogues, Anthony. "Michael Manley, Equality, and the Jamaican Labour Movement." *Caribbean Quarterly* 48, no. 1 (2002): 77–93.

Bonilla, Yarimar. *Non-Sovereign Futures: French Caribbean Politics in the Wake of Disenchantment.* Chicago: University of Chicago Press, 2015.

Boyce Davies, Carole, and Elaine Savory Fido, eds. *Out of the Kumbla: Caribbean Women and Literature.* Lawrenceville, NJ: African World Press, 1990.

Brand, Dionne. *Bread out of Stone: Recollections, Sex, Recognitions, Race, Dreaming, Politics.* Toronto: Coach House Press, 1994.

———. *Chronicles of the Hostile Sun.* Toronto: Williams-Wallace Publishers, 1984.

———. *In Another Place, Not Here.* New York: Grove Press, 1996.

———. *A Map to the Door of No Return: Notes to Belonging.* Toronto: Doubleday, 2001.

Brathwaite, Kamau. *M/R.* New York: Savacou North, 2002.

———. *Roots.* Ann Arbor: University of Michigan Press, 1993.

Brizan, George. *Grenada: Island of Conflict.* London: Macmillan Education, 1998.

Calliste, Agnes. "Women of 'Exceptional Merit': Immigration of Caribbean Nurses to Canada." *Canadian Journal of Women and Law* 6, no. 1 (1993): 85–102.

Carby, Hazel. *Reconstructing Womanhood: The Emergence of the Afro-American Woman Novelist.* Oxford: Oxford University Press, 1987.

Carpentier, Alejo. *The Kingdom of This World.* 1949. Translated by Harriet de Onís. New York: Farrar, Straus and Giroux, 2006.

Chile, Dame Sarah. "Cotay Si, Cotay La: What Is ah Likkle 'Coop' for Us?" *Torchlight* 22, no. 44 (June 17, 1979).

Coard, Bernard. *The Grenada Revolution: What Really Happened?* Kingston, Jamaica: McDermott Publishing, 2017.

Collins, Merle. *Angel.* 1987. Leeds: Peepal Tree Press, 2011 (rev. ed.).

———. *Because the Dawn Breaks! Poems Dedicated to the Grenadian People.* London: Karia Press, 1985.

———. *The Colour of Forgetting.* London: Virago Press, 1995.

———. *Lady in a Boat.* Leeds: Peepal Tree Press, 2003.

———. "Tout Moun ka Pléwé (Everybody Bawling)," *Small Axe: A Caribbean Journal of Criticism* 11, no. 1 (2007): 1–16.

Collins, Patricia Hill. "Mammies, Matriarchs, and Other Controlling Images." In *Black Feminist Thought: Knowledge, Consciousness, and the Politics of Empowerment,* 76–106. New York: Routledge, 2009.

Cox, Edward L. "Fedon's Rebellion 1795–96: Causes and Consequences," *Journal of Negro History* 67, no. 1 (Spring 1982): 7–19.
Crenshaw, Kimberlé. "Demarginalizing the Intersection of Race and Sex: A Black Feminist Critique of Antidiscrimination Doctrine, Feminist Theory and Antiracist Politics." *University of Chicago Legal Forum* 140, no. 1 (1989): 139–67.
Cummings, Ronald. "Between Here and 'Not Here': Queer Desires and Postcolonial Longings in the Writings of Dionne Brand and José Esteban Muñoz." *Journal of Postcolonial Writing* 55, no. 3 (2019): 308–22.
———. "Queer Theory and Caribbean Writing." In *Routledge Companion to Anglophone Caribbean Literature*, edited by Michael Bucknor and Alison Donnell, 323–31. New York: Routledge, 2011.
Dalleo, Raphael. *Caribbean Literature and the Public Sphere: From the Plantation to the Postcolonial*. Charlottesville: University of Virginia Press, 2011.
Das, Veena. *Life and Words: Violence and the Descent into the Ordinary*. Berkeley: University of California Press, 2006.
Davis, Angela Y. *Are Prisons Obsolete?* New York: Seven Stories Press, 2003.
de la Fuente, Alejandro. *A Nation for All: Race, Inequality, and Politics in Twentieth-Century Cuba*. Chapel Hill: University of North Carolina Press, 2001.
Donnell, Alison. *Twentieth-Century Caribbean Literature: Critical Moments in Anglophone Literary History*. New York: Routledge, 2006.
Dubois, Laurent. *A Colony of Citizens: Revolution and Slave Emancipation in the French Caribbean 1784–1804*. Chapel Hill: University of North Carolina Press, 2004.
Duffus Commission. *Report of the Duffus Commission of Inquiry into the Breakdown of Law and Order and Police Brutality in Grenada*. St. George's, Grenada: Duffus Commission, 1975. http://ufdc.ufl.edu/AA00010419/00001.
Dunkley, D. A. 2011. "Hegemony in Post-Independence Jamaica." *Caribbean Quarterly* 57, no. 2 (June 2011): 1–23.
Echavez See, Sarita. *The Decolonized Eye: Filipino American Art and Performance*. Minneapolis: University of Minnesota Press, 2009.
Edmondson, Belinda. *Making Men: Gender, Literary Authority, and Women's Writing in the Caribbean*. Durham, NC: Duke University Press, 1999.
Ellis, Nadia. *Territories of the Soul: Queered Belonging in the Black Diaspora*. Durham, NC: Duke University Press, 2015.
Fanon, Frantz. *Black Skin, White Masks*. 1952. Translated by Richard Philcox. New York: Grove Press, 2008.
———. *The Wretched of the Earth*. 1961. Translated by Richard Philcox. New York: Grove Press, 2004.
Farrell, William E. "U.S. Allows 15 Reporters to Go to Grenada for Day." *New York Times*, October 28, 1983.
*Forward Ever: The Killing of a Revolution*. Dir. Bruce Paddington and Luke Paddington. New York: Third World Newsreel, 2013.

Francis, Donette. *Fictions of Feminine Citizenship: Sexuality and the Nation in Contemporary Caribbean Literature*. New York: Palgrave Macmillan, 2010.
Franklyn, David. *Mission Betrayed*. St. Peter, Barbados: Caribbean Chapters, 2012.
Freeman, Elizabeth. *Time Binds, Queer Temporalities, Queer Histories*. Durham, NC: Duke University Press, 2010.
García, Cristina. *Dreaming in Cuban*. New York: Ballantine Books, 1992.
Georgia Writers' Project, Work Projects Administration, Savannah Unit. *Drums and Shadows: Survival Studies among the Georgia Coastal Negroes*. 1940. Athens: University of Georgia Press, 1986.
Gilmore, Ruth Wilson. *Golden Gulag: Prisons, Surplus Crisis, and Opposition in Globalizing California*. Berkeley: University of California Press, 2007.
Glissant, Éduoard. *Monsieur Toussaint: A Play*. 1961. Translated by Michael Dash. Washington, DC: Three Continents Press, 2005.
———. *Poetics of Relation*. 1990. Translated by Betsy Wing. Ann Arbor: University of Michigan Press, 1997.
Gomez, Michael A. *Exchanging Our Country Marks: The Transformation of African Identities in the Colonial and Antebellum South*. Chapel Hill: University of North Carolina Press, 1998.
Gopinath, Gayatri. *Impossible Desires: Queer Diasporas and South Asian Public Cultures*, Durham, NC: Duke University Press, 2005.
Gordon, Ken. *Getting It Write: Winning Caribbean Press Freedom*. Kingston, Jamaica: Ian Randle Publishers, 1999.
*Grenada Revolution Online*. "Bloody Sunday, 18 November 1973." Edited by Ann Elizabeth Wilder. 2001. http://www.thegrenadarevolutiononline.com/bloodysunday.html.
Grenade, Wendy C. ed. *The Grenada Revolution: Reflections and Lessons*, Jackson: University Press of Mississippi, 2015.
Gunning, Sandra, Tera Hunter, and Michele Mitchell, eds. *Dialogues of Dispersal: Gender, Sexuality, and African Diasporas*. Oxford: Wiley-Blackwell, 2004.
Halberstam, Judith. *In a Queer Time & Place: Transgender Bodies, Subcultural Lives*. New York: New York University Press, 2005.
Hall, Stuart. "Cultural Identity and Diaspora." In *Identity: Community, Culture, Difference*, edited by Jonathan Rutherford, 222–37. London: Lawrence and Wishart, 1990.
Haynes, Tonya. "Interrogating Approaches to Caribbean Feminist Thought." *Journal of Eastern Caribbean Studies* 42, no. 3 (2017): 25–58.
Hirsch, Marianne. *The Generation of Postmemory: Writing and Visual Culture after the Holocaust*. New York: Columbia University Press, 2012.
Hodge, Merle. "Caribbean Women and Politics." *Torchlight* 22, no. 45 (June 21, 1979), 4.
Hoffman, Sarah Z. "HIV/AIDS in Cuba: A Model for Care or an Ethical Dilemma?" *African Health Sciences* 4, no. 3 (December 2004): 208–9.

Hosein, Gabrielle Jamela, and Jane Parpart, eds. *Negotiating Gender, Policy and Politics in the Caribbean: Feminist Strategies, Masculinist Resistance and Transformational Possibilities.* London: Rowman and Littlefield, 2017.

*The House on Coco Road.* Dir. Damani Baker. Los Angeles: Array, 2017.

Hudson, Peter James. "Imperial Designs: The Royal Bank of Canada in the Caribbean." *Race & Class* 52, no. 1 (2010): 33–48.

Jacobs, Curtis. "The Jacobins of Mt. Qua Qua: Fedon's Rebellion in Grenada, 1762–1796." Ph.D. diss., University of the West Indies, 2000.

James, C. L. R. *The Black Jacobins: Toussaint L'Ouverture and the San Domingo Revolution.* 1963. New York: Vintage Books, 1989.

Kelley, Robin D. G. *Freedom Dreams: The Black Radical Imagination.* Boston: Beacon Press, 2002.

Kempadoo, Kamala. *Sexing the Caribbean: Gender, Race and Sexual Labour.* New York: Routledge, 2004.

Kincaid, Jamaica. *A Small Place.* New York: Farrar, Straus and Giroux, 1988.

King, Rosamond. *Island Bodies: Transgressive Sexualities in the Caribbean Imagination.* Gainesville: University Press of Florida, 2014.

Klein, Naomi. *The Shock Doctrine: The Rise of Disaster Capitalism.* New York: Picador, 2008.

Kushner, Rachel. "Is Prison Necessary? Ruth Wilson Gilmore Might Change Your Mind." *New York Times*, April 17, 2019.

Lacey, Terry. *Violence and Politics in Jamaica, 1960–70: Internal Security in a Developing Country.* London: Frank Cass, 1977.

Lambert, Laurie. "The Revolution and Its Discontents: Grenadian Newspapers and Attempts to Shape Public Opinion during Political Transition." In "The Invasion of Grenada 30 Years On: A Retrospective," special issue, *Round Table: The Commonwealth Journal of International Affairs* 102, no. 2 (2013): 143–53.

———. "Worlds Real and Invented: The Grenada Revolution and the Caribbean Literary Imaginary." Ph.D. diss., New York University, 2013.

Lamming, George. "The Education of Feeling." In *The George Lamming Reader: The Aesthetics of Decolonisation*, edited by Anthony Bogues, 11–22. Kingston, Jamaica: Ian Randle Publishers, 2011.

———. *In the Castle of My Skin.* 1953. Ann Arbor: University of Michigan Press, 1991.

———. "Maurice Bishop Lives: Address by George Lamming at the Memorial Service for Maurice Bishop and Colleagues at Trinity Cathedral, in Trinidad, December 1983." In *In Nobody's Backyard: Maurice Bishop's Speeches, 1979–1983: A Memorial Volume.* Edited by Chris Searle, 1–6. London: Zed Books, 1984.

———. *The Pleasures of Exile.* Ann Arbor: University of Michigan Press, 1992.

———. *The Sovereignty of the Imagination—Conversations III: Language and Politics of Ethnicity.* Philipsburg, St. Martin: House of Nehesi, 2009.

Layne, Ewart. *We Move Tonight: The Making of the Grenada Revolution*. CreateSpace Independent Publishing Platform, 2014.
Levi, Darrell E. *Michael Manley: The Making of a Leader*. Athens: University of Georgia Press, 1990.
Lewis, Linden, ed. *Caribbean Sovereignty, Development and Democracy in an Age of Globalization*. New York: Routledge, 2015.
Lewis, Patsy. "A Response to Edward Seaga's *The Grenada Intervention: The Inside Story*." *Social and Economic Studies* 62, nos. 3–4 (2013): 83–111.
———. "Revisiting the Grenada Invasion: The OECS's Role and Its Impact on Regional and International Politics." *Social and Economic Studies* 48, no. 3 (1999): 85–120.
Lewis, Patsy, Gary Williams, and Peter Clegg, eds. *Grenada: Revolution and Invasion*. Mona, Jamaica: University of the West Indies Press, 2015.
*Life and Debt*, directed by Stephanie Black. New York: New Yorker Films, 2001.
"Local Feminists' Dream." *Torchlight* 22, no. 44 (June 17, 1979).
Lorde, Audre. "I am Your Sister." *Women & Therapy* 6, no. 4 (1988): 25–30.
———. *Sister Outsider: Essays and Speeches*. Berkeley, CA: Crossing Press, 1984.
Lovelace, Earl. *Is Just a Movie*. London: Faber and Faber, 2011.
———. *Salt*. London: Faber and Faber, 1996.
MacCannell, Juliet Flower. *The Regime of the Brother: After the Patriarchy*. New York: Routledge, 1991.
Manley, Beverley. *The Manley Memoirs*. Kingston, Jamaica: Ian Randle Publishers, 2008.
Margaret Thatcher Foundation. Archive. https://www.margaretthatcher.org/archive.
Marryshow, Theophilus Albert. *Cycles of Civilization*. St. George's, Grenada: Printed at the office of *The West Indian*, 1917. Microform.
McClintock, Anne. *Imperial Leather: Race, Gender and Sexuality in the Colonial Contest*. New York: Routledge, 1995.
McKittrick, Katherine. *Demonic Grounds: Black Women and the Cartographies of Struggle*. Minneapolis: University of Minnesota Press, 2006.
Meeks, Brian. *Caribbean Revolutions and Revolutionary Theory: An Assessment of Cuba, Nicaragua and Grenada*. 1993. Mona, Jamaica: University of the West Indies Press, 2001.
———. *Narratives of Resistance: Jamaica, Trinidad, and the Caribbean*. Mona, Jamaica: University of the West Indies Press, 2000.
"Meeting of Coordinating Council of Delegates: Agenda," *New Jewel*, May 19, 1974, 1.
Mohammed, Patricia, ed. *Gendered Realities: Essays in Caribbean Feminist Thought*. Mona, Jamaica: University of the West Indies Press, 2002.
Mohanty, Chandra Talpade. "Under Western Eyes: Feminist Scholarship and Colonial Discourse." *Boundary 2: A Journal of Postmodern Literature and Culture* 12 (Spring and Fall 1984): 333–58.

Moraga, Cherríe, and Gloria Anzaldúa, eds. *This Bridge Called My Back: Writings by Radical Women of Color.* Albany: SUNY Press, 2015.
Morrison, Toni. *Song of Solomon.* New York: Penguin Books, 1977.
Moss, Stephen. "The Oxford Poetry Job Would Have Been Too Much Work." Interview with Derek Walcott. *Guardian.* May 3, 2012.
Moten, Fred. *In the Break: The Aesthetics of the Black Radical Tradition.* Minneapolis: University of Minnesota Press, 2003.
Moya, Paula M. L. "The Search for Decolonial Love: An Interview with Junot Díaz." *Boston Review,* June 26, 2012.
Muñoz, José Esteban. *Cruising Utopia: The Then and There of Queer Futurity.* New York: New York University Press, 2009.
Naipaul, V. S. *Guerrillas.* 1975. New York: Vintage, 1990.
———. "An Island Betrayed," *Harper's,* March 1, 1984, 61–72.
Neptune, Harvey. *Caliban and the Yankees: Trinidad and the United States Occupation.* Chapel Hill: University of North Carolina Press, 2007.
"NJM Bishop to Attend Pan-African Congress." *Torchlight,* May 26, 1974.
Nixon, Angelique. *Resisting Paradise: Tourism, Diaspora, and Sexuality in Caribbean Culture.* Jackson: University Press of Mississippi, 2015.
Noguera, Pedro. *The Imperatives of Power: Political Change and the Social Basis of Regime Support in Grenada from 1951–1991.* New York: Peter Lang, 1997.
Palmer, Colin. *Eric Williams and the Making of the Modern Caribbean.* Chapel Hill: University of North Carolina Press, 2006.
Phillip, Nicole Laurine. *Women in Grenadian History, 1783–1983.* Mona, Jamaica: University of the West Indies Press, 2010.
Pinto, Samantha. *Difficult Diasporas: The Transnational Feminist Aesthetic of the Black Atlantic.* New York: New York University Press, 2013.
Porter, John. *The Vertical Mosaic: An Analysis of Social Class and Power in Canada.* Toronto: University of Toronto Press, 1965.
Posmentier, Sonya. *Cultivation and Catastrophe: The Lyric Ecology of Modern Black Literature.* Baltimore, MD: Johns Hopkins University Press, 2017.
Purcell, Joan M. *From Wilderness to Promise: A Spiritual Perspective of Grenada's History.* Maitland, FL: Xulon Press, 2014.
———. *Memoirs of a Woman in Politics: Spiritual Struggle.* Bloomington, IN: AuthorHouse, 2009.
Puri, Shalini. *The Grenada Revolution in the Caribbean Present: Operation Urgent Memory.* New York: Palgrave Macmillan, 2014.
"Rastas to Protest." *Torchlight,* October 10, 1979, 1.
Reddock, Rhonda E., ed. *Interrogating Caribbean Masculinities: Theoretical and Empirical Analyses.* Mona, Jamaica: University of the West Indies Press, 2004.
"Remember Bloody Sunday." *Free West Indian,* November 17, 1979.
Roberts-Squires, Maria. *October, All Over.* London: Heinemann, 2005.
Robinson, Cedric. *Black Marxism: The Making of the Black Radical Tradition.* Chapel Hill: University of North Carolina Press, 1983.

Roumain, Jacques. *Masters of the Dew*. 1944. Translated by Mercer Cook and Langston Hughes. Pompano Beach, FL: EducaVision, 2012.

Rosenberg, Leah. *Nationalism and the Formation of Caribbean Literature*. New York: Palgrave Macmillan, 2007.

Rothberg, Michael. "Decolonizing Trauma Studies: A Response." *Studies in the Novel* 40, no. 1/2 (2008): 224–38.

Salkey, Andrew. "After the Counter-Revolution, After the Invasion." In *In the Border Country and Other Stories*. London: Bogle-L'Overture Press, 1998.

———. *Georgetown Journal*. London: New Beacon Books, 1972.

———. *Havana Journal*. London: Penguin Books, 1971.

———. *In the Border Country and Other Stories*. London: Bogle-L'Ouverture Press, 1998.

———. "Maurice." *Black Scholar* 15, no. 1 (May/June 1984): 15.

Sananas, Rebecca. "Love, Loss and Beauty Pageants: Inside a Cuban HIV Sanitarium." National Public Radio, March 26, 2016.

Sandiford, Wayne. "Economic Growth and Development during the Grenada Revolution." Paper presented at a conference, "The Grenada Revolution 40 Years After: Commemoration, Celebration and Critique." True Blue, Grenada, May 27, 2019.

Saunders, Patricia. *Alien-nation and Repatriation: Translating Identity in Anglophone Caribbean Literature*. Lanham, MD: Lexington Books, 2007.

Scoon, Paul. *Survival for Service: My Experiences as Governor General of Grenada*. Oxford: Macmillan Caribbean, 2003.

Scott, David. "The Fragility of Memory: An Interview with Merle Collins." *Small Axe: A Caribbean Journal of Criticism* 14, no. 1 (March 2010): 79–163.

———. *Omens of Adversity: Tragedy, Time, Memory, Justice*. Durham, NC: Duke University Press, 2014.

———. "The Sovereignty of the Imagination: An Interview with George Lamming." *Small Axe: A Caribbean Journal of Criticism* 6, no. 2 (September 2002): 72–200.

Sharpe, Christina. *In the Wake: On Blackness and Being*. Durham, NC: Duke University Press, 2016.

Sheller, Mimi. *Aluminum Dreams: The Making of Light Modernity*. Cambridge, MA: MIT Press, 2014.

Smith, Faith, ed. *Sex and the Citizen: Interrogating the Caribbean*. Charlottesville: University of Virginia Press, 2011.

Sommer, Doris. *Foundational Fictions: The National Romances of Latin America*. Berkeley: University of California Press, 1991.

Spivak, Gayatri. *A Critique of Postcolonial Reason: Toward a History of the Vanishing Present*. Cambridge, MA: Harvard University Press, 1999.

———. "Three Women's Texts and a Critique of Imperialism." *Critical Inquiry* 12 (Autumn 1985): 243–61.

Stephens, Michelle A. *Black Empire: The Masculine Global Imaginary of Caribbean Intellectuals in the United States, 1914–1962*. Durham, NC: Duke University Press, 2005.
"Still United in Our Cultural Heritage." *Free West Indian,* June 2, 1979, 6–7.
Stone, Carl. *Class, Race, and Political Behavior in Urban Jamaica*. Mona, Jamaica: Institute of Social and Economic Research, University of the West Indies, 1973.
———. *Stratification and Political Change in Trinidad and Jamaica*. Beverly Hills, CA: Sage Publications, 1972.
Taubman, Philip. "The Reason for Invading." *New York Times,* November 1, 1983.
Thomas, Deborah A. *Exceptional Violence: Embodied Citizenship in Transnational Jamaica*. Durham, NC: Duke University Press, 2011.
———. "Silence, Taboo, and Everyday Practices of Revolution: What Sovereignty Feels Like." Paper presented at the New York University African-Diaspora Forum, October 22, 2014.
Tinsley, Omise'eke Natasha. *Thiefing Sugar: Eroticism Between Women in Caribbean Literature*. Durham, NC: Duke University Press, 2010.
Trouillot, Michel Rolph. *Global Transformations: Anthropology and the Modern World*. New York: Palgrave Macmillan, 2003.
Visser, Irene. "Decolonizing Trauma Theory: Retrospect and Prospects." *Humanities* 4, no. 2 (2015): 250–65.
———. "Trauma and Power in Postcolonial Literary Studies." In *Contemporary Approaches in Literary Trauma Theory,* edited by Michelle Balaev, 106–30. New York: Palgrave Macmillan, 2014.
Walcott, Derek. "Good Old Heart of Darkness." Derek Walcott Papers, MS Collection 136, box 1, folders 30–31. Thomas Fisher Rare Book Library, University of Toronto, Toronto, Canada.
———. *Henri Christophe* (1949). In *The Haitian Trilogy: Plays: Henri Christophe, Drums and Colours, and the Haytian Earth*. New York: Farrar, Straus and Giroux, 2002.
———. *Selected Poems*. Edited by Edward Baugh. New York: Farrar, Straus and Giroux, 2007.
———. "To Die for Grenada." Derek Walcott Papers, MS Collection 136. Thomas Fisher Rare Book Library, University of Toronto, Toronto, Canada.
———. *What the Twilight Says: Essays* (New York: Farrar, Straus and Giroux, 2014).
Walcott, Rinaldo. *Queer Returns: Essays on Multiculturalism, Diaspora, and Black Studies*. London: Insomniac Press, 2016.
Walker, Alice. *In Search of Our Mothers' Gardens*. Orlando, FL: Harcourt Brace Jovanovich, 1984.
Watson, Jini Kim, and Gary Wilder. *The Postcolonial Contemporary*. New York: Fordham University Press, 2018.

Wilson-Tagoe, Nana. *Historical Thought and Literary Representation in West Indian Literature.* Gainesville: University Press of Florida, 1998.

Young, Robert J.C. *White Mythologies: Writing History and the West.* New York: Routledge, 1991.

Young Leaders of Presentation Brothers College. *Under the Cover of Darkness.* Grenada: Ministry of Education, 2002.

# Index

Advisory Council, 166
African diaspora, 47; black radical tradition on, 22, 187n52; Brand on writers and, 133–35, 137–38, 140; to Canada, 148; Caribbean writers of, 125–27; as flying home, 148; home movies documenting, 175–76; Purcell including, 153–54; revolution and, 36; writers of, 126–27
"aftermath without end," 22, 92, 121
"After the Counter-Revolution, After the Invasion" (Salkey), 35, 79, 103–4
Allende, Salvador, 119, 139, 196n21
American imperialism, 60; black women's resistance to, 177; Christianity and, 162–63; colonialism replicated by, 21; as disarticulated, 116; economic aid and, 31; foreign journalists excluded by, 101; Grenadians on, 88, 117–18; Haughton caution on, 176; journalism supporting, 102; Lorde on, 24; rejection of, 25, 51–52; Scott on, 15, 149, 167; sovereignty limited by, 19, 101–2, 137–38; trauma from, 113–14; Walcott on, 93, 98–101
ancestral knowledge, 37–38; adversity handled through, 63–64; Brand on failure and, 138–39; Carib memories and prophecies as, 55, 58, 61–63; "Dream Mourning" and, 67; "Morning Glory" and, 68–69; women carrying, 61. See also generations
*Angel* (Merle), 35–76, 104, 107, 174, 191n27
archives, 182; gaps in, relating to Grenada Revolution, 16; gender and, 5–6, 140; home movies as, 175–76; literature adding to, 16–17; as patriarchal construct, 16; women missing in, 7–8

Baker, Damani, 173–82, 204n3
Barbados, 4, 33–34, 81, 85–86, 100, 118–20
*Because the Dawn Breaks* (Merle Collins), 70
Bishop, Alimenta (Ma), 179–82, *180*
Bishop, Ann, 179–82
Bishop, Maurice, 2, 6, 187n54; assassination of, 10–11, 12–13, 32–33, 87, 120–21, 136, 185n29; Baker on, 204n3; elder vision and poetry on, 37–38; fatal missteps by, 34; Grenada 17 and assassination of, 75–76, 105, 151–52, 154, 166, 168–70, 204n27; Grenadians and tension with, 87; as historical leader, 4, 108; house arrest of, 31; joint leadership and, 31, 87, 180–81; Lamming eulogy on, 88–89; Marryshow and Lenin linked by, 77–78; military installation decision by, 31–32, 189n69; NJM at odds with, 31, 73–74, 197n29; Purcell on, 159, 161–62; women's rights championed by, 28
black feminism, 18, 105, 177, 187n52
*Black Jacobins, The* (James), 3–4, 88, 199n57
blackness, 46–48, 174
Black Power movement, 1, 25; antiblackness response to, 174; blackness and, 46; black radical tradition and, 26, 111; Caribbean revolution with, 174; Merle Collins, character exploring, 46–47;

Black Power movement (*continued*)
coup by, 90; macho masculinity of, 6, 114, 141; politics of, 47; population forgotten by, 146; PRG support by, 23; United States and, 8, 173, 176; Walcott on, 96; women expanding, 175

black queer women, 8, 17, 36, 141

black radical tradition, 18, 124, 126; Black Power and, 26, 111; Caribbean feminism and, 146–50; Caribbean mother character in, 105; connections to, 23, 187n52; disillusionment with, 139; generations and genders in, 36; Grenada Revolution and, 22–23, 35, 111, 187n54; limits of, 114, 140; as male, heterocentric, 79, 141, 149; Marxism and, 187n52; NJM and, 80, 90; queer women into, 141, 150; Salkey on, 103; West Indies Federation in, 77; women and, 132–33, 141, 146–47, 150, 182

Bonilla, Yarimar, 26–27

Brand, Dionne: on ancestor magic, 138–39; on Black Power macho, 6, 114; on black queer women, 17, 36; Canada and, 111, 125, 198nn39–40; in Caribbean feminism, 113; on communism, 129–30, 190n18, 199n56; Cuban Revolution and family of, 127–31, 137, 199n56; on diasporic writer and revolution, 133–35, *134*, 137–38, 140; on gender, 125–26, 131, 133, 135–36, 140, 144; as Grenada Revolution writer, 7, 9, 18, 28, 110–50, 131–32, 184n21; humanizing vignettes from, 124–25; movement and, 126–29; on NJM problems, 124, 198n36; on queerness, 131, 135, 140, 147, 149; on revolution limits, 111, 136; on sexuality, 125–26, 134, 140–41, 144; on sovereignty, 35–36; on terror, 142–43; on *Torchlight*, 118–20; trauma in poetry and, 112; from Trinidad, 110–11, 125; U.S. invasion viewed by, 114–15; women and revolution by, 136; on writing and Revolution, 131–32. Works: *Bread out of Stone*, 35–36, 112, 125–27, 140, 201n80; *Chronicles of the Hostile Sun*, 17, 35, 110, 122, 142; "Diary—The grenada crisis," 121; *In Another Place, Not Here*, 35–36, 112, 140–48, 201n80; "Military Occupations," 120; "Night—Mt. Panby Beach—25 March 1983," 117–18; "Nothing of Egypt," 126, 136–37; "On eavesdropping on a delegation of conventioners at Barbados Airport," 118–20

*Bread out of Stone* (Brand), 35–36, 112, 125–27, 140, 201n80

British parliamentary system, 23, 78–79, 153, 167

Canada, 111, 114, 125, 141, 148, 198nn39–40

Caribbean, 3; Black Power movement and the, 174; black queer women and the, 8, 17, 36, 141; Brand on the, 111; Cold War and U.S. pressure on the, 100, 103, 114, 124, 130; colonialism, solutions to by Caribbean writers, 81; Cuba and risk for the, 86; cycles and the, 192n52, 193n5; education as, 81–82; Grenada policed by the, 33–34; hurricanes in the, 70–71; men, 88; near-invisibility and representations of queerness in, 142; revolution trauma for the, 72–73; sexual citizenship of the, 144–45; tourism industry dangers in the, 120, 197n23

Caribbean Community (CARICOM), 30

Caribbean feminism, 8–9, 107, 113, 146–50

Caribbean feminist literary criticism, 5, 7–8

Caribbean radical tradition: of black radical tradition, 22–23; generations and genders in, 36; Marryshow related to, 77–78; NJM ideology versus, 80

Caribbean women, 13; Brand as queer, 131; demands on, 28; Lorde on, 25; male editor on, 28–29, 188n67; in NJM, 15–16; oppression of, 1–2; politics letting down, 18; queer, 8, 141

Caribbean women writers, 2, 126–27, 139; on Grenada Revolution, 7, 13, 16, 28, 173, 184n21; histories revised by, 30; on nation-building and revolution, 5; on revolution, 5, 27–28; trauma seen by, 5–6

Caribbean writers, 2, 126–27, 139: of the diaspora, 125–27; Lamming as elder statesman and, 81; Lamming's, Walcott's, and Salkey's interest in, 80; poetry and mythology by, 95; PRG censoring,

92–97, 120, 194n22; sovereignty and, 87; trauma focus by, 108
CARICOM (Caribbean Community), 30
Centre for Popular Education (CPE), 23
Charles, Eugenia, 33
Chile, 98, 119–20, 139, 196n21
Christianity, 36, 152, 162–63, 165, 168–71, 202n7
*Chronicles of the Hostile Sun* (Brand), 17, 35, 110, 122, 143
Coard, Bernard, 3, 123–24, 151, 163, 168; Ann Bishop on, 180, 180–81; Maurice Bishop, joint leadership with, 31, 87, 180–81
Coard, Phyllis, 28, 31, 123–24, 151, 168, 197n29
Cold War: Cuban Revolution and, 127, 129; Grenada Revolution in, 6, 27, 167; Grenadians opting out of, 48; Non-Aligned Movement and, 22, 48, 83, 116–17; rejection of, 144, 149; U.S. pressure over, 100, 103, 114, 124, 130
Collins, Merle: Black Power explored by, 46–47; Caribbean feminism of, 107; on conflict genealogy, 38; early life of, 40, 189n4; education of, 189n4; as feminist disruptor, 39; on Gairy, 45; as Grenada Revolution writer, 7, 9, 28, 184n21; hurricane poetics of, 192n49; on NJM, 190n14; on radicalism cycles, 35–55; representations of women by, 107. Works: *Angel*, 35–55, 104, 107, 174, 191n27; *Because the Dawn Breaks*, 70; *The Colour of Forgetting*, 35, 37–40, 55–64, 107, 174, 191n35; "Dream Mourning," 53, 64–68, 181, 191n27; "I d Open the Gate," 75–76; *Lady in a Boat* by, 39, 64–76, 65; "October, All Over," 71–74; "Shame Bush," 75
Collins, Patricia Hill, 8
colonialism: arson and resistance to, 41; capitalism in, 48; Caribbean solutions to, 81; Christianity and, 162–63; Dalleo on Caribbean and, 201n87; English, 4; escape as difficult from, 110–11; genre and, 20; media and, 118–19; "Night—Mt. Panby Beach—25 March 1983" on, 117–18; oppressive replications of, 21; Purcell's desire for order of, 154–57; racism and, 23; revolution as response to, 20–21, 186n47; Scott on, 15; sexism and patriarchy from, 8; "thiefing sugar" and resistance to, 144; trauma and, 12–14, 121; violence from, 10–12; Walcott on, 95–96
*Colour of Forgetting, The* (Merle Collins), 35, 37–40, 55–64, 107, 191n35
communism: Brand on, 129–30, 190n18, 199n56; Bernard Coard and rumor about, 163; as criminal, 167; Manley and, 48, 190n18; masculinity and, 130; U.S. fantasy on, 137; young generation on, 48–49. *See also* Cold War
CPE (Centre for Popular Education), 23
Creft, Jacqueline, 28, 32, 123, 188n67, 197n29
Crenshaw, Kimberlé, 8, 184n22
Cuba, 21, 33, 49, 98, 114, 196n21, 197n30
Cuban Revolution, 3, 25; Brand family and, 127–31, 137, 199n56; Caribbean people risk from, 86; Cold War and, 127, 129; Grenada implicated with, 97, 117; PRG supported by, 23; racism in, 21, 98
cycles, 35–55, 113, 192n52, 193n5

Dalleo, Raphael, 201n87
David, Christine, 28
Davis, Angela, 175
"Diary—The grenada crisis" (Brand), 121
Dominica, 33
"Dream Mourning" (Merle Collins), 53, 64–68, 181, 191n27

Eastwood, Clint, 200n69
economic aid, 31
education: in agricultural science, *11;* billboard for, *89;* as Caribbean, 81–82; Lamming on, 35, 79, 81–82; NJM training teachers in, 23–24, *24;* PRG promoting, 28; UWI for, 40, 47, 77, 153–54
"Education Is Production Too!," 81
"Education of Feeling, The" (Lamming), 35, 79

Fanon, Frantz, 43, 79, 128
Fedon, Julien, 77–78, 192n3
feminism: Maurice Bishop championing, 28; black feminism and, 18, 105, 177, 187n52; Caribbean feminism and, 8–9, 107, 113, 146–50; citizenship and,

feminism (*continued*)
8, 140–41, 204n2; Merle Collins and disruptive, 39; liberation and, 145; on revolution, 132–33; as women voices, 56

*Fictions of Feminine Citizenship* (Francis), 8, 140–41, 204n2

"From Toussaint L'Ouverture to Fidel Castro" (James), 3–4

*From Wilderness to Promise* (Purcell), 153–54, 202n7

Gairy, Eric, 3, 11–12, 37–38, 41, 46–48, 79; Baker on, 204n3; Merle Collins on, 45; nurses against, 6, 7; Purcell on, 154–55, 157–58; Salkey on, 104

gender, 186n35, 198n36; analysis by, 2, 15; archives and, 5–6, 140; Brand on, 125–26, 131, 133, 135–36, 140, 144; Grenada Revolution and, 2–3, 15; idealized and proscribed concepts of, 184n8; Lamming, Salkey, and Walcott on politics and, 18–19; leadership roles and, 184n10; literature recognizing, 17; marginalized by, 25, 28; masculine identity in, 4, 57, 76–77, 86; men and, 1–2, 4, 28–29, 44–45, 56–57, 61, 88, 188n67; patriarchy and, 15–16; politics of, 5–6, 9, 19, 105, 140; Purcell and, 18, 152–53; queerness and, 8; revolution and politics of, 9, 17, 182; revolution with sexuality and, 144–45, 149; sovereignty imagined in, 27. *See also* queerness; women

generations: ancestral knowledge of, 53, 55–56, 58, 61–64, 67–69, 138–39; Baker on, 204n3; black radical tradition and, 36; Brand on failure and, 138–39; Caribbean mother character in, 105; class tensions among, 81; Merle Collins on conflict between, 38; communism as issue between, 48–49; connections seen by, 51; "Dream Mourning" and, 64; Gairy and loyalty by, 47–48; *The House on Coco Road* including, 175; Marxism, rejection of, and, 10, 48, 50; political violence experienced between, 42–43; queerness and, 149; testimony of, 177–79; U.S. invasion destruction and, 16; values transmitted in, 60–61; of women and revolution, 39–40; young as intoxicated by the new, 66, 68

genres: acceptance of, 17; Merle Collins ignoring, 39; colonial and revolutionary violence in, 20; Latin America and romance, 183n8; Naipaul on murder, 89–90; nationhood and romance, 183n8; Puri on, 14–15, 189n3; revolution through, 20–22; Walcott and tragedy as, 103; women defining, 178–79

"Good Old Heart of Darkness" (Walcott), 35, 79, 91–102, 94, 157

Grenada: Caribbean nations policing, 33–34; Cold War rejected by, 144, 149; Cuban Revolution implications for, 97, 117; on English colonialism, 4; Non-Aligned Movement and, 22, 48, 83, 116–17; political violence and, 41–42; Purcell averting violence in, 152; sovereignty and, 111; tourism dangers for, 120, 197n23; U.S. influencing, 167–68

Grenada 17: assassinations by, 75–76, 204n27; Purcell on, 152, 154, 166, 168–70; trial and conviction of, 105, 151

Grenada Revolution, 12; archival gaps on, 16; assassinations and freedom lost by, 164; Baker on, 204n3; black radical tradition within, 22–23, 35, 111, 187n54; Bloody Sunday and Bloody Monday of, 9–10; Brand writing on, 7, 9, 18, 28, 110–50, 131–32, 184n21; by Caribbean women writers, 13, 16, 173; in Cold War, 6, 27, 167; Merle Collins writing on, 7, 9, 28, 184n21; day of, 22; elder vision and poetry on, 37–38; for emancipation, 139; Fedon and, 77–78, 192n3; future inspired by, 126, 128; genres showing, 20–22; Grenada 17 after, 75–76, 105, 151–52, 154, 166, 168–70, 204n27; Grenadian response after, 107–8; Grenadians plotting out, 50; Grenadians reclaiming, 76; Haughton experience of, 174–77; Hodge and, 92, 95; hurricanes and secret of, 74; inability and bondage by, 126; Lamming eulogy on, 88–89; literature on, 34; Lorde on, 24, 92; Marryshow and, 77–78; Meeks on, 14, 186n35; *Memoirs of a Woman in Politics* and, 36, 151–52, 154–71; "Military Occupations" and end of, 120; moneyed class versus lower class in, 28–30; narratives revised on, 18; NJM and chaos in, 32, 34, 69, 73, 87, 159, 161; poetry on, 115–16; political change and, 27; for political control, 3; politics and violence in, 41–42; Purcell on violence and, 158, 171; RMC after, 32–34, 102, 121, 156, 161, 164, 168, 197n29; sexuality and gender of, 2–3, 15; as trauma, 158; U.S. claims about, 121–22; violence investigated in, 45, 190n12; violent ending of, 124–25; volunteers during, 30–31; Walcott frustrations on, 91–94, 98–99, 103; women of, 1–2, 7–8, 68, 132–33, *134;* women writers on, 7, 13, 16, 28, 173, 184n21; writers on, 2; and young as intoxicated by the new, 66, 68

*Grenada Revolution in the Caribbean Present, The* (Puri), 14–15, 201n94

Grenadians: on American imperialism, 88, 117–18; Maurice Bishop and tension with, 87; Black Power forgetting, 146; Cold War opt-out by, 48; collective shame of, 11–13, 39, 52, 75, 88, 99, 100, 151, 156, 164; French and deaths of, 38, 55–56, 59, 133, 147–48; Gairy and, 79; Grenada Revolution plotted out by, 50; Grenada Revolution reclaimed by, 76; Grenada Revolution response and, 107–8; Haughton similarities to, 176; invasion shock for, 122–23; Naipaul disregard for, 90–91; NJM disconnect with, 80–81, 97; political control betraying, 43; politics mishandled hurting, 51; Purcell disavowing, 162, 165; Salkey on resilience and, 105; "shoot-to-kill" curfew influencing, 32, 52, 121, 156, 168; traumatic history and, 64; on U.S. invasion, 20, 122–23, 167; violence employed by, 43; and volunteers during Grenada Revolution, 30–31; as women laborers, 133–34, *134*

Haitian Revolution, 3, 25, 77–78, 96, 111, 192n3

Haughton, Fannie, 173–82

*Heartbreak Ridge* (Eastwood), 200n69

Hodge, Merle, 28, 92, 95, 188n67

*House on Coco Road, The* (Baker), 173–82

hurricanes: Caribbean renewal after, 70–71; Merle Collins, poetics on, 192n49; as metaphor of Grenada Revolution, 74; "October, All Over" and, 71–74; politics and, 71–72; Puri on history and, 14–15, 192n49; volcano violence and, 62–63

"I d Open the Gate" (Merle Collins), 75–76

*In Another Place, Not Here* (Brand), 35–36, 112, 140–48, 201n80

*In Search of Our Mothers' Gardens* (Walker), 204n1

intersectionality, 8, 141, 184n22

"Island Betrayed, An" (Naipaul), 79, 89

Jamaica: Bernard Coard and Phyllis Coard, living in, 151, 168; Merle Collins studying in, 189n4; literature of, 4; Manley of, 48, 119, 190nn17–18, 196n21; media destabilizing, 119; PRG supported by, 23; Seaga of, 33; socialism failure in, 139; soldiers from, 33–34, 100; Trinidad and, 81, 190n15

James, C. L. R., 3–4, 88, 129–30, 187n52, 199n57

justice, 168–69, 204n24

*Lady in a Boat* (Merle Collins), 39; "Dream Mourning" in, 53, 64–68, 181, 191n27; "Morning Glory" in, 68–70; poetry of mourning and loss in, 64–76; "Se Mwe Nutmeg (Is Me, Nutmeg)" in, 64, *65*

Lamming, George, 18–19, 35, 79–88, 107–8

land, 35, 57–59

leadership: Maurice Bishop and Bernard Coard's joint, 31, 87, 180–81; Maurice Bishop, exhibiting male, 4, 108; from blackness, 46; Merle Collins on, 49; gender and roles of, 184n10; Grenada Revolution with male, 10

Lenin, Vladimir, 78–80, 82

liberation, 80–81, 83–87

literary nationalism, 4, 23, 35

literature: archives, masculinity and, 16–17; of Barbados, Jamaica, and Trinidad, 4; Brand and humanizing, 124–25; elder vision and poetry, 37–38; gender in, 17; history documented in, 113; on land ownership, 35; liberation and local, 80–81, 83–87; mother character

literature (*continued*)
  in Caribbean, 105; NJM promoting local, 23; on people's revolution, 34; poetry and, 53–55, 70, 95, 112, 115–16; revolution and, 21–22, 186n48; on rural women, 35; on trauma, 20, 186n48; women defining, 178–79; women voices in, 17, 56
Lorde, Audre, 143–44; on Caribbean feminism, 8; Grenada Revolution favor by, 24, 92; *Sister Outsider*, 24; on U.S., 24–25, 188n58

"Mammies, Matriarchs, and Other Controlling Images" (Patricia Hill Collins), 8
Manley, Michael, 48, 119, 190nn17–18, 196n21
Marryshow, T. A., 77–81, 166, 192n1, 193n5
Marxism: black radical tradition and, 187n52; fervor for, 81–87; Jamaica and, 139; Lamming on, 79–80, 82–88, 92; Naipaul on, 90, 92; NJM on, 10, 25, 27, 64, 80; older generation rejecting, 10, 48, 50; Purcell on, 163; Rasta on, 97–98; Walcott on, 79–80, 92–93, 98
masculinity: aggression and, 4, 57, 76–77, 86; Black Power on, 6, 114, 141; as black radical, 79; challenge and trope of, 18; communism and, 130; expectations related to, 135–36; as gender identity, 4, 57, 76–77, 86; idealized and proscribed concepts of, 184n8; Lamming on, 84–86; literature countering, 16–17; loss of masculine authority, 35; Walcott on gentlemanliness and, 103
Maternity Leave Law, 28, 161
media: American imperialism and, 101–2; Chile influenced by, 119–20, 196n21; colonialism and, 118–19; Jamaica destabilized by, 119; Murdoch and, 118, 196n18; PRG battling, 92–97, 120, 194n22; on Rasta, 96–97. *See also Torchlight*
Meeks, Brian, 14, 186n35
*Memoirs of a Woman in Politics* (Purcell), 36, 152–71
men, 1–2, 4; Caribbean, 88; on Caribbean women, 28–29, 188n67; as open and communicative, 56–57, 61; warned of violence, 44–45, 56, 61. *See also* patriarchy
military: Maurice Bishop confronting, 31–32, 189n69; Maurice Bishop executed by, 10–11, 12–13, 32–33, 87, 120–21, 136, 185n29; fatal missteps by, 34; Jamaica, Barbados sending, 33–34, 100; RMC and curfew by, 32, 52, 121, 156, 168; on U.S. invasion, 33
"Military Occupations" (Brand), 120
"Morning Glory" (Merle Collins), 68–70
movement, 126–29, 132
Murdoch, Rupert, 118, 196n18

Naipaul, V. S., 4, 79, 81, 89–92
National Performing Company, 188n57
National Women's Organization (NWO), 6, 28
New Jewel Movement (NJM): Maurice Bishop at odds with, 31, 73–74, 197n29; Brand on problems and, 124, 198n36; Caribbean and black radical tradition versus, 80, 90; Caribbean women in, 15–16; Merle Collins on, 190n14; elder vision and poetry on, 37–38; fatal missteps by, 34; Grenadians disconnect with, 80–81, 97; Lenin connection by, 78; for Marxism, 10, 25, 27, 64, 80; member deaths of, 32; "Morning Glory" and metaphor of, 69; natural chaos metaphor for, 69; overzealousness conceded by, 159; Purcell support and rejection of, 151, 155–57, 159; relationships disintegrating in, 73; secrecy by, 87; socialism pursued by, 23; teachers trained by, 23–24, 24; top-down political control of, 14, 30; U.S. invasion against, 33; on violent revolution, 9–10, 185n27; women and, 6, 50
"Night—Mt. Panby Beach—25 March 1983" (Brand), 117–18
NJM. *See* New Jewel Movement
Non-Aligned Movement, 22, 48, 83, 116–17
"Nothing of Egypt" (Brand), 126, 136–37
NWO (National Women's Organization), 6, 28

OAS (Organization of American States), 28, 188n67
"October, All Over" (Merle Collins), 71–74

"October 19th, 1983" (Brand), 123–25
OECS (Organization of Eastern Caribbean States), 100, 164, 188n56, 203n15
*Omens of Adversity* (Scott), 15, 40, 186n35, 204n27
"On eavesdropping on a delegation of conventioners at Barbados Airport" (Brand), 118–20
oppression, 1–2, 10, 21, 147
Organization of American States (OAS), 28, 188n67
Organization of Eastern Caribbean States (OECS), 100, 164, 188n56, 203n15

patriarchy, 8, 14; archives by, 16; black radical tradition and, 141, 149; expectations by, 135–36; gender and, 15–16; of Grenada Revolution, 12; men and, 1–2, 4, 28–29, 44–45, 56–57, 61, 88, 188n67; Purcell on, 152–53; queerness and outlaw in, 141, 150; repetition of violence from, 15; women and violence of, 12, 21
People's Revolutionary Army (PRA), 2, 11, 22, 32, 97, 153
People's Revolutionary Government (PRG): Maurice Bishop at odds with, 31, 73–74, 197n29; collapse of, 112; critics harassed by, 10; Cuba supporting, 23; "Education Is Production Too!" conference of, 81; education promoted by, 28; Jamaica supporting, 23; journalistic censorship by, 92–97, 120, 194n22; Maternity Leave Law and, 28, 161; "On eavesdropping on a delegation of conventioners at Barbados Airport" on, 118–20; Purcell on, 155, 161, 163, 166; Rasta community harassed by, 93, 98; *Torchlight* closed by, 96–97, 118, 159, 193n18, 196n22; U.S. and documents of, 113, 195n6
Phillip-Dowe, Nicole Laurine, x, 186n35
Pitt, Claudette, 28
poetry, 53–55, 70, 95, 112, 115–16
political control, 3, 93
political violence: generations and, 42–43; Grenada and, 41–42; Grenada Revolution and investigation of, 45, 190n12; making sense of, 74; memories of, 59; Pax and peace in relation to, 191n35; personal power grab as, 46; trauma from, 20–21, 43–44, 186n47, 187n48

politics: of Black Power movement, 47; British parliamentary system, 23, 78–79, 153, 167; CARICOM pressure on, 30; escape from colonialism and, 110–11; Gairy and, 3, 41, 46; of gender, 5–6, 9, 17, 19, 105, 140, 182; Grenada Revolution and, 27; Grenadians betrayed by, 43; Hodge activity in, 28, 92, 95, 188n67; hurricanes versus, 71–72; Lamming on gender and, 18–19; moneyed class versus lower class in, 28–30; NJM with top-down, 14, 30; parish council meeting, 37; power mishandled in, 51; Purcell and, 17–18, 162, 164–66; queer love as, 146; revolution and, 9, 17, 36, 182; Salkey on gender and, 18–19; sexuality and, 9, 79, 140; triumph connection for, 52; women influenced by, 1–2
PRA. *See* People's Revolutionary Army
PRG. *See* People's Revolutionary Government
Purcell, Joan: Advisory Council silence by, 166; African diaspora and, 153–54; on authoritarian leaders, 152–53; on Maurice Bishop, 159, 161–62; on Christianity, 36, 152, 162–63, 165, 168–71, 202n7; for colonial order, 154–57; on democracy path, 164–66; *From Wilderness to Promise*, 153–54, 202n7; on Gairy, 154–55, 157–58; on gender, 18, 152–53; on Grenada, 17, 152, 154, 166, 168–70; on Grenada Revolution violence, 158, 171; Grenadian efforts disavowed by, 162, 165; on justice and clemency, 169; life of, 153–54; Marxism unnerving, 163; *Memoirs of a Woman in Politics*, 36, 151, 154–71; NJM supported and rejected by, 151, 155–57, 159; not leftist black feminism, 18; on personal isolation, 160–61; politics contradiction by, 162; on PRG, 155, 161, 163, 166; revolution rejected by, 157–59, 161; U.S. passivity by, 164; on women in politics, 17–18
Puri, Shalini: on dilated time, 121; on genres, 14–15, 189n3; *The Grenada Revolution in the Caribbean Present*, 14–15, 201n94; on hurricane historiography, 14–15, 192n49; on silencing, 201n94

queerness, 10; alternative temporalities for, 131, 200n59; "beyond the quagmire" and, 126–27; black radical tradition and, 141, 150; Brand and, 131, 135, 140, 147, 149; Brand on black women, 17, 36; Caribbean, black women, and, 8, 141; desire recognition and, 143; Grenada Revolution and, 112, 140–46; historical sense in, 149; *In Another Place, Not Here* on, 112, 140–46; love and, 146; near-invisibility of, 142; patriarchy on, 141, 150; property-status rejected with, 143–44; as radical act, 149; radical movements shaped by, 135, 145–46; as sovereignty, 144–45, 149

racism, 21, 23, 98, 141, 177; of U.S., 24–25, 114, 175
Rasta: on Marxism, 97–98; newspaper headline on, 96–97; PRG harassing, 93, 98
Reagan, Ronald, 33, 99, 108, 117, 121–22, 194n32, 204n3
"regime of the brother," 3, 183n6
resistance, 41, 93, 143–44, 177, 197n30
revolution: "aftermath without end" and, 22, 92, 121; "After the Counter-Revolution, After the Invasion" and, 103–4; *Angel* on cycles and, 35–55; black freedom in, 111; Brand on, 111, 136; Brand on diasporic writers and, 133–35, 137–38, 140; as break and cycle, 113; Caribbean and trauma of, 72–73; Caribbean women writers on, 5, 27–28; diasporic kinship and inheritance in, 36; exclusionary and oppressive policies of, 147; feminism on, 132–33; future (im)possibilities in, 35; gender and sexuality in, 144–45, 149; genre with, 20–22; literature and, 21–22, 186n48; love as best of, 148; multigenerational women experiences in, 39–40; Naipaul against, 89–90; "October, All Over" on, 71–74; politics and, 3, 36; politics of gender and, 9, 17, 182; as process, 132; Purcell rejecting, 157–59, 161; questioning of, 52–53; as repetition, 25; as response to colonialism, 20–21, 187n48; sexuality and, 9, 79; society and economy after, 46, 190n15; trauma from, 113–14;

as violent weapon, 98; women and, 49–50, 135, 145–46; women writers on harm and, 27
Revolutionary Military Council (RMC), 33–34, 102, 161, 164, 197n29; shoot-to-kill curfew by, 32, 52, 121, 156, 168

Salkey, Andrew, 18–19, 35, 79–80, 103–9
Scott, David: on "aftermath without end," 22, 92, 121; on American imperialism, 15, 149, 167; on Merle Collins, 40; *Omens of Adversity,* 15, 40, 186n35, 204n27
Seaga, Edward, 33
"Se Mwe, Nutmeg (Is Me, Nutmeg)" (Merle Collins), 64, 65
sexuality, 10; analysis of, 15; Brand on, 125–26, 134, 140–41, 144; Caribbean citizenship and, 144–45; Grenada Revolution and, 2, 15; politics of, 9, 79, 140; queerness and, 143; revolution with gender and, 144–45, 149; violence relating to, 57
SGPWA (St. George's Progressive Women's Association), 28
shame: Grenadians feeling, 11–13, 39, 52, 75, 88, 99, 100, 151, 156, 164; "Shame Bush," 75
"Shame Bush" (Merle Collins), 75
silencing: political trauma after, 21, 187n48; PRG forcing Rasta, 93, 98; Purcell and, 160–61, 166; Puri on, 201n94; over sexuality and queerness, 10; "Shame Bush" on, 75; shame ensuring, 12–13
*Sister Outsider* (Lorde), 24
"Sky Red," 41
slave revolts, 3, 25, 77–78, 96, 111, 192n3
sovereignty, 5, 12; American imperialism limiting, 19, 101–2, 137–38; Brand on, 35–36; from Caribbean poetics, 87; gender and imagining, 27; Grenada Revolution for, 139; Grenada without, 111; Lorde on, 24; queerness as, 144–45, 149; romance genre for, 183n8; as self-determination, 26–27; U.S. violating, 147, 164
St. George's Progressive Women's Association (SGPWA), 28
Stroude, Tessa, 28

teachers, 23–24, *24*
time: Grenada Revolution and, 126, 128; literature documenting, 113; Puri on dilated, 121; queerness and alternative, 131, 200n59; revolution and, 35
Tinsley, Omise'eke Natasha, 143–44
*To Die for Grenada* (Walcott), 102–3
*Torchlight* (newspaper), 187n54; Brand on, 118–20; PRG closing, 96–97, 118, 159, 193n18, 196n22; on women, 28–29
tourism, 120, 197n23
transnational black radicalism, 36
trauma: Brand and poetry relating to, 112; Caribbean revolution amd, 72–73; Caribbean women writers on, 5–6; Caribbean writers focusing on, 108; from colonial period, 12–14; Grenada Revolution conflated as, 158; Grenadians and, 64; imperialism and revolution and, 113–14; literature on, 20, 186n48; "October 19th, 1983" on, 123–25; from political violence, 21, 43–44, 187n48; political violence and, 20–21, 43–44, 186n47, 187n48; postcolonial, 121; repetition of, 51–52, 99, 105
Trinidad, 1, 4; Brand from, 110–11, 125; Hodge from, 95; Jamaica and, 81, 190n15; James on U.S. and, 129–30, 199n57; Naipaul from, 89; social and economic sameness in, 190n15; U.S. military on, 129–30, 199n57

United Nations, 34, 164
United States: advantage taken by, 34; Black Power movement and, 8, 173, 176; Cold War pressure by, 100, 103, 114, 124, 130; communism fantasy by, 137; on Cuba, 33, 49, 114; Grenada influenced by, 167–68; Grenada Revolution claims by, 121–22; James on Trinidad and, 129–30, 199n57; Lorde on, 24–25, 188n58; PRG documents and, 113, 195n6; racism of, 24–25, 114, 175; on RMC resistance, 197n30; sovereignty violated by, 147, 164; Trinidad and military of, 129–30, 199n57. *See also* American imperialism
United States invasion, 112, 120–21, 203n20; Barbados soldiers in, 33–34, 100; Brand viewing, 114–15; day of, 22; documents destroyed in, 16; Grenadians on, 20, 122–23, 167; Lorde on, 24–25; military on, 33; Mt. Panby Beach and, 117–18; as not necessary, 164; OECS inviting, 100, 164, 188n56, 203n15; psychological operations by, 166; Purcell passivity on, 164; Salkey scorning, 105; small-nation practices versus, 59–61
University of the West Indies (UWI), 40, 47, 77, 153–54

violence: Brand on terror and, 142–43; Benard Coard and, 123–24; from colonialism, 10–12; executions as, 10–11, 12–13, 32–33, 87, 120–21, 136, 185n29; fear ecology as, 12; Gairy and state-sponsored, 11–12; genre and, 20–22; Grenada and political, 41–42; Grenada Revolution ending in, 124–25; Grenadians employing, 43; marginalized gender as, 25, 28; NJM on Revolution and, 9–10, 185n27; patriarchy repeating, 15; poem on, 53–55; Purcell on, 158, 171; revolution and, 98; Scott on, 15; as silencing, 10, 12; submerged volcano as, 62–63; successive encounters of, 57; woman averting, 152; women warning about, 44–45, 56, 61. *See also* political violence

Walcott, Derek: on American imperialism, 93, 98–101; on black power, 96; for Caribbean writers, 80; on colonial periods, 95–96; essay on revolution not completed by, 91–92, 99; on gender politics, 18–19; and genre of tragedy, 103; on gentlemanliness and masculinity, 103; "Good Old Heart of Darkness," 35, 79, 91–102, *94*, 157; Grenada Revolution frustrations of, 91–94, 98–99, 103; on Haitian Revolution, 96; on Marxism, 79–80, 92–93, 98; and preservation of poetry, 95; *To Die for Grenada*, 102–3
Walker, Alice, 204n1
West Indies Federation, 23, 77, 199n57
whiteness, 57
Williams, Dessima, 28, 188n67
women, 13; and aftermath of revolution, 39; ancestral knowledge through, 61; archives missing on, 7–8; Baker on, 204n3; Black Power expansion by, 175; black radical tradition and, 132–33,

women (*continued*)
141, 146–47, 150, 182; Brand on revolution and, 136; Caribbean feminist literary criticism on, 5, 7–8; Caribbean writers as, 2, 5–7, 13, 16, 27–28, 30, 173, 184n21; by Merle Collins, 107; and commonsense approaches, 49; against Gairy, 6, 7; Grenada Revolution and, 1–2, 68, 132–33, *134;* Grenadians and labor by, 133–34, *134;* Haughton similarities to, 176; *In Another Place, Not Here* on, 140; intuition of, 181–82; literature on rural, 35; literature recognizing, 17, 56; marginalization of, 68; as mothers, 178–79; on NJM, 6, 50; as nurses protesting, 6, 7; patriarchal violence on, 12, 21; persistence and reinvention of, 108–9; political movements influenced by, 1; political violence as concern of, 41–42; Purcell on politics and, 17–18; resistance to imperialism by, 177; revolution and, 49–50, 135, 145–46; Salkey and, 104–9; story defined by, 178–79; *Torchlight* on, 28–29; trauma and silencing of, 15; trauma and women writers, 5–6; violence averted by, 152; voices of, 56; warnings about violence, 44–45, 56, 61

writers: of African diaspora, 126–27; on Grenada Revolution, 2; healing from, 139; home movies and, 175–76. *See also* Caribbean writers

RECENT BOOKS IN THE SERIES
# New World Studies

*Comrade Sister: Caribbean Feminist Revisions of the Grenada Revolution*
Laurie R. Lambert

*Cultural Entanglements: Langston Hughes and the Rise of African and Caribbean Literature*
Shane Graham

*Water Graves: The Art of the Unritual in the Greater Caribbean*
Valérie Loichot

*The Sacred Act of Reading: Spirituality, Performance, and Power in Afro-Diasporic Literature*
Anne Margaret Castro

*Caribbean Jewish Crossings: Literary History and Creative Practice*
Sarah Phillips Casteel and Heidi Kaufman, editors

*Mapping Hispaniola: Third Space in Dominican and Haitian Literature*
Megan Jeanette Myers

*Mourning El Dorado: Literature and Extractivism in the Contemporary American Tropics*
Charlotte Rogers

*Edwidge Danticat: The Haitian Diasporic Imaginary*
Nadège T. Clitandre

*Idle Talk, Deadly Talk: The Uses of Gossip in Caribbean Literature*
Ana Rodríguez Navas

*Crossing the Line: Early Creole Novels and Anglophone Caribbean Culture in the Age of Emancipation*
Candace Ward

*Staging Creolization: Women's Theater and Performance from the French Caribbean*
Emily Sahakian

*American Imperialism's Undead: The Occupation of Haiti and the Rise of Caribbean Anticolonialism*
Raphael Dalleo

*A Cultural History of Underdevelopment: Latin America in the U.S. Imagination*
John Patrick Leary

www.ingramcontent.com/pod-product-compliance
Lightning Source LLC
Chambersburg PA
CBHW021854230426
43671CB00006B/389